FIRESIDE

OTHER BOOKS BY STANLEY W. ANGRIST

Direct Energy Conversion, 2nd Edition

(with A. S. Weinstein)
An Introduction to the Art of Engineering

(with L. G. Hepler)
Order and Chaos: Laws of Energy and Entropy

(for young people)
How Our World Came to Be

Other Worlds, Other Beings

Sensible Speculating in Commodities

☐ Or How to Profit in the Bellies, Bushels and Bales Market

by STANLEY W. ANGRIST

A Fireside Book
Published by Simon and Schuster

A Fireside Book
Published by Simon and Schuster
A Gulf+Western Company
Rockefeller Center, 630 Fifth Avenue
New York, New York 10020

ISBN 0-671-21342-3
ISBN 0-671-22428-X pbk.
Library of Congress Catalog Card Number 72-83910
Designed by Irving Perkins
Manufactured in the United States of America

3 4 5 6 7 8 9 10

1 2 3 4 5 6 7 8 9 10 pbk

Contents

Foreword

□

This book is about commodity trading, and no one would be more surprised than I if you made a million dollars in the commodity market after reading it. That is not to say, however, that it won't help you make some money in commodities futures—it's just that it's hard to *earn* a million dollars no matter which way you approach the problem. (I have used the word *earn* in order to exclude the case of the person who wakes up one morning and discovers that sweet old Aunt Agatha who passed away last month remembered you in her will to the tune of a million crisp ones. Such people didn't, in most cases, earn anything—they just were lucky enough to have the right relatives succumb at the right time.) But I digress. Money can be, and is, made in the commodity market every day of the week. And, in fact, in some ways it is an easier market to know than the stock market because there are only twenty-five or so actively traded commodities compared with more than four thousand actively traded stocks in the listed and unlisted markets. It is the purpose of this book to explain how you —someone who perhaps has never even heard of the commodity futures market—can learn to cope with the ins and outs of a market that is known to send thousands of investors a year back to savings and loan associations with what remains of their trading capital after only six weeks of pork bellies or wheat or whatever.

Commodity trading is not for the fainthearted, but I believe that any stock-market investor who lived through the great bear market of 1970 would agree that a strong constitution is also an important asset for a stock trader. The striking difference between commodity trading and stock trading is that profits can accrue at a much faster rate in commodities than in stocks. By much faster I mean ten or twenty times as fast; it is not uncommon for a reasonably competent commodity trader to make 300 percent on a single trade in two months time or less. But, of course, the commodities market is also willing to take money away from its participants much faster than the stock market—*if you let it.*

That brings us to the subject of this book—how do you get as many 300 percent profitable trades per year while not giving back to the market all your profits plus a large part of your initial capital? You do it by following a few simple rules—rules that you must learn and follow without exception. This book will detail those rules, as well as the mechanics of trading commodities, and several useful techniques that can be used to put you in and take you out of speculative positions at appropriate times.

I believe that once you have read and thought about the rules and techniques given here, and then actually try them for a while yourself, you might come around to my point of view that while anyone cannot make a million dollars, a sensible commodity speculator might make himself \$5,000 to \$50,000 a year *without* a recently deceased Aunt Agatha or a roaring bull market on Wall Street.

STANLEY W. ANGRIST

Pittsburgh, Pennsylvania
October 1972

CHAPTER **1**

Why You Should Consider Speculating in Commodities

"Both he who chooses heads and he who chooses tails are equally at fault. They are both in the wrong. The true course is not to wager at all."

—Blaise Pascal, seventeenth-century French mathematician, physicist and founder of the theory of probability.

□

Unfortunately none of us is in a position to accept Pascal's advice. We live in a world which forces us to wager—that is to take risks—and most of us have learned to cope with a modest amount of such activity fairly well. Commodity markets are set up to allow a large number of people to share risks which, prior to the organization of such markets, was borne by only a few individuals. And it should be obvious that if the market is willing to allow you to bear a risk it is also willing to allow you to be rewarded.

Commodity speculation is a high-risk activity. But it should be clear that in any market in which the risks are so high there must also be extremely high rewards for those able to forecast price movements with some accuracy. *True* stories of people who have turned $5,000 into $30,000 or more in the commodity market in three months abound. It can be done, and it is done with some regularity. However, a U.S. Department of Agriculture survey of 8,782 speculators in the grain-futures markets showed that only 25 percent made a net profit. Why is the percentage so low? The answer to that question is not obvious, but I believe that by the time you have finished reading this book you will understand why so few traders are successful. More importantly, you will know enough about commodity trading so that you can avoid the most common mistakes made by almost all beginning traders.

You do not need to be rich to speculate in commodities. On the contrary, because of the low margins required on commodity positions there is no area of speculation in which your money will go farther. This book is written from the point of view of an individual who wants to speculate and can risk losing $3,000. If you can afford to lose this amount, but are willing to follow several simple rules that almost all new commodity traders break every day that they trade, then you stand to make rewards many times higher than those that are available through other investment opportunities.

Risk-bearing

We must all do it every day. If you purchase a house, there is the risk that it might burn. You transfer a portion of that risk to an insurance company who for an annual premium agrees to pay you a previously agreed-on sum in the event that the house does burn. You expose yourself to risk any time you choose to own anything that can be lost. In fact, the idea that ownership and risk go together was the driving force that brought commodity futures markets into being.

Just living involves a risk. And thus a large number of people in the United States make a conscious effort to share that risk by purchasing life insurance. A life insurance policy is a bet on a dead (no pun intended) certainty—if kept in force long enough the company must lose the bet (but not necessarily any money). The uncertainty or risk arises in whether the insured will die sooner or later. The risk of financial hardship that the insured's family would suffer if he were to die, thus ending his income production, is partially transferred to the insurance company, which bears this risk for the reward of an annual premium.

But why this discussion of risk-bearing? Because that is what commodity speculation is all about. People speculate on commodities (or on anything else for that matter) because they hope to make a profit. They expect to be rewarded because of their willingness to bear a risk—in the same way that your insurance company expects to receive an annual premium as its reward for bearing the risk that you might die prior to your expected lifetime of seventy or so years.

Financial Risk-bearing

Why must anyone bear any risk at all when it comes to the financial side of his life? Because there is no way to escape risk-bearing, whether you want to or not. If you put your money into a checking account where it does not gather interest, it depreciates in value every year by whatever the rate of inflation is for that year. If the inflation rate is 5 percent, then $1,000 in your checking account today will be worth only $950 in goods and services next year on this date. You have, whether you like it or not, borne the risk of inflation.* While it's true that as long as you had your money in a checking account you could lose no more than what inflation took from you, it is also true that such funds were incapable of increasing in value.

If you put your $1,000 into an insured savings account that paid interest at 5 percent per year, at least you might offset, more or less, the inflation rate, which is assumed to be 5 percent in this discussion. Next year your savings account would show a balance of $1,050, which would still buy you about $1,000 worth of this year's goods and services.

If you wanted to expose yourself to a little more risk you might buy reasonably good-grade corporate bonds paying between 7 and 8 percent per year in interest. Though not quite as secure as a Government-insured savings account, a bond investment would let you net some return over and above the inflation rate. Economists say that an 8 percent bond gives a real rate of return of 3 percent during a period of 5 percent inflation.

If you had even a larger taste for risk, you might decide that the only way to beat inflation would be to buy common stocks. Several studies have been done on rates of return in the stock market, but

* Of course, in the event that our economy entered into a strong deflationary period, money in a checking account would actually be able to buy *more* goods and services after a year. This country has not seen such a period since the 1930s.

one of the most thorough was done by the Center for Research in Security Prices at the Graduate School of Business of the University of Chicago. This study found that the average rate of return for all common stocks on the New York Stock Exchange from January 1926 through December 1960—assuming reinvestment of all dividends and after payment of all commissions—was 9.0 percent per year compounded annually. During most of that time period inflation was not running at a 5 percent rate and thus the average real rate of return over that 34-year period might have been close to 6 or 7 percent. Stock market wizards argue that 9 percent is too low an expected rate of return because an average investor does not buy every stock on the board; no, sir, the astute investor, according to the wizards, just buys those stocks that triple in two years. (*Hoo-ha!*) Be that as it may, lots of people view the stock market as a hedge against inflation, and for some, no doubt, it is.

That brings us to the commodity market as a means of increasing one's capital and thus staying ahead of inflation. What rate of return might be expected if one engages in sensible commodity speculation? Well, since I have already pointed out that 75 percent of over 8,000 grain traders studied by the U.S. Agriculture Department lost money, obviously lots of traders had negative rates of return. But since they made lots of mistakes that my trading rules will stop you from making, let's forget about the losers for the moment. Most successful commodity speculators believe that if they do not make 50 percent per year on their money in bad years and more than 100 percent in good years, then they have been wasting their time. Hold on a minute. Why are stock-market investors satisfied with a 9 percent or so return, whereas a commodities speculator feels that he needs a return of 50 percent or more? The answer to that question boils down to the old saw that says without risk there is no reward; and furthermore, the greater that risk the greater the potential reward.* The commodity market is considerably riskier than the stock market, and thus people will not venture into it unless they believe they can get a much bigger re-

* Suppose that I ask you to make a sales pitch for Israel Bonds to two audiences. The first audience is a local United Jewish Appeal dinner. The second speaking engagement I have arranged for you is the Pan-Arab Conference for Ministers of War at the Cairo Hilton. You would be foolish, and I would be naive, to think that you would face these same audiences for the same speaking fee.

ward. But there are two important differences between the stock market and the commodity market that should be made clear: one involves moral attitudes and the other is concerned with the psychological attitudes of people who are in those markets.

ME, A SPECULATOR?

If you approached the average buyer of common stocks and asked him if he considered himself a speculator, he would probably answer in a slightly insulted tone of voice that he certainly was not. Speculation is considered by many to be a practice that while not strictly illegal, is a less than reputable activity. The typical purchaser of common stocks considers himself an *investor* and not a *speculator.* The word sounds better; it even has an almost noble ring to it. What speculators do is for themselves, while what investors do is for the good of society—at least a little. Or so my stock-market-investing friends tell me. This self-righteous attitude tends to make stock buyers feel good, but unfortunately their claims do not bear close examination.

An investment is frequently defined by those who consider themselves economically rigorous as the placement of money into a property, which could be a building, shares of a company, a debt issue of a company, or the like, from which one intends to receive earnings. These earnings might be paid as rent, dividends, or interest. A speculation is defined by this same group as the placement of money into a property without hope of receiving any (or, at best, small) earnings, but with only the hope of receiving a profit based on an expectation of a *price change.* The distinction is clear enough—a true investor pays little or no attention to changes in price, but only looks at earnings. A true speculator adopts the exactly opposite attitude.

Now let us examine the portfolios of the average common-stock buyer. For years Avon Products has been a very popular stock among both big and little investors. During the six-year period between 1966 and 1971 it earned between $1.00 and $1.75 per share, while selling within a range of between $38 and $102 per share. Thus, during this period it has sold at a price-to-earnings ratio of about 50. The stock in 1971 was paying a dividend of a $1.30 per share which at a price of $100 per share gives it a return *as an investment* of 1.30 percent. Are the purchasers of Avon Products shares investors or speculators? The answer is clear. If they are interested in investments they can surely do better than 1.30 percent. They buy Avon because historically Avon has a good record of increasing in price; Avon is not bought for its dividends but for its potential change in price. It is a speculation. The stock market is full of such investments—Control Data, Itek, Jim Walters, Polaroid and Xerox. All these New York Stock Exchange "investments" and thousands more on the American Stock Exchange and in the over-the-counter market are bought daily by people and institutions who would be grossly insulted if you accused them of speculating. But if the shoe fits . . .

Clock Watching in Investing and Speculating

Most of the people who take up speculation in commodities come to it after they have tried their hand in the securities market. Thus they bring with them a set of attitudes and a way of operating that may have served them well in their financial lives. It is sad but true that most of these attitudes don't work very well in the commodities market; thus it is not uncommon for a fairly successful stock trader to bomb out of the commodities market in six weeks. Most of these new commodity traders bog down because of their old attitudes toward time—especially when they tenaciously hold on to the belief that they will come out all right "in the long run." The one idea that a new commodities-market trader must fix firmly in his mind is: *In the commodity market there ain't no such thing as the long run.*

Say you buy some XYZ Corporation stock for $50 and the market starts to go into a sinking spell; XYZ sells off to $40. You reason that since XYZ, in your opinion, was a good buy at $50, it is even a better buy at $40. If you have the funds you buy some more at $40, and if you don't you hold your XYZ stock, because in the *long run* it will sell for $60 or $70 a share. It is true that lots of professional stock traders would find this strategy repugnant; if XYZ sinks $2 or $3 they would sell out and wait to buy in again when they thought that a bottom had been reached. That is, they are like commodity traders in that they don't believe in the long run.

In fact, to survive even briefly in commodity trading you must adopt the attitude of the professional stock trader. Even before you take up a commodity position you must decide firmly at what price you will admit that you have made a mistake.

The necessity of recognizing mistakes and closing out losing positions is an attitude that not everyone possesses. Avoidance of taking a loss in the stock market is achieved by some investors by holding onto stocks for years; they reason that if they wait long enough the market will reverse its original judgment of their opinion. This strategy can clearly not be followed in the commodities market as no contract ever has more than eighteen months to run before it expires. Since a commodity trader cannot wait too long for the market to bail him out of his mistakes, many positions must be closed out with losses. It is for this reason that most commodity traders are happy to be right on only four out of every ten trades. Not only are they happy but they find that such a percentage gives them a nice return on their money. How they can make money on a 40 percent success record will be explained in later chapters. The ability to eat humble pie six days out of every ten is not everyone's idea of a well-balanced diet.

All commodity contracts have a time limit built into them. A buyer of a December corn contract is a person who must do one of two things before a certain known date in December arrives: (1) Take delivery of 5,000 bushels of corn, or; (2) Sell his contract before that date arrives. Thus if a buyer of December corn at $1.50 per bushel sees the price of corn drop to $1.45 per bushel he can ill afford to sit around and wait for corn prices to come back. They just might not do it before the contract expires. Therefore the only prudent thing a buyer of a December corn contract can do is set the price at which he will sell out and admit his error. You cannot conclude that corn is necessarily a better buy at $1.45 than it was at $1.50—you can only conclude that you should have sold it short instead of having bought it at $1.50. Even if you had excess funds you probably would not want to buy another contract of corn at $1.45 to "average down" your corn price. For once a trend starts in a commodity it is more likely to persist than to reverse. It is a well-established fact among commodity traders that people who "average down" generally "average out" of the market very quickly.

John Maynard Keynes, the distinguished British economist, summarized the situation very well when he was discussing land as a vehicle for speculation. He recognized that there was only a fixed amount of land on the earth and that the earth's population was increasing; therefore, in the long run, land must be an excellent speculation. He then went on to say that in the long run we are all dead.

CHAPTER **2**

How Futures Markets Evolved

□

Trade is now recognized as one of the most important communal activities that man engages in. Even in primitive societies one man might have owned something that another man needed or wanted. The method used to satisfy that need was probably pretty simple (and unfortunately it is still more widely practiced than we care to admit) ; many needs were satisfied simply by theft. The virtue of theft was that it required no meetings of the minds between a buyer and seller, no medium of exchange, and no complicated bookkeeping system to keep track of the transaction. It still possesses those virtues today. In ancient times and even now it was frequently accompanied by violence between the old owner of the property in question and the man who hoped to become the new owner. One measure of a society's advancement is the extent to which it has given up theft as a means of satisfying wants. In most societies today, buying and selling of goods by means of a medium of exchange (money) has replaced theft and bartering of goods as methods of satisfying needs.

The First Markets

The first and still most common transaction that involves both goods and money is the so-called "spot" sale. The seller offers his goods to the buyer and a price is negotiated "on the spot." In these early exchanges of goods and money the transaction took place immediately. Traveling merchants wandered from town to town and country to country, sometimes alone and sometimes in groups, offering their wares by the spot-sale method on a door-to-door basis. In time both the local merchants and the traveling ones convinced the local rulers of the towns and cities to grant them permission to organize formal trading centers where for a specific time each year they could display their merchandise for inspection and sale; at the same time the traveling merchants would buy local products for resale elsewhere. These centers, in time, developed into periodic fairs. It was not long before the medieval fair of the Middle Ages became a highly organized and efficient institution for the marketing of products throughout Europe and the British Isles.

Although almost all of the trading at these fairs was in merchandise immediately available, and thus constituted "spot" sales, at times contracts were drawn up to sell merchandise "to arrive" or "for delivery" at some future time. These contracts were the crude beginnings of what is now called a futures market.

The Early Futures Markets

Farmers and those who utilize what the farmers produce—food processors—began to realize the inadequacies of trade fairs in handling the buying and selling of farm products. They frequently found themselves in feast-or-famine situations. In the fall, at harvest time, grains such as wheat or corn might be offered at prices as low as 15 cents per bushel and still no buyers might be found. Grain merchants and millers who had a need for grain had bought all that they could use now or store for future use. The newly harvested grain setting out in barges or wagons would soon deteriorate. In the spring and summer, before the new crop had been harvested, exactly the opposite situation held. Wheat that might have sold for 15 cents in October could not be purchased at $1.50 or even $3 per bushel. This inability to distribute the crop through the year worked against both the farmer and the processor. The risks borne by both groups were tremendous and many members felt that they would gladly share the risk with others if a system could be worked out to do so.

As early as 1840 grains began to trade on a deferred basis in

Chicago. The actual operation of such trading was rather simple. After harvesting his crop and loading it on to a wagon or river barge bound for Chicago, the farmer would take the fastest transportation available to Chicago. In this way he would arrive before his shipment.

At the Haine's Feed Store on the banks of the Chicago River, grain processors, brokers and merchants would congregate. For several hours each day they would negotiate with farmers for their crops which they needed for their flour milling and other activities. If a farmer had a harvest on the way he would offer his crop on a "to arrive" basis, since he could not physically deliver the grain on the day that the sale took place.

A firm price was set for the sale. But it was entirely possible that between the time the sale took place and delivery was effected the price might rise. In such a case it would be to the seller's advantage to default and not deliver his crop against the sale. On the other hand, if prices fell during the waiting period it would be to the buyer's advantage to default and not pay for the high-priced grain, but to buy grain at the lower prices now available. Some sort of insurance was obviously needed to protect both buyers and sellers against a default on the part of the opposite party.

The Evolution of Margin

It was this state of affairs that caused "margin" to come into use in the grain trade. After a buyer and seller had agreed on a price for the grain, they would each deposit a mutually acceptable amount of cash with a disinterested third party. In case either side defaulted, the margin deposit would be paid to the injured party in order to reimburse him for any inconvenience or financial loss that he might have suffered because of the default.

Margin then acts as a performance bond and not as a down payment; such payments bind the buyer into accepting delivery and paying for the agreed upon goods in full. The margin binds the seller to making good on his delivery promise. Margin today still serves as a performance bond; however, it is no longer held by a disinterested third party but by a clearinghouse which acts as an intermediary between buyers and sellers. Unlike margin on a commodity transaction, margin in the case of stocks and bonds *is* a down payment, and thus interest must be paid on the balance owed the broker.

It was not too long after trading of grain began at Haine's Feed Store that a new group of buyers and sellers appeared on the scene. This group had no need for the actual grain themselves, nor did they have the land or skill to produce it. They were the grain speculators. "Long" speculators would buy to-arrive offerings of the farmers, hoping that in the interim between their purchases and the arrival of the grain, prices would increase and offer the "longs" an opportunity to sell out at a profit. The "short" speculators acted in just the opposite fashion by selling to-arrive grain for delivery in thirty, sixty, or ninety days in the hope that prices would fall enabling the "shorts" to buy the cash grain that they needed to deliver against their earlier sales at a price less than what they sold the grain for initially. If they were able to make such purchases, they stood to make a profit. Neither the longs nor the shorts had any interest in taking delivery or making delivery; these individuals were merely assuming the risks of price fluctuation over a specified period of time in the hope of profiting from a change in price. All speculators today play exactly the same role. They agree to bear a risk hoping to be rewarded for that risk-bearing by the profit that can be made if they correctly estimate the direction in which prices move.

The informal arrangements which were used to distribute risks soon evolved into formal ones in a number of locations. In 1848 the Chicago Board of Trade was organized to handle grain trading. Today it is the oldest, largest and most important commodity futures exchange in the world. The New York Produce Exchange was organized in 1862, followed by the New York Cotton Exchange in 1870 and the New York Coffee Exchange in 1885. Today there are more than ten active commodity exchanges in the United States. Their importance in facilitating the efficient use and distribution of a large number of agricultural and industrial commodities can hardly be overstated. In 1971 the value of commodities traded on all the exchanges in the United States was estimated at $150 billion (more than $70 billion of that amount was on the Chicago Board of Trade), compared with $103 billion value of the securities traded on the New York Stock Exchange.

CHAPTER 3

Hedgers, Speculators, and Gamblers

□

It is a common misconception among people who have only a passing knowledge of the futures market to assume that only gamblers venture into such markets. In truth, there is no room at all for gamblers in such markets. Indeed, there may be ill-informed speculators, but whether they like it or not, such individuals serve a useful economic function—and that function has nothing at all to do with gambling. In this chapter I shall outline the roles played by hedgers and speculators in futures markets and show how neither, in their activities, possess the characteristics commonly associated with gambling.

What Does a Hedger Do?

The single most important purpose for the futures market is to provide price insurance to those people who produce and use certain fundamental commodities. As a commodity speculator you will be buying and selling from hedgers at various times and therefore it is important that you understand how your role differs from theirs.

First, most of the people who produce commodities, such as farmers, and those who use them, such as grain processors, have no interest in speculation. They have enough to worry about without guessing about the direction which prices will move in the future. Therefore they seek to protect themselves from this uncertainty.

Consider the case of a flour miller who signs a contract to deliver to a bakery all the flour that can be made from 50,000 bushels of wheat. Since he has been in business a number of years, he knows his costs well. He knows his labor costs, depreciation costs, and maintenance costs. He knows the minimum number of dollars he must make from this milling job as profit in order to remain in business. He can also call up a local grain merchant and find out the price of wheat *today*. But he does not and cannot know what wheat will cost him when he goes to fill his contractual obligations in about a year; and yet he has committed himself to deliver flour at that time *at a fixed price*.

Thus driven by uncertainty about the future, he seeks a way to guarantee that the price of wheat will not cause him to lose money on the milling job. First, he assumes that wheat will cost the same a year from today as it does today; then he fixes his price of wheat by buying ten wheat futures contracts that come due in a year. Each futures contract obligates the seller to deliver 5,000 bushels of wheat to the miller on the day the contract expires. Suppose he pays $1.60 per bushel for wheat when he buys his futures contracts. Twelve months pass and the price of "cash wheat" is $1.50 per bushel; he buys the wheat he needs at this price from a grain merchant who has the actual commodity ready for delivery. He then sells his futures contract on the Board of Trade at the same price ($1.50), taking a 10 cents per bushel loss on the futures contract wheat. But since he is able to buy cash wheat 10 cents cheaper than what he estimated ($1.60) a year ago, the profit on the cash part of the transaction offsets the loss on the futures part of the transaction.

If wheat prices had gone up 10 cents per bushel, then the gain on the miller's futures contracts would have offset any losses he would have suffered when he had to buy the higher-priced wheat in the cash market. In either case, the miller does not have to worry about wheat prices, as he has *hedged* his position. He is then said to be a *commercial hedger* or a *hedge buyer* in the futures market.

Hedging is also carried out by firms which are in the business of storing and merchandising commodities traded on various exchanges. These could include, no doubt, the grain merchant from whom the flour miller in the example above bought his cash grain to fill his milling order. Hedging is important to anyone who must own or store, over an extended period of time, large stocks of a commodity whose price may be subject to fluctuation. These price fluctuations create unavoidable risks to the owners and users of commodities. Usually those in the business of storing, processing and merchandising cash commodities in large volume have neither the taste nor the assets to assume those risks. They are in a competitive business which generally operates on an extremely narrow profit margin; these small profit margins can be wiped out by unpredictable price changes. Thus they seek ways to reduce or transfer their risks by utilizing hedges.

Who Are Those Men in the White Hats?

Why, son, those are speculators. And by and large, they do far more good than harm. Let us look at the evidence to support that statement. Speculators frequently buy commodities when actual users of the commodity have little desire to buy, and they sell when actual producers of the commodity have little incentive to sell. Their activity is not a simple economic contrivance but is a practice that has risen out of the risks inherent in a highly unpredictable business. The speculators' willingness to buy or sell at nearly any time acts as a leveling or damping influence in the marketplace, and is indeed the most effective countermeasure for the excesses which otherwise always develop in the face of surpluses that cannot be used or supplies not adequate to meet demands.

It is the primary function of the commodity speculator—or trader, if you prefer—to assume the risks that commercial hedgers do not wish to bear. Critics of speculation argue that during the course of a year sometimes as much as twenty times the crop size is actively traded on a futures exchange. Thus, the critics reason, are not speculators taking on far more risk than is necessary to absorb the risks connected with hedging transactions? The answer to this criticism can be found in one word: *liquidity*. In order for hedging risks to be readily and easily absorbed, there must be a volume of trading well in excess of that required to absorb the hedges. If speculators were scarce and the market thin, then some flour millers might have to wind up doing business directly with wheat farmers, which could cause price disadvantages for each of them at different times of the year. The presence of speculators in a market ensures that purchases and sales can be made on an almost continuous basis in a market with great liquidity.

The Speculator vs. the Gambler

I have claimed great virtues for speculators, but there are many people who believe that the speculator is no different in his actions than the bettor at the race track. Both seek situations in which uncertainty prevails and then choose to wager sums on the outcome of an uncertain event.

The argument that speculators and gamblers engage in the same type of activity is weak in at least two respects. The gambler creates his own risks by sitting down at a poker table or going out to the track and laying bets, whereas the speculator merely assumes existing risks arising out of natural or economic forces. But that is not enough of a distinction—a critic of speculation might argue that one who bets at a race track creates no risk but merely tries to profit from the uncertain factors inherent in horse racing, such as the relative speed of a number of animals. But that argument is weak in that a financial risk is created that would otherwise not exist until a bet is placed. A commodity speculator, however, accepts the transfer of a risk that already exists when he agrees to take a position in a commodity. Price risks really exist for producers and consumers of commodities, whether or not speculators agree to bear them.

The other important point that must be noted is that every contract entered into on a commodity exchange by every trader, whether he be a hedger or a speculator, is, unlike a gambling debt, an obligation enforceable by law to deliver or to accept and pay a fixed price for a stated quantity of a given commodity at a definite time. This fact, already alluded to earlier in the discussion of liquidity, is indeed critical. It is of critical importance because each purchase or sale of a commodity contract temporarily adds to the apparent demand or apparent supply of the commodity.

A commodity trader, whether he likes it or not, at the instant he makes a trade becomes a part of the marketing machinery for the commodity he is trading. Whether he is buying from a selling hedger or selling to a hedging buyer, he takes on the price-insurance function that was discussed earlier. If he chooses, he can accept delivery of the commodity—or he might make delivery of the commodity to a buyer if he were a seller.* Or he might step out of the transaction by making an offsetting sale if he is long, or an offsetting purchase if he is short and thus avoid the delivery aspect of his trade completely. Nevertheless, as long as a commodity trader is long or short a given commodity, he is part of the distributive system of that commodity and he is performing a useful economic function.

Speculators have been attacked at one time or another by every group that has anything to do with production and consumption of commodities. Producers of commodities traditionally attack speculators when commodity prices are low, such as occurred in the 1930s. And, of course, as commodity prices rise, it is generally the consumers of the commodities who level their fire at the speculators as the cause of rising prices.

Most economists agree† that by and large speculators are neither the cause of higher or lower prices. Paul Samuelson, one of the practitioners of the dismal science, as Thomas Carlyle dubbed economics, summarized the activities of speculators well when he wrote that:

> . . . to the extent that speculators can form accurate guesses today about the future *scarcity* of a commodity, they will tend to buy it now for *future* delivery, thereby causing (1) a withdrawal of present supply, (2) an increase of present price, (3) an increase in amount stored, (4) an increase in future supply, (5) a reduction in future price—or in all a relative stabilization of price and consumption over time.

Defense of speculators by economists and, in at least one case, by a distinguished Justice of the Supreme Court, Oliver Wendell Holmes, will not cause criticism of speculators to cease. However, it is probably safe to conclude that any one group that down through the years has been the target of so many diverse interests simply cannot be all bad.

* We need not concern ourselves here with what a commodity trader might want to do with 5,000 bushels of soybeans, or how he might arrange to deliver 69,120 square feet of ½-inch-thick plywood.

† As contradictory a statement as can be written. Rarely do two economists agree on anything. It is common knowledge that if you locked the ten best-known economists in the United States in the master clock room at the Naval Observatory in Washington and told them that they could not come out until they could agree on what time it is, there is a good chance they would all have reached retirement before they would have reached a consensus.

CHAPTER **4**

Which Commodities Are Traded and Where?

□

There are about fifty different commodities traded on exchanges throughout the world. This leaves a large number of very important commodities that are not traded in any organized market. Why is it that coffee is traded in both New York and London but tea is not traded anywhere? Why is it that you can buy a futures contract on apples but not bananas? What reasons can be advanced to justify the trading of soybean oil but not crude oil? The answers to these questions cannot be found in the relative importance or value of the commodity in question. There are probably more bananas produced in the world than apples. Crude oil is far more important to the world's economy than is soybean oil. And tea is undoubtedly drunk by more people throughout the world than is coffee. The reasons why some commodities are traded but others are not depends basically on six factors. A commodity might possess five of these factors but not the sixth, and thus will not be traded.

Six Factors that a Tradable Commodity Needs

Free Flow of the Commodity to Market. One of the first tests that is generally applied to a commodity to see whether or not it can be traded is whether its flow to market is natural. Is the supply of the commodity that is to be traded in the world's markets subject to artificial restraints by either government or private agencies? Trading of any commodity on a futures exchange would be impossible if the supply or price of that commodity were under effective control and could be increased or reduced at the will of any government, corporation, cartel or individual. The market in this case would be incapable of acting as a price-making machine; instead it would serve as a handmaiden to the true controller of the supply or price of the commodity. It is this test that has eliminated crude oil as a commodity that might be traded on a futures basis. Given the interference of various government agencies, both here and abroad, on the production and importation of crude oil, which essentially acts to control its price, a futures market in crude oil would be an exercise in futility.

A Large Supply and Demand. In addition to coming to market freely the commodity must also be in ample supply and demand. For example, if artichokes met all the other tests for a tradable commodity, they would still fail the supply-and-demand test. Compared to the staple commodities both their supply and demand are small. Under such conditions it would not be too difficult for a small number of speculators to gain effective control of an artichoke futures market. It would soon cease to be a free market but would be a captive trading arena subject to the whims of its controllers. No amount of fundamental or technical analysis can assist a speculator in a market controlled by a small group that is not subject to market forces. Those traders not privy to the next market action of the control group would become the unwilling victims of this group. Speculators as a group are, if nothing else, risk takers, but all of them prefer, at least, to play in an honest game.

A Homogeneous Trading Unit. Neither hedgers nor speculators buy a specific lot of a commodity when they purchase a futures contract on an exchange. They buy or sell only a specified amount which meets established grades or descriptions published by the exchange where trading in that commodity takes place. A grain elevator storing thousands of bushels of Number 1 soft spring wheat which may belong to several owners has the same commodity in it from top to bottom. A buyer who takes delivery from that elevator couldn't care less whose wheat is actually delivered to him when he sends his trucks to pick it up. The contents of the elevator are homogeneous. Any commodity that is produced in such a way that large quantities of it are not homogeneous would not be suitable for trading on exchanges.

Standardization of Grades. It would seem reasonable that any commodity which is homogeneous must be capable of being divided into standard grades. Natural variation will cause one lot of a commodity to be different in some important ways from other lots of that same commodity. For example, not all two-by-fours are of the same quality, but standards have been established so that their quality can be *judged objectively*. If a building contractor buys a lumber-futures contract and accepts delivery of it when the contract expires, he knows exactly what he may expect to get when his lumber arrives. The specification on the futures contract require, in part, that the lumber shall be:

> . . . kiln dried or air dried construction grade not to exceed 35% standard grade random lengths 2 × 4s manufactured in California, Idaho, Montana, Nevada, Oregon and Washington. The lumber shall meet the requirements of Simplified Practice Recommendation 16-53. . . . The moisture content of at least 95% of the pieces shall not exceed 19.0% as determined by moisture meter readings in accordance with . . .

And so on. Everything the contractor might possibly want to know about the lumber he bought is spelled out in the details of the futures contract, which is available from the exchange where that contract is traded. This requirement that a commodity be gradable, by the way, is the one that precludes tea from being traded. It turns out that the establishment of commercial grades for this commodity is a matter that involves not only expert opinion but individual taste as well. It has been concluded that the subjective factors in tea grading are so wide-ranging that agreed-on standards could probably not be arrived at.

Commodity Must Be Storable. Because commodity contracts always call for delivery of the commodity some number of months in the future, it must be capable of being stored for considerable periods of time. Only if it is storable can it be available to market in times of scarcity. A purchaser who buys a contract expecting to take delivery must have some reason to believe that the commodity will remain substantially unchanged in quality until the delivery date. In essence, today's surplus supply of the commodity must be capable of becoming the essential supply of tomorrow. Apples pass this test, but bananas fail as a possible trading medium.

Uncertainty of Supply and Demand. It should be obvious by now that there could be no commodity market if certainty prevailed. If supply and demand are certain, then prices can be adjusted without recourse to an organized market. Moreover, if either supply or demand alone is certain, the problem of price adjustment is more difficult, but no elaborate market machinery is required to bring about the appropriate price adjustments. It is only under those conditions where supply and demand are both large and uncertain, subject to wide fluctuations from season to season or from year to year, that a free market will operate successfully. In no other market in the world is the daily battle between the bull (who believes prices are going up) and the bear (who believes prices are going down) as clearly exposed as in the commodity markets. The constantly uncertain and shifting demand facing a changing market supply operates to make for an irregular but continual variation in prices. Without this uncertainty the market may be replaced by "administered prices," which use some other method of allocating the world's tradable resources.

Commodities in Which Exchange Trading Is Conducted

Considering the six tests that a commodity must pass before it is traded on an exchange, it may seem surprising that more than fifty different commodities are traded throughout the world. It is also worth noting that some commodities are traded on more than one exchange, though the contract specifications might not be the same on the commodity. For example, cocoa, coffee and copper are all traded on exchanges in both London and New York. Wheat is traded in Chicago, Kansas City and Minneapolis.

The list of traded commodities is impressive and should be large

Table 1

Commodity Futures Specifications--Part I

Commodity	Exchange Trading Hours (New York Time)	Margin-Regular† Initial Maintenance	Margin-Spread† Initial Maintenance	Non-Member Commissions (Round Turn) Regular	Spread	Day Trade
Broilers, Iced	Chicago Board of Trade 10:15 am-2:05 pm	$ 300.00 200.00	$100.00 50.00	$30.00	$36.00	$20.00
Cattle, Live*	Chicago Mercantile Exchange 10:05 am-1:40 pm	400.00 250.00	250.00 100.00	40.00	43.00	25.00
Cocoa	New York Cocoa Exchange 10:00 am-3:00 pm	750.00 450.00	300.00 150.00	60.00**	70.00**	30.00**
Copper	Commodity Exchange Inc. 9:45 am-2:10 pm	1000.00 750.00	200.00 150.00	36.50	51.40	18.50
Corn*	Chicago Board of Trade 10:30 am-2:15 pm	400.00 300.00	100.00 50.00	30.00	36.00	20.00
Cotton*	New York Cotton Exchange 10:30 am-3:00 pm	800.00 600.00	300.00 175.00	46.00**	56.00**	23.50**
Eggs, Fresh*	Chicago Mercantile Exchange 10:15 am-1:45 pm	500.00 300.00	200.00 150.00	40.00	43.00	25.00
Hogs, Live*	Chicago Mercantile Exchange 10:20 am-1:50 pm	400.00 300.00	200.00 100.00	35.00	38.00	22.00
Lumber	Chicago Mercantile Exchange 10:45 am-2:15 pm	450.00 250.00	200.00 100.00	40.00	43.00	25.00
Oats*	Chicago Board of Trade 10:30 am-2:15 pm	300.00 200.00	100.00 50.00	25.00	36.00	17.00
Orange Juice, Frozen Concentrate*	New York Cotton Exchange 10:15 am-2:45 pm	600.00 450.00	200.00 150.00	45.00	54.00	25.00
Platinum	New York Mercantile Exchange 9:45 am-1:30 pm	650.00** 420.00	100.00**	45.00	45.00	22.50
Plywood	Chicago Board of Trade 11:00 am-2:00 pm	500.00 300.00	100.00 50.00	30.00	40.00	20.00

†Margins are listed for illustrative purposes only. Brokerage houses may set margins at any value they want above the exchange minimum. Both exchanges and brokerage houses may change their margins on individual commodities at any time.

*Under Commodity Exchange Authority Control.

**Varies with price level.

Table 1

Commodity Futures Specifications--Part I (Continued)

Commodity	Exchange Trading Hours (New York Time)	Margin-Regular† Initial Maintenance	Margin-Spread† Initial Maintenance	Non-Member Commissions (Round Turn)		
				Regular	Spread	Day Trade
Pork Bellies, Frozen* Chicago	Chicago Mercantile Exchange 10:30 am-2:00 pm	$ 750.00 500.00	$400.00 200.00	$45.00	$48.00	$27.00
Potatoes, Maine*	New York Mercantile Exchange 10:00 am-2:00 pm	300.00 200.00	100.00 100.00	30.00	32.00	15.00
Silver (New York)	Commodity Exchange Inc. 9:30 am-2:15 pm	1000.00 750.00	150.00	45.00**	63.00**	22.50**
Silver (Chicago)	Chicago Board of Trade 9:30 am-2:25 pm	500.00 400.00	100.00 50.00	30.00	32.00	15.00
Silver Coins	New York Mercantile Exchange 9:25 am-2:15 pm	800.00 640.00	400.00 320.00	35.00	35.00	17.50
Soybeans*	Chicago Board of Trade 10:30 am-2:15 pm	750.00 500.00	150.00 100.00	30.00	36.00	20.00
Soybean Meal*	Chicago Board of Trade 10:30 am-2:15 pm	500.00 400.00	100.00 50.00	33.00	44.00	22.00
Soybean Oil*	Chicago Board of Trade 10:30 am-2:15 pm	500.00 400.00	150.00 100.00	33.00	44.00	22.00
Sugar, World #11	New York Coffee & Sugar Exchange 10:00 am-3:00 pm	500.00 250.00	200.00 100.00	42.00	42.00	21.00**
Wheat,* Soft Red	Chicago Board of Trade 10:30 am-2:15 pm	600.00 500.00	200.00 100.00	30.00	36.00	20.00
Wheat,* Hard Red	Kansas City Board of Trade 10:30 am-2:15 pm	750.00 500.00	100.00 50.00	30.00	36.00	20.00
Wheat,* Spring	Minneapolis Grain Exchange 10:30 am-2:15 pm	750.00 500.00	100.00 50.00	30.00	33.00	20.00

†Margins are listed for illustrative purposes only. Brokerage houses may set margins at any value they want above the exchange minimum. Both exchanges and brokerage houses may change their margins on individual commodities at any time.

*Under Commodity Exchange Authority Control.

**Varies with price level.

enough to satisfy the taste of any speculator. Furthermore, the list is not a static one; new commodities are always being added to it and others removed as interest in a given commodity wanes or trade conditions no longer make commodity trading feasible for that substance.

For example, in 1971, trading commenced in feeder cattle, milo, propane, silver coins, and tomato paste. In recent years trading has been abandoned in onions and lard. The list of commodities available for trading in 1971 looked like this: apples, barley, frozen boneless beef, iced broilers, live steers, feeder cattle, live cattle, cocoa (New York and London), coffee (New York and London), copper (New York and London), cotton, cottonseed oil, currency (pound sterling, Canadian dollar, West German deutsche mark, French franc, Italian lira, Japanese yen, Swiss franc), fresh eggs (Chicago and New York), fish meal, flaxseed, frozen skinned hams, live hogs, lead, lumber, mercury, milo, oats (Chicago and Winnipeg), frozen orange juice, palladium, black pepper, platinum, plywood (Chicago and New York), frozen pork bellies (Chicago and Minneapolis), Idaho potatoes (Chicago and New York), Maine potatoes, propane, rapeseed, rubber, rye, silver (Chicago, London, and New York), silver coins, soybeans (Chicago and New York), soybean meal, soybean oil (Chicago and London), sugar (New York and London), sunflower-seed oil, tomato paste, tin (New York and London), wheat (Chicago, Kansas City, and Minneapolis), and zinc.

The size* of the above list may seem formidable to the new commodity trader, but take heart—in my opinion, more than half of the above commodities can be ignored as trading vehicles. You may safely rule out those commodities traded only on foreign exchanges such as barley, flaxseed, lead, rapeseed, rubber, rye, sunflower seed oil, and zinc. Furthermore, there are a number of commodities that do not enjoy much of a public or small-speculator market; such commodities, in my opinion, are best left to the professionals. In Table 1, I have put down a list of those commodities which I believe are suitable for a beginning commodity trader. I admit that this list reflects my personal biases and that some traders might argue with the commodities I have elected to include, but I

* Remember there are more than 1,500 issues listed on the New York Stock Exchange and more than 1,000 on the American Stock Exchange.

believe that the list is more than adequate to satisfy all but the most active traders.

Useful Trading Facts

Tables 1 and 2 include a number of useful bits of information that you would want to know before you assumed a position in one of the commodities listed. Working from left to right in each table we will consider each column in turn. The first column after the name of the commodity gives the name of the exchange where the commodity is traded and the hours (based on New York time) during which trading takes place. For example, the iced-broilers contract is traded on the Chicago Board of Trade between 10:15 A.M. and 2:05 P.M.

The next column in Table 1 lists margin requirements for a single contract. These are margins as set forth by a commodities brokerage house at the time of this writing and are subject to change at any time. Each exchange sets minimum margins, and no member firm can ask its customers to put up less than this amount on a contract. Member firms can and do ask customers to put up more than the exchange minimum if the margin clerk perceives the exchange's minimum margin does not offer adequate protection to the firm. The first margin listed is the initial margin required on a new position, while underneath this margin is listed the maintenance margin down to which your equity could fall before you would be asked to supply additional funds to restore your margin to its initial value. For example, if you wanted to go long or short an iced-broilers contract, you would be asked to put up $300; but if the price moved the wrong way and reduced the equity in your account to only $200, then your broker would ask you to sell out or supply him with another $100 to restore your margin to its original value of $300.

The next column is the margin required on a spread position. The subject of spreads will be treated in detail in Chapter 12. Briefly, however, a spread is an arbitraging operation between various delivery months or between interrelated commodities. That is, if a trader believes the price of July soybeans will gain on the price of September soybeans, he might simultaneously buy July and sell September beans. Because such a position is perceived to have

Table 2

Commodity Futures Specifications--Part II

Commodity	Contract Size	Whose Price Changes By	Will Produce a Profit or Loss Per Contract of	Daily Trading Limits From Last Close	Max Range
Broilers, Iced	28,000 lbs.	0.025 cent per pound* 0.20 cent per pound 2.00 cent per pound	$ 7.00 56.00 560.00	2 cents	4 cents
Cattle, Live	40,000 lbs.	0.025 cent per pound* 0.20 cent per pound 1.00 cent per pound	10.00 80.00 400.00	1 cent	2 cents
Cocoa	30,000 lbs.	0.01 cent per pound* 0.20 cent per pound 1.00 cent per pound	3.00 60.00 300.00	1 cent	2 cents
Copper	25,000 lbs.	0.01 cent per pound* 0.20 cent per pound 2.00 cent per pound	2.50 50.00 500.00	2 cents	4 cents
Corn	5,000 bushels	1/8 cent per bushel* 1/2 cent per bushel 8 cent per bushel	6.25 25.00 400.00	8 cents	16 cents
Cotton	50,000 lbs.	0.01 cent per pound* 0.20 cent per pound 2.00 cent per pound	5.00 100.00 1000.00	2 cents	4 cents
Eggs, Fresh	22,500 dozen	0.05 cent per dozen* 0.20 cent per dozen 2.00 cent per dozen	11.25 45.00 450.00	2 cents	4 cents
Hogs, Live	30,000 lbs.	0.025 cent per pound* 0.20 cent per pound 1.50 cent per pound	7.50 60.00 450.00	1.50 cent	3 cents
Lumber	100,000 board feet	10 cents per 1000 bd. ft.* $2.00 per 1000 bd. ft. $5.00 per 1000 bd. ft.	10.00 200.00 500.00	$5.00 per 1000 bd. ft.	$10.00 per 1000 bd. ft.
Oats	5,000 bushels	1/8 cent per bushel* 1/2 cent per bushel 6 cent per bushel	6.25 25.00 300.00	6 cents	12 cents
Orange Juice, Frozen Concentrate	15,000 lbs.	0.05 cent per pound* 0.20 cent per pound 3.00 cent per pound	7.50 30.00 450.00	3 cents	3 cents

*Minimum fluctuation.

Table 2
Commodity Futures Specifications--Part II (Continued)

Commodity	Contract Size	Whose Price Changes By	Will Produce a Profit or Loss Per Contract of	Daily Trading Limit From Last Close	Max Range
Platinum	50 troy ounces	10 cents per ounce* $ 2.00 per ounce $10.00 per ounce	$ 5.00 100.00 500.00	$10.00	$10.00
Plywood	69,120 square feet	10 cents per 1000 sq. ft.* $2.00 per 1000 sq. ft. $7.00 per 1000 sq. ft.	6.91 138.24 483.84	$7.00 per 1000 sq. ft.	$14.00 per 1000 sq. ft.
Pork Bellies	36,000 lbs.	0.025 cent per pound* 0.20 cent per pound 1.50 cent per pound	9.00 72.00 540.00	1.50 cent	3 cents
Potatoes, Maine	50,000 lbs.	0.01 cent per pound* 0.20 cent per pound 0.35 cent per pound	5.00 100.00 175.00	35 cents per 100 pounds	70 cents per 100 pounds
Silver (New York)	10,000 troy ounces	0.10 cents per ounce* 2.00 cents per ounce 10.00 cents per ounce	10.00 200.00 1000.00	10 cents	10 cents
Silver (Chicago)	5,000 troy ounces	0.10 cents per ounce* 2.00 cents per ounce 10.00 cents per ounce	5.00 100.00 500.00	10 cents	20 cents
Silver Coins	10 bags each containing $1000 face amt.	$ 1.00 per bag* $ 50.00 per bag $100.00 per bag	10.00 500.00 1000.00	$100.00 per bag	$200.00 per bag
Soybeans	5,000 bushels	1/8 cent per bushel* 1/2 cent per bushel 10 cent per bushel	6.25 25.00 500.00	10 cents	20 cents
Soybean Meal	100 short tons	5 cents per ton* 20 cents per ton $5.00 per ton	5.00 20.00 500.00	$5.00	$10.00
Soybean Oil	60,000 lbs.	0.01 cent per pound* 0.20 cent per pound 1.00 cent per pound	6.00 120.00 600.00	1 cent	2 cents
Sugar	112,000 lbs.	0.01 cent per pound* 0.20 cent per pound 0.50 cent per pound	11.20 224.00 560.00	0.50 cent	1 cent
Wheat (all contracts)	5,000 bushels	1/8 cent per bushel* 1/2 cent per bushel 10 cent per bushel	6.25 25.00 500.00	10 cents	20 cents

*Minimum fluctuation.

lower risk than an outright long or short position—and sometimes it has lower risk and sometimes it doesn't—the broker asks you to put up only $150 margin on the spread and then maintain an equity of at least $100 on each spread.

The last set of columns lists the commissions for trading one contract of the commodity. All commodity commissions are quoted on a round-turn basis. That is, no commission is paid until a position is closed out, and then one commission covers *both* the purchase and the sale of the contract. Some commodity commissions depend upon the price of the commodity, and such commissions are marked in the table with a double asterisk. You should check with your broker to get the exact commission at the prevailing price if you are interested in trading such commodities. The spread commission is the round-turn charge for handling *both* sides of a spread. That is, though the commission is $30 for buying and then at a later date selling one contract of July soybeans, it is only $36 to simultaneously buy a July soybeans contract and sell a September contract and then at some later date make the necessary offsetting trades to close out such a position (sell a July and buy a September contract).

The next column gives the commission for initiating and closing out a position in a single day. For example, if you bought and sold a cocoa contract within a single trading session you would pay only $30 instead of the regular $60 commission.

Table 2 gives the other pertinent facts that you would want to know if you were trading commodities. The second column in this table gives the contract size. That is, a contract of iced broilers is 28,000 pounds, while a lumber contract is 100,000 board feet. You will note that all the grains are traded in units of 5,000 bushels.

The next column lists price changes, with the first row for each commodity giving the minimum price change that can take place. Thus, the price for iced broilers cannot change less than 0.025 cents per pound; and such a change represents a profit or loss per contract of $7.00. A lumber contract is 100,000 board feet, while prices are quoted per 1,000 board feet. The least amount the price of lumber can change by is 10 cents per 1,000 board feet, which represents a profit or loss of $10 per contract. A price change of $2 per 1,000 board feet means a profit or loss of $200 per contract.

All commodities have a maximum amount by which their price

per unit can move from the previous day's closing price. These maximum moves are called "daily limits," and they came into being because from time to time dramatic news developments occur, such as war scares, crop catastrophes or blights; and under such stimuli commodity prices generally experience exceptionally sharp price movements. Exchanges have adopted daily limits to prevent unnecessarily large fluctuations caused by hysteria or exaggerated hopes or fears. These limits are listed for each commodity in the table under the heading "Daily Trading Limits." Remember, the first number is the maximum amount that the commodity's unit price can change from the previous day's closing price. For example, the price of live hogs cannot increase *or* decrease by more than 1.50 cents per pound from the previous day's close; thus the maximum *daily price range* is 3 cents. By the way, you should be aware of the exceptions to these daily limits; the daily limits on some commodities do not hold during the last few days of trading of a contract. Since we are speculators and not hedgers, which means we have no interest in making or taking delivery, we are well advised to avoid holding a contract into its delivery month. In each case I have shown in the price-change column the greatest number of dollars you can make or lose if the commodity's price were to change by the daily limit. Thus if lumber were to rise or fall $5 per 1,000 board feet, it would produce a profit or loss of $500.

Price Quotations

Table 2 lists the smallest price change per unit of commodity traded. If you wish to test your understanding of that table, I suggest that you examine the commodities page of a newspaper that publishes commodity quotations. Both *The Wall Street Journal* and *The New York Times* give fairly good coverage of the more actively traded commodities. Many local newspapers also devote a column or two to commodity prices. Figure 1 is a reproduction of the commodity prices for July 21, 1971 from *The Wall Street Journal*. Note that no units of trading are given. You must refer to Table 2 until you have enough familiarity with commodities to figure out what the numbers mean. You might also notice that sometimes two prices are given under the column headed "Close."

Futures Prices

Wednesday, July 21, 1971

	Open	High	Low	Close	Change	Season's High	Season's Low
CHICAGO—WHEAT							
July	152	152½	147¾	148⅛-¼	−5⅞to5¾	168⅞	142
Sept	151	153¼	150½	152⅞-¾	⅛+to unch	170½	149⅝
Dec	154	156½	153¼	156-156⅛	−¼to⅛	173½	153¼
Mar'72	156¼	158⅜	155⅝	158	−¼	175⅜	155
May	155½	157½	154	156¾-⅝	unch to−⅛	174⅛	153½
CORN							
July	145½	146⅛	139⅛	140-139⅛	−7⅛to8	168	134½
Sept	142¼	142¾	140	140¾-141½	−3to2¼	165	139½
Dec	137	137½	134½	136⅛-136	−2⅝to2¾	162⅞	134½
Mar'72	139¾	141⅛	138¼	140½-⅝	−2½to2⅜	167¼	138¾
May	142¾	143¼	141¼	143-142¾	−2to2¼	168⅞	141¼
OATS							
July	69	69¼	64	64½-66	−5⅛to3⅝	85	64
Sept	67½	67⅞	66½	67-67⅛	−1to⅞	76⅝	65¼
Dec	69⅝	69¾	68½	68⅝-¾	−1⅛to1	79½	68⅛
Mar	71	71	69¼	69¾	−1½	80	69¼
May	70¾	70¾	69½	70	−1½	80¼	69½
SOYBEANS							
July	341	346¼	341	346-346¾	+4¼to5	351½	289
Aug	342½	346⅜	342¼	344⅞-¾	+2⅛to2	351⅜	286½
Sept	339¾	344	339	342½-¾	+1⅝to1⅞	349½	279
Nov	332¾	336	332¾	334-334⅜	+¼to⅝	342¼	275½
Jan'72	336¼	339	336¼	337¾-⅞	+½to⅝	346	280
Mar	339¼	342	339	340½-¾	+⅝to⅞	348⅞	288½
May	341¾	344	341¼	343	+⅞	351¼	299¼
SOYBEAN OIL							
July	14.85	15.14	14.75	14.80-.76	− .10to.14	15.40	9.59
Aug	14.48	14.73	14.39	14.53-.51	+ .05to.03	14.98	9.60
Sept	14.06	14.35	14.00	14.17-.15	+ .09to.07	14.65	9.90
Oct	13.74	13.95	13.62	13.79-.80	+ .04to.05	14.28	10.05
Nov	13.42	13.56	13.29	13.44-.47	+ .03to.06	13.99	9.93
Dec	13.23	13.44	13.17	13.33-.30	+ .02to−.01	13.87	9.77
Jan'72	13.10	13.32	13.10	13.17	− .04	13.77	9.68
Mar	13.00	13.21	12.98	13.07-.06	− .04to.05	13.65	10.03
May	12.98	13.10	12.86	12.92-.91	− .07to.08	13.54	10.25
SOYBEAN MEAL							
July	87.50	88.15	87.20	87.65-.50	+ .15to unch	89.40	76.50
Aug	87.60	88.40	87.40	87.70-.75	− .05to unch	89.95	76.95
Sept	86.65	87.10	86.45	86.65-.55	unch to−.10	89.10	76.25
Oct	84.10	84.50	84.00	84.30b	+ .10	86.90	73.90
Nov	83.20	83.90	83.20	83.70b	+ .20	86.35	74.25
Dec	83.00	83.70	82.85	83.40-.35	+ .05to unch	86.60	73.50
Jan'72	82.85	83.70	82.85	83.15-.20	unch to+.05	86.30	73.90
Mar	84.10	84.10	84.00	84.00-.10	+ .05to.15	86.70	74.50
May	84.50	85.15	84.50	84.80b	+ .30	87.50	77.50
ICED BROILERS							
July	28.02	28.05	27.95	28.05	+ .05	31.27	27.92
Aug	28.02	28.10	27.70	27.75	− .35	31.05	27.70
Sept	27.45	27.45	27.22	27.25	− .20	29.80	27.22
Nov	26.95	26.95	26.80	26.80	− .20	29.00	26.50
Dec	27.60	27.60	27.35	27.35	− .20	27.70	27.35
Jan'72	28.30	28.30	28.00	28.02	− .23	28.35	28.00
PLYWOOD							
July	95.20	97.20	95.20	96.70	+1.90	112.00	79.70
Sept	97.50	98.90	97.10	98.20-98.	+1.7to1.5	111.50	81.60
Nov	98.80	100.10	98.40	99.50-.20	+1.2to.9	112.00	83.20
Jan'72	99.80	100.80	99.80	100.50-.40	+1.1to1.	110.00	90.00
Mar	101.40	102.50	101.30	102.00	+1.00	102.50	91.20
May	102.00	104.00	102.00	103.40-.30	+1.1to1.	104.00	92.80
CHICAGO—SILVER							
Aug	155.40	156.20	155.30	155.50-.40	+ .50to.40	205.70	154.50
Oct	157.90	158.50	157.70	157.70	+ .40	208.50	156.50
Dec	160.40	160.70	160.00	160.10	+ .60	208.00	158.50
Feb'72	162.90	162.90	162.20	162.30	+ .50	202.30	161.30
Apr	165.20	165.20	164.60	164.70	+ .60	192.60	166.10
June	167.50	167.50	167.10	167.10	+ .60	192.60	166.10
Aug	170.20	170.20	169.50	169.70	+ .90	187.30	168.30
Oct	172.00	172.10	171.90	172.00	+ .90	178.80	170.80
KANSAS CITY—WHEAT							
July	144	144¼	143	143¾	−1½	160¼	137
Sept	144½	145¼	144⅜	145-145⅛	−½to⅜	163	143¼
Dec	147½	148⅛	147¼	148	−¼	161	145¾
Mar'72	148½	149¾	148½	149½	....	163	148
May	148¾	148¾	147⅝	148½	−⅜	161⅝	147⅝
MINNEAPOLIS—WHEAT							
Sept	159	159¼	158⅜	159	−¾	174½	158⅛
Dec	162	162	160¾	161¾	−¾	173½	160¾
WINNIPEG—RAPESEED (VANCOUVER)							
July	324⅛	328	324⅛	328b	+1	332⅝	266
Sept	309¼	313⅛	309	313b	+2⅞	317½	258
Nov	301	305¾	301	305⅜-¾	+3¼to3⅝	310	246⅞
Jan'72	295⅞	299⅝	295⅞	299⅜a	+2⅜	305⅛	262½
Mar	291½	292¾	291⅜	292⅛a	+3⅛	298	270
RYE							
July	105	105¾	105	105¾b	+¾	120	102¾
Oct	106⅛	107⅜	106	107⅜	+1⅛	121¾	101¼
Dec	106	106¾	105½	106¾	+1	115	105½
May'72	107⅛	108⅛	107	108⅛b	no comp	108⅛	107
OATS							
July	76¼	76¼	76¼	76¼b	....	91½	72½
Oct	74¾	74¾	74¼	74½	−⅛	80½	73
Dec	74½	74½	74⅛	74⅛	−½	76¾	74⅛
BARLEY							
July	119¾	199¾	118	118	−1⅞	134	114¼
Oct	115½	115½	114¾	115a	−½	129	110⅞
Dec	114½	114½	113⅛	113¾	−¾	118¾	111
May'72	112½	112½	110	110⅛b	−2¼	117½	110
FLAXSEED							
July	241½	243¾	241⅜	243⅜b	+1¾	263	241⅛
Oct	246⅞	248⅞	246⅝	248⅝	+1⅝	264¾	245½
Nov	246¾	248½	246¾	248⅜a	+1⅝	260⅝	244½
Dec	245⅝	248	245⅝	248b	+2	260⅞	243½
May'72	255⅞	258	255¾	258b	+2⅛	256⅞	254⅝

	Open	High	Low	Close	Change	Season's High	Season's Low
CATTLE (CHICAGO MERCANTILE EXCHANGE)							
Aug	32.80	33.17	32.72	32.80-.75	+ .25to.20	33.17	28.25
Oct	31.10	31.35	31.00	31.12-.10	+ .25to.23	31.47	27.90
Dec	30.77	30.95	30.70	30.77-.75	+ .07to.05	30.95	27.90
Feb'72	31.20	31.40	31.20	31.27	+ .12	31.40	28.25
Apr	31.12	31.32	31.10	31.25	+ .18	31.50	30.35
Sales estimated at: 3,599 contracts.							
FRESH EGGS							
July	32.75	33.05	32.60	32.90-33.05	.35to.20	35.60	27.75
Aug	34.30	34.30	33.75	33.95	− .35	38.85	32.55
Sept	38.70	38.95	38.55	38.70-.75	− .10to.05	40.25	37.25
Oct	37.65	37.75	37.30	37.75	− .20	39.25	36.85
Nov	39.75	39.75	39.50	39.70	− .05	40.85	35.40
Dec	39.40	39.40	39.10	39.25	....	39.90	38.50
Sales estimated at: 746 contracts.							
FROZEN PORK BELLIES							
July	22.12	22.82	22.12	22.80-.75	+ .90to.85	36.20	21.15
Aug	20.30	20.60	20.30	20.47-.42	+ .20to.15	35.20	19.90
Feb'72	28.45	28.60	28.20	28.47-.42	+ .17to.12	36.80	28.20
Mar	28.55	28.67	28.30	28.52-.55	+ .12to.15	36.50	28.25
May	29.00	29.30	29.00	29.15	+ .15	35.75	28.97
July	29.60	29.77	29.55	29.70	+ .13	36.60	29.50
Aug	28.62	28.82	28.57	28.72-.75	+ .17to.20	36.40	28.50
Sales estimated at: 4,336 contracts.							
HOGS							
Aug	20.60	20.75	20.57	20.60-.65	unch to+.05	23.85	18.62
Oct	19.35	19.60	19.35	19.35	+ .03	22.70	18.55
Dec	19.62	19.80	19.52	19.57-.52	unch to−.05	23.90	19.20
Feb'72	21.30	21.50	21.30	21.45	+ .20	24.78	20.70
Apr	21.20	21.40	21.20	21.25	+ .28	24.95	20.50
June	23.15	23.15	23.15	23.15		25.25	23.05
July	23.40	23.40	23.40	23.40	− .10	25.25	23.20
Sales estimated at: 616 contracts.							
POTATOES (IDAHO RUSSET)							
May'72	5.50	5.50	5.50	5.50	....	5.65	5.45
Sales estimated at: 2 contracts.							
LUMBER							
Sept	111.00	111.00	110.40	110.90	+1.10	118.10	84.60
Nov	107.50	107.70	106.80	107.40	+ .70	117.00	89.40
Mar72	107.60	108.30	107.60	108.30	+ .70	113.00	103.80
Sales estimated at: 161 contracts.							
NEW YORK—SILVER							
July	155.40	155.60	155.10	155.40	+1.10	221.80	154.70
Aug	155.70	155.70	155.60	155.60	+1.20	161.40	155.60
Sept	156.70	157.00	156.10	156.60	+1.20	206.00	156.00
Dec	160.00	160.50	159.50	160.10	+1.20	210.00	159.30
Jan72	161.00	161.50	161.00	161.20	+1.20	210.80	160.60
Mar	163.30	164.00	163.10	163.60	+1.20	104.80	163.00
May	165.70	166.10	165.70	166.00	+1.20	191.30	165.50
July	168.70	168.80	166.00	168.40	+1.20	192.50	167.70
Sept	170.60	171.00	170.40	170.80	+1.20	190.70	170.10
Sales: 1,924 contracts.							
COPPER							
Sept	49.35	49.65	49.05	49.35	+ .50	59.50	45.10
Oct	49.40	49.50	49.30	49.40	+ .75	59.40	45.75
Dec	49.40	49.80	49.15	49.55	+ .85	58.95	45.85
Jan'72	49.75	49.80	49.45	49.75	+ .80	58.60	46.10
Mar	49.90	50.25	49.80	50.15	+ .75	58.45	47.55
May	50.00	50.35	49.95	50.30	+ .90	58.30	48.35
July	50.55	50.55	50.25	50.45	+ .90	56.00	48.40
Sales: 1,224 contracts.							
SUGAR NO. 11 (WORLD CONTRACT)							
Sept	4.14	4.27	4.12	4.26	+ .13	5.24	3.63
Oct	4.14	4.26	4.13	4.26	+ .12	5.16	3.68
Mar'72	4.27	4.41	4.26	4.41	+ .15	5.00	3.92
May	4.28	4.39	4.27	4.39	+ .12	5.00	4.27
July	4.29	4.41	4.29	4.41	+ .15	4.88	4.25
Sept	4.32	4.32	4.32	4.39b	+ .13	4.71	4.27
Oct	4.32	4.30	4.30	4.39b	+ .13	4.51	4.26
Sales: 1,062 contracts.							
COCOA							
July	25.25	25.85	25.25	25.57	− .08	37.00	21.75
Sept	25.55	25.82	25.50	25.52	− .13	37.12	22.18
Dec	25.30	25.54	25.27	25.31	− .06	36.97	22.57
Mar'72	25.60	25.85	25.60	25.61	− .09	34.25	23.05
May	25.95	26.18	25.95	26.00	− .06	31.30	23.38
July	26.40	26.40	26.30	26.30	− .06	28.28	23.65
Sept	26.55	26.75	26.55	26.61	− .05	27.35	23.95
Sales: 569 contracts.							
ORANGE JUICE (FROZEN CONCENTRATED)							
Sept	57.80	58.95	57.75	58.25	+ .75	66.70	36.50
Nov	56.15	56.95	56.05	56.45	+ .65	66.75	37.10
Jan'72	53.20	54.20	53.20	53.85	+ .95	64.05	45.00
Mar	53.60	54.15	53.40	53.75b	+ .85	63.00	46.30
May	53.60	54.20	53.45	53.85b	+ .95	62.95	46.65
Sales: 950 contracts.							
COTTON							
Oct	30.64	30.82	30.48	30.56	+ .03	33.75	24.00
Dec	31.26	31.43	31.06	31.16-.19	− .04to.01	34.40	25.56
Mar'72	32.07	32.20	31.85	31.93	− .05	35.10	28.10
May	32.33	32.40	32.20	32.20b	− .10	35.40	28.11
July	32.05	32.33	32.00	32.09b	− .01	35.50	27.74
Oct	30.00	30.25	30.00	30.08	+ .08	31.60	28.30
Dec	30.01	30.10	29.70	29.95b	− .05	30.94	29.00
PLATINUM							
Oct	114.50	115.30	114.40	114.40	+ .40	169.00	96.00
Jan72	116.00	117.00	115.80	116.10	+ .60	155.00	97.60
Apr	117.20	118.00	117.20	117.40	+ .40	131.50	103.00
July	118.50	118.50	118.20	118.20	+ .70	121.70	105.00
Oct	120.00	120.00	119.10	119.10	+ .10	123.00	112.20
Sales: 1,081 contracts.							
POTATOES (MAINE CONTRACT)							
Nov	2.80	2.80	2.80	2.80	+ .05	2.85	2.52
Mar'72	3.10	3.14	3.10	3.13	+ .07	3.17	2.90
Apr	3.26	3.30	3.26	3.30	+ .05	3.36	3.13
May	3.84	3.87	3.83	3.86	+ .03	3.98	3.64
Sales: 163 contracts.							

a-Asked. b-Bid. n-Nominal.

FIGURE 1. Price quotations for some of the more popular commodities as they appear daily in *The Wall Street Journal.*

For example, November soybeans are shown as closing at 334–334⅜. That means that at the closing bell two trades were taking place simultaneously: one was for soybeans at $3.34 per bushel and the other at $3.34⅜ per bushel.

Sometimes a small *b* or *a* will appear after a closing price. If a quotation has a *b* after it that means somebody wanted to buy or was bidding at that price. If an *a* appears after a quotation, that is what a seller was asking for that commodity at the close. Figure 1 shows that July oats in Winnipeg were being bid for at 76⅛ cents per bushel at the close.

Also appearing in the *Journal* and the *Times* is a table headed "Cash Prices," which is illustrated in Figure 2. These are the prices that were actually being paid to obtain physical delivery of the goods listed. Of course, when a contract is ready to expire, the futures price for that contract should approach the cash price. Thus the last days of trading before a contract expires can produce some wild price swings in that contract. Since July 21, 1971, was the last day of trading for the grains on the Chicago Board of Trade, note what happened to the July prices. July corn, for example, closed down more than 7 cents per bushel. You might have noticed in Figure 1 that July corn went off the board at about $1.40 per bushel while cash corn traded that same day in Chicago at $1.47¾. This curious discrepancy will be discussed when the fundamental supply-and-demand situation is analyzed in a later chapter.

What if you want to know prices during the day? The simplest way to get them is to call your broker and he will give them to you. Most brokerage houses that do a substantial business in commodities can get the prices of the major commodities on their desk-top quoting machines used to quote stock prices. Some of the larger houses have board rooms where the prices are posted on the more popular contracts. (You are probably better off not sitting in a board room and watching the prices of the commodities you are interested in. Unless you have a will of iron, it will just cause you to make foolish trades.*) Getting the prices you are interested in once or twice a day is more than enough.

* Given enough time it will also probably cause you to become addicted to a wide range of antacids and a frequent visitor to physicians who practice internal medicine.

Cash Prices

Wednesday, July 21, 1971
(Quotations as of 4 p.m. Eastern time)

	Wed.	Tues.	Yr. Ago
FOODS			
Flour, hard winter NY cwt	n$6.85	$6.85	$6.55
Coffee, Santos 4s NY lb	a.43	.43	.54¼
Cocoa, Accra NY lb	n.28¼	.28⅜	.33¼
Sugar, Refined NY lb	.1270	.1270	.1205
Sugar, Raw NY lb	.0858	.0857	.0814
Butter, Fresh A-92 sc NY lb	.68½-¾	.68¾	.70¾
Eggs, Lge white, Chgo., doz	.33	.31½	.41
Broilers, Dressed "A" NY lb	.31	.31½	.26¾
Pork Bellies, 10-12 lbs., Chgo., lb	.21½	.22½	.40
Hogs, Omaha avg cwt	19.10	19.55	24.45
Steers, Chicago choice avg cwt	33.15	32.85	31.00
Pepper, black NY lb	a.46	.46	.62
GRAINS AND FEEDS			
Wheat, No. 2 ord hard KC bu	1.51¼	1.51⅝	1.36½
Corn, No. 2 yel Chicago bu	1.47¾	1.52	1.37
Oats, No. 1 wh. hvy, Chgo., bu	n.70	.71¼	.66½
Rye, No. 2 Minneapolis bu	.98	1.00	1.11
Barley, top qlty., Mpls., bu	1.35	1.35	1.20
Soybeans, No. 1 yel Chicago bu	n3.46¼	3.44¼	2.95¾
Flaxseed, Minneapolis bu	n2.66	2.66	2.85
Bran, Buffalo ton	44.00	44.00	40.00
Linseed Meal, Minneapolis ton	n63.50	63.50	65.00
Cottonseed Meal, Memphis ton	n76.00	75.50	79.00
Soybean Meal, Decatur, Ill. ton	n84.00	84.00	81.50
FATS AND OILS			
Cottonseed Oil, crd Miss Vly lb	a.16¾	.16¾	.14
Corn Oil, crude Chicago lb	a.19¼	.19¼	.15
Soybean Oil, crd Decatur, Ill. lb	n.1487	.1490	.1199
Peanut Oil, crd Southeast lb	.18½	.18¾	.15½
Coconut Oil, crd Pac Cst lb	a.13¾	.13¾	.16¼
Lard, Chicago lb	n.1200	.1200	.1125
Tallow, bleachable, NY lb	b.07¼	.07¼	.08¼
Linseed Oil, raw NY lb	a.1021	.1021	.1230
TEXTILES AND FIBERS			
Cotton, 1 1-16 in. mid Memphis lb.	.2725	.2725	.2625
Print Cloth, 64x60 38½ in. NY yd	.17	.17	.16¼
Print Cloth, 78x78 48-in. NY yd	.28	.28	.24¼
Sheetings, 56x60 40-in.NYyd	.22¾	.22¾	.21½
Burlap, 10 oz. 40 in. NY yd	n.1840	.1855	.1495
Wool, fine staple terr. Bstn, lb	.58	.58	.99
Rayon, Satin Acetate NY Yyd	.24½	.24½	.24
METALS			
Steel Scrap, 1 hvy melt Cng. ton	30.50	30.50	42.50
Copper, per lb	.52¾-.53	.52¾-.53	.60-¼
Copper Scrap, No. 2 wire NY lb	n.37	.37½	.47½
Lead, NY lb	.14-.14½	.14-.14½	.15½
Zinc, per lb	.16	.16	.15½
Tin, NY lb	1.66½	1.66½	1.65¼
Aluminum, ingot, NY lb	.29	.29	.29
Quicksilver, NY 76 lb flask	n300.00	300.00	410.00
Silver, (H&H) NY oz.	1.557	1.546	1.725
MISCELLANEOUS			
Rubber, smoked sheets NY lb	n.17	.16⅝	.20
Hides, light native cows Chgo lb	n.15	.15	.14½
Gasoline, 92 oct. mid-Cont. gal	.13¼	.13¼	.13¼
Fuel Oil, No. 2 mid-Cont. gal	.09¾	.09¾	.09½

a-Asked. b-Bid. n-Nominal.

FIGURE 2. Cash prices for the more important agricultural and industrial commodities as they appear daily in *The Wall Street Journal.*

Volume and Open Interest

Two terms that produce some confusion in the minds of new traders are *volume* and *open interest.* In order to understand these terms it is necessary to realize that there must be a seller for every buyer of a futures contract. Whether one is buying oats from a cash grain dealer or on the futures market, the oats must be bought from a seller.

Let us consider what happens when a trader decides to take a position in May oats which opens for trading in May of the year preceding the harvest. That is, May 1972 oats start trading in May 1971. Imagine that Trader Horse offers to buy one contract–5,000 bushels–at 70 cents from Trader Feeder on the first day of trading in the May oats contract. The transaction is carried out on the Chicago Board of Trade by their respective floor brokers and the price at which the transaction took place is posted on the board. Toward the end of the session Trader Horse decides he does not want to own any oats overnight, so he offers to sell his oats at 70½ cents but finds no buyers. He lowers his price until Trader Feeder is induced into buying back the contract at 69¼ cents per bushel. The offsetting trade is carried out. (Keep in mind that it would be very unusual to have only 10,000 bushels traded during a day but it does happen, especially when trading just begins in a contract.)

After the first trade is made, the *open interest* in May oats stands at 5,000 bushels since the open interest reflects only *one side* of all positions held. But then Trader Horse closes out his position at the close by selling it back to Trader Feeder. At the end of the day both Trader Feeder and Trader Horse have "offset" their positions. At this stage of trading nobody is due to receive or deliver any oats when the May oats contract expires in a year. That is, at the close of business on this day open interest is zero in the May oats contract. However, note that the *volume* of trading is 10,000 bushels, which represents the amount of oats that changed hands during the session. If Trader Horse had elected to keep his oats overnight, the volume of trading would have been 5,000 bushels and the open interest would have been 5,000 bushels. This subject will be discussed again in Chapter 10, which covers the use of open interest and volume as technical trading aids.

Figure 3 is a tabulation of the volume and open interest for a

Volume and Open Interest

The Commodity Exchange Authority reported grain futures trading on the Chicago Board of Trade as of the close of business Tuesday, July 20, 1971 (in thousands of bushels):

	July	Sept.	Dec.	Mar'72	May	Total
Wheat	1,425	3,435	3,875	1,300	615	10,650
Corn	7,530	9,820	39,120	7,045	2,765	66,280
Oats	370	500	540	75	85	1,570

Soybeans: July, 3,675; August, 20,035; September, 8,-560; November, 43,580; January, 7,775; March, 5,470; May, 3,870; Total, 92,965.

Soybean oil trading totaled 7,489; soybean meal trading totaled 2,373.

Open Interest (in thousands of bushels):

	Wheat	Corn	Oats	Soybeans	r-Meal	s-Oil
July	1,465	9,055	515	3,110	513	656
August	....	....	....	47,195	5,753	7,707
September	29,550	36,980	3,415	32,410	3,567	4,740
October	....	....	....	....	2,870	3,629
November	....	....	....	117,425	515	1,415
December	38,990	121,015	4,045	....	5,351	4,247
January'72	....	....	....	37,170	3,197	2,962
March	14,515	47,525	900	34,690	1,846	3,228
May	6,580	29,395	305	25,560	1,328	2,254
Total	91,100	243,970	9,180	297,560	24,940	30,838

r-In hundreds of tons. s-In tank cars of 60,000 pounds.

Open contracts for July 20 and changes from Monday: **Frozen Pork Bellies** (36,000 pounds each), July 692, Aug. 8,045, Feb. 5,116, March 1,253, May 426, July 728, Aug. 682. Total 16,942, off 380. **Cattle** (40,000 pounds each), Aug. 4,-659, Oct. 3,014, Dec. 2,128, Feb. 1,287, April 307. Total 11,-395, up 124. **Fresh Eggs** (600 cases each), July 108, Aug. 197, Sept. 2,058, Oct. 70, Nov. 404, Dec. 87. Total 2,924, off 106. **Maine Potatoes** (50,000 pounds each), Nov. 172, March 363, April 302, May 1,811. Total 2,648, up 14. **World Sugar No. 11** (112,000 pounds each), Sept. 1,613, Oct. 2,108, Jan. 140, March 2,846, May 1,071, July 627, Sept. 220, Oct. 217. Total 8,842, off 177. **Cocoa** (30,000 pounds each), July 37, Sept. 1,938, Dec. 3,163, March 2,774, May 1,852, July 1,707, Sepy. 221. Total 11,692, up 65. **Copper** (25,000 pounds each), July 84, Sept. 2,574, Oct. 309, Dec. 2,223, Jan. 675, March 1,419, May 820, July 213. **Total** 8,314 off 90. **Silver** (10,000 troy ounces each), July 182, Aug. 7, Sept. 7,202, Dec. 6,801, Jan. 3,990, March 6,627, May 4,828, July 4,598, Sept. 2,140. Total 36,375 off 9. **Orange Juice** (15,000 pounds each), July 179, Sept. 2,733, Nov. 1,580, Jan. 1,276, March 891, May 493, July 42, Sept. 25, Nov. 25. Total 7,244, up 98. **Cotton** (500-pound bale), Oct. 194,200, Dec. 808,500, March 246,500, May 67,900, July 63,100, Oct. 56,000, Dec. 25,700. Total 1,461,900, off 17,700.

FIGURE 3. Tabulation of the volume of trading, open interest and changes in open interest for some of the more widely traded commodities as appears in *The Wall Street Journal.* These data are normally one day behind the price quotation data, that is, not until the July 22 edition of the paper will open interest data for July 20 appear.

number of different commodities. It usually runs one day behind the price data. On July 20, 1971, the volume of trading in May oats was 85,000 bushels, which is equivalent to 17 contracts (85,-000/5,000) changing hands. The open interest in May oats on July 20, 1971 oats was 305,000 bushels which is equivalent to 61 contracts of 5,000 bushels each.

Note that as a contract comes closer to its maturity date the open interest generally begins to fall. This is caused by the fact that most speculators have no interest in taking delivery or making delivery. So they begin to make offsetting trades—that is, the longs begin to sell their contracts to the shorts so that both types of speculators can remove themselves from the delivery process. Longs who do not sell their contracts before the last day of trading must be prepared to pay for and accept delivery of their contracts. Shorts who do not buy in to offset their earlier sales must be prepared to deliver the actual commodity to an authorized warehouse. As mentioned earlier, we have no intention of ever becoming involved in making or taking delivery. Indeed, we will sleep better if we never have any positions in a contract during the entire month in which that contract expires.

CHAPTER **5**

How to Open a Trading Account

□

Now that you have explored the subjects of why you should consider trading commodities, how and why commodity markets evolved, and which commodities are traded, you may have decided that you would like to try trading for yourself. In these next two chapters we shall explore the mechanics of trading—that is, What are the things you must do to open an account and carry out a trade?

Opening a Commodities Account

If you already have a securities account with a reasonably good-sized brokerage house, opening a commodities account will entail only signing a couple of additional forms. If you do not have a securities account, opening a commodities account will require seeking out a broker who handles such accounts. All the major stock-brokerage houses will also be glad to service your commodities account. Furthermore, there are a number of brokerage firms in the larger cities that do nothing but commodities trading. Generally, both the larger stock-exchange member firms and the commodity brokerage firms are members of the Chicago Board of Trade and other major commodity exchanges.

You will find that not all brokerage houses give the same quality service—some have well-managed commodity divisions while others seem to treat commodity trading as an unimportant sideline. It is up to you to determine if you are getting good service. By that I mean efficient execution of orders, timely receipt of accurate confirmations, and prompt, complete monthly statements. You want to devote your time and energy to commodity trading and not to correcting errors in your account. Of course, mistakes can and do happen but you should be able to get them fixed by a single phone call to your broker. If you find that it is taking you more than that, then you should have a different broker. The only certain way to determine that you are getting good service from a broker is to try several. You should not hesitate to move your account if you believe that your account is not being serviced at a high level of quality. As a commodity trader you must believe that action in the marketplace speaks louder than irate phone calls and letters. A broker will receive the message loud and clear that he has not performed up to your expectations if you close your account and take it elsewhere. Remember, it is your money that pays for the operation of his whole business and there is no need for you to settle for less than first-rate service.

Once you have selected a brokerage house, you should then become acquainted with an account executive or broker who is familiar with commodity transactions. It would be wise to have a brief chat with him while you explain your trading methods and objectives to him. If at that time he does not volunteer his philosophy about commodity trading, you might ask him his views; if your philosophies are very far apart, you might consider using a different account executive.

Margin Requirements

Once you have opened your account, you will be expected to place in it a margin deposit against which you may begin to trade. Few firms will consider letting you place on deposit less than $1,000. In my opinion you would be wise not to consider trading until you can put down a deposit of at least $3,000. The reasons for this will be more fully developed later in the book, but briefly they are: Trading in commodity markets is a high-risk activity fraught with opportunities to lose money; therefore it is preferable to take more than one position at a time. The only sensible way to do this is to have on deposit more than the minimum amount required.

The amount of margin required to hold a position depends on the commodity to be traded. It is usually, however, no more than 10 percent of the value of the contract. For example, if corn is selling for $1.50 a bushel, then a 5,000-bushel contract has a value of $7,500. Most brokers would require that you deposit no more than $500 per contract, which is a margin of 6.67 percent. How much margin is actually required on each position is set by the brokerage house. However, the exchanges themselves will set a minimum margin for each commodity traded on that exchange; brokerage houses cannot set a margin level below the exchange limit. For example, a brokerage house might ask $600 for a live-hog contract while the exchange has a required margin of at least $400. No two brokerage houses have the same margin requirements on all commodities. The commodities manager in each house makes a judgment on the risk inherent in each commodity and sets the margin accordingly. Furthermore, depending on the volatility of a commodity, margin requirements may be changed. Inactive commodities might have their margins lowered, while more active ones might have theirs increased. Some typical margins as required by one brokerage house are given in Table 1.

There is another reason why you should deposit more than the minimum margin required to hold a given position: margin calls—that is, a call for additional funds. Most commodity houses have a rule that says, Once a position has moved against you so that 25 percent of your margin has been impaired, you must restore your account to full margin. Suppose you buy a contract for March copper at 51 cents per pound and the broker asks you to deposit $1,000 in margin on the 25,000 pound contract. If copper drops one cent to 50 cents per pound you would be holding a paper loss of $250 and your margin would have been impaired by 25 percent. Thus you would receive a margin call for $250 if you had no other funds in your account. However, if you had originally deposited $1500 with your broker and held no other positions, you would not be bothered by a margin call.

Margin calls are no fun. They frequently come at a time when you have no excess funds in your checking account, or when you are planning to go on vacation or do something else that absorbs excess funds. Therefore I strongly recommend that if you deposit $3,000 in your account, do not trade commodities that require more than $2,200 in margin. That cushion will give you more than $800 of peace of mind. And you will be surprised how much this slack in your account will improve your trading decisions. Sure, you can learn to live with your back to the wall, but I believe there are enough hazards in trading commodities without adding the one of perpetually sweaty palms.

One other word of caution which for most people will probably be superfluous: Trade only with those funds you can afford to lose. That is, commodity trading is not investing for income; there is no assurance that even one of the next three trades you make is going to be profitable. So don't use funds that you need to meet your daily living expenses. Use risk capital only—funds that you have set aside over and above what is required for necessities and that you can afford to lose. Don't use funds that will cause you to reduce your standard of living if you lose them. And don't use borrowed money. There is nothing that is more liable to impair your judgment than the thought in the back of your mind that if this position doesn't work out that you will be saddled with a $3,000 debt that will take you two years to pay off out of your regular income.

Segregation of Margin Funds. Commodities are divided into two categories by law in the United States—regulated and unregulated. Regulated commodities are, for all intents and purposes, most of the foodstuffs traded on the Chicago Board of Trade and the Chicago Mercantile Exchange. (They are marked with a star in Table 1 in Chapter 4.) Margin funds for these commodities must be segregated from the other funds the brokerage house might be holding. They cannot be put into the operating funds of the brokerage house as can be done with margin money put up by customers on stocks and bonds. Such funds may be used by the broker to pay the expenses of running his business such as rent, salaries and the like. As long as the brokerage house meets the ratio of liabilities to assets required by the Securities and Exchange Commission, it may use its customers' "free credit balances" in any way it sees fit. The broker is still legally liable for the balance, but not all of the actual funds carried as free credit balances in its customers' accounts will necessarily be available on any given day.

Not so with funds deposited for margin against positions in regulated commodities. Those funds can only be used to pay for your commissions and for covering whatever losses you might sustain. In the event of a brokerage-house failure, security margin funds may be lost, but commodity funds cannot be. The Commodity Exchange Authority requires that the broker have those funds on hand for as long as they are in the broker's custody. Sometimes traders who deal in both commodities and securities transfer all funds not in actual use to their regulated commodities account, thereby gaining the security provided by the Commodities Exchange Act.

Your Broker's Role

People do have different expectations of their brokers. Some people plan to depend on them for all their trading advice; at the other extreme, there are those who want them to fill their orders and nothing else. Still others want their brokers to hold their hands once they have taken a position and reassure them that they have made the right move. You will have no difficulty in finding a broker to fill whatever role you wish to assign him. Remember, he needs your business to make a living.

In my opinion it is not wise to expect too much of your broker. You should not expect him to produce a string of winning recommendations that will make you a millionaire in ninety days. If he were able to do that, he would not be your broker; he would be sunning himself on a yacht in the Caribbean with a ship-to-shore telephone giving buy and sell orders to *his* broker. However, if you have sold cotton short and his firm receives a wire during the day that the largest swarm of boll weevils ever seen by man or beast is now munching its way through the cotton belt, it is not unreasonable to expect a good broker to at least try to phone you and let you know this news. He does have a commodity wire in his office where he receives this kind of news, and you don't have one in your office or home, so it would be a help to get this kind of information without having to wait to read it in the paper the next day.*

But what about asking your broker whether or not you should go long soybeans? Well, there is certainly no harm in asking and listening to his answer. Frequently, an honest broker will simply say he has no opinion on a given position.† Another broker might say that he will ask his commodity research department for an opinion on soybeans. Such an act could be extremely helpful, and you should certainly try to get all the opinions you can before taking a position. But remember, commodity brokers are very likely to have customers on both sides of a position. Three minutes after you decide to go long soybeans, another customer might call up and say he wants to go short soybeans. You should keep in mind, however, that the only purpose of a brokerage house is to place orders (hopefully profitable ones) for its customers. Thus such houses will always be buying *and* selling for their customers. Your broker gets the same fraction of the $30 commission for your trade whether you go long or short 5,000 bushels of soybeans, and whether your trade shows a $500 profit or a $500 loss. Of course he wants you to make a profit, because then you will trade more with him, but it is not necessary for you to show a profit for him to earn his commission.

Discretionary Accounts. Sometimes new traders feel so awed by what they don't know about commodities trading that they will seek out a brokerage house that accepts discretionary accounts. In this kind of account the customer signs a release that gives his broker a free hand. It is a kind of power of attorney that gives the broker the right to buy and sell on behalf of the customer *with* or *without* the customer's knowledge or approval.

The Chicago Board of Trade has set up some rules to protect customers who use discretionary accounts. Commodities traded on the Chicago Board of Trade by brokers for their discretionary accounts must be personally supervised by a partner in the brokerage house. Though a discretionary-account customer does not make

* Whether you would actually act on this kind of news is another matter that will be taken up in other chapters. Even if the broker phoned you immediately, in many cases the prices would already have reflected the news.

† Any broker who has an opinion on every position is probably not worth having.

trading decisions, he does receive confirmations, purchase and sales slips, and monthly statements as if he were making his own trades. Should you open a discretionary account? In my opinion the answer to that question should be No. It is expecting a tremendous amount of a broker, and if he makes a couple of bad trades, it is far too easy for you to simply say that he doesn't know what he is doing and close the account.

Moreover, the chances of your learning very much if you have a discretionary account are almost nil. The broker has all the responsibility and you have none. You don't have to read and you don't have to think—like magic the broker will take care of everything. I write on this subject from experience. One time I encountered a broker who believed he had an excellent system for trading commodities. Indeed, in a period of generally rising prices, it worked pretty well and his track record was quite impressive. He was convinced, and I must confess that I was too, that his system was bound to produce profits. He would not, of course, divulge any but the most vague details of how his system worked. I opened a discretionary account and started to make plans on what I was going to do with the profits. His confidence was almost overwhelming, for he had just completed a string of three very profitable months. He told me that because he had a number of clients with discretionary accounts and because his system generally produced profits, he did not use stop-loss orders to take his clients out of positions that were going against them. It seemed reasonable to me at the time—though it was really insane. I went long two copper contracts and they moved against me by 5 cents per pound ($1,250 per contract) in one case and 3 cents per pound ($750 per contract) in the other. These losses nearly wiped me out in my first two trades. Each of those positions should have had sell or stop-loss orders entered no more than 2 cents per pound below where I got into them. Within a few weeks I began to enter stop-loss orders on every position I had with him and I soon realized that I didn't need a discretionary account. Neither do you.

Women Commodity Traders

The above might seem like a peculiar title for a section heading but I am afraid it is a necessary one. It has been reported in the financial press that some brokerage houses refuse to open a commodities-trading account for a woman unless her husband agrees to be responsible for her losses. Such houses have argued that women are too emotional to trade commodities and that the brokers have suffered losses because women clients have refused to cover losses that accrued in their accounts.

No doubt some women commodity traders have caused brokerage houses to suffer losses, but that fact in no way justifies refusing to open an account for a woman commodity trader. If the brokerage house requires a margin deposit before trading commences and then automatically sells out its clients if their positions deteriorate there is no reason for a brokerage house to suffer any losses, regardless of the sex of its clients. To refuse to open a trading account for a woman in my opinion is unfair, ridiculous and possibly illegal.

It is probably true that some women should not trade commodities, just as some men should not trade them; some people are simply temperamentally not suited to such activity. In my observations, the emotional qualifications for taking risks are not exclusive to either sex. The only test that a brokerage house should apply to its clients is whether or not the client has deposited sufficient funds to open an account, and whether the client has signed the proper forms for opening such an account. To require more is to discriminate on grounds that are patently irrelevant. Furthermore, to refuse to open an account for a financially responsible woman might well be in violation of many civil rights acts that have been passed by a number of states in recent years; these laws forbid discrimination on the basis of race, national origin, or sex. Brokerage houses are supposed to serve the public in the same way a restaurant serves the public. No restaurant today can legally apply artificial and irrelevant criteria to potential customers who expect to be served upon entering. And so it would seem that no brokerage house can legally apply similar criteria based on sex to its potential commodity traders.

In the event that any female reader of this book encounters such discrimination at a brokerage house she should do three things: first, locate a brokerage house that will accept her as a client (and there are many), and then inform the manager of the branch that refused her of the name of the brokerage house where she will be doing her trading in the future; and then, just for fun, tell the branch manager that she is going to file a discrimination complaint with the state attorney general. If enough women follow these three steps, whether they actually file a complaint or not, discrimination based on sex will soon come to an end insofar as commodity trading goes.

CHAPTER **6**

Completing a Trade

□

You are now just about at the point where you would like to begin trading. If you have had some experience in trading stocks, you will not find very much in this chapter new to you. However, it may serve as a good review, since commodity traders use many more different types of orders than do stock traders. Knowing which order to use when, will come only with experience, but at least for now you should know which orders are available to you. But before we tackle the subject of orders, we should consider the meaning of the words "long" and "short," which I have already used a number of times in the preceding chapters. While every stock trader knows what it means to be long—that is to own stock in a company—not one in ten can accurately explain the meaning of being short. Since the short side of the market is at least as important as the long side, if not more so, it is this subject that we will take up first.

He Who Sells What Isn't His'n Must Buy It Back or Go to Prison

This verse represents most persons' total understanding of a short sale. But its content is as wobbly as its grammar. A short seller believes the price of the thing he is trading is going to fall, while a trader who goes long or buys believes the price of his trading vehicle is going to rise. Just so your trading will not be inhibited, I will let you in on the well-established fact that short sellers do not go to prison any more often than do longs.

More than 95 percent of the people who invest in the stock market are long whenever they are in the market. That is, they believe stock prices are going to rise and so they buy shares of the companies that they believe will rise the most. A few of the more adventuresome dare to take up short positions from time to time. A short seller of a stock is one who believes that the price of that stock is going to fall rather than rise. If the XYZ Company's shares are selling at 50 but you believe that they should be selling for 35, then you may sell shares you don't own (but which your broker will borrow for you) at 50 with the hope that at some time in the future you will be able to return the borrowed shares with stock you bought at some lower price, say 35. The only way your broker can borrow those shares for you to sell is to give the lender of those shares the market value of those shares in cash (supplied by you) for the length of time you are borrowing them. During the interval you have the shares borrowed, you must continue to pay any dividends the company may declare to the original owner of the stock from whom you have borrowed your shares. The borrowed stock comes from the portfolio of those people who have margin accounts at their brokers. When you open a margin account you sign a form that says you don't mind if your stock is loaned out to short sellers. You will never know, of course, whether any stock you own is out on loan or not unless you go to New York every day and ask to see your certificates, which are supposedly in your broker's vaults. Brokers like to lend out stock for short sales because they can turn idle stock certificates into investable cash by such a loan.

Now let us consider the analogous situation in the commodities market. If you believe that the price of plywood will rise between now and next July you are said to be "bullish" on plywood and may buy a contract for July plywood—you are then "long" plywood. If it does go up you may then sell out at a profit—or if you are in the construction business you may elect to take delivery of the plywood when the contract expires.

In the event that you believe plywood prices will fall (and thus are a bear on plywood) between now and next July, you may decide to sell a July plywood contract. You are then "short" plywood. If between now and the time the contract expires the price falls, you may "cover" your short sale by buying a cheaper plywood contract to offset your short position. If the price does fall once you have shorted it, you may offset at a profit; if you fail to offset by the time the contract expires, you must be prepared to make delivery of what the contract requires. Note how much simpler an operation short selling is in the commodities market than in the stock market.

Short selling over the years has been viewed as an inherently evil activity and has been the object of many legislative attacks. The attacks have been mostly made by people who believe that it artificially holds down prices; critics of short selling never want to recognize that, during times of inflation, short selling may inhibit higher prices for producers of a commodity, but at the same time it also keeps prices lower for consumers of that commodity.

A short sale temporarily increases the supply of a commodity, but as has been pointed out earlier, for every seller there must be a buyer. If demand cannot absorb the volume of selling, prices recede; but if buying power is sufficient to absorb the volume of selling, prices will advance, and the shorts will be forced to buy back their contracts at a higher price, thus contributing more fuel to the advancing prices. At any rate, speculators who are short must at some time offset their position by means of a purchase before the contract expires. A market which is falling in which heavy short sales have been made has had its fall cushioned in advance, since all speculative short sellers are buyers at some time in the future. As prices begin to fall, the buying of short sellers as they take their profits tends to offset the panicky selling of the longs who bought at higher prices.

Some, but not all, of the studies done on commodity traders have found that, in general, the speculative public is long rather than short. There are probably good psychological reasons for this optimistic outlook with regard to prices. Unfortunately, such an outlook causes these speculators to lose more money than they make. The Commodity Exchange Authority in the survey cited in Chapter 1 notes: "The study confirms the commonly held impressions that the amateur speculator is more likely to be long than short in the futures market. . . . Short positions of speculators tended to show profits more frequently than long positions."

Since the market does not necessarily have an upward bias, it is thus foolish to bias trading decisions in the long direction. Economic forces can cause declining prices as well as rising prices. Moreover, it has been well established that profits on short positions tend to accumulate faster than profits on long positions. This occurs because the time required for prices to fall is usually shorter than the time required to build them up. Since it is just as easy to sell short as to buy long, prudent speculators* always give careful consideration to those commodities they believe are overpriced.

Orders—Instructing Your Broker

Since I hope that in the previous chapter I dissuaded you from opening a discretionary account, the only way left for you to get into the commodity market is by placing your own orders. A large number of different orders are available to you, but I will not try to cover all of them. I will explain the orders that are used most of the time by most commodity traders.

It is extremely important that you place your orders with care; therefore it will pay you to learn well the terminology of the more common orders. Misphrasing could cause you to be taken into or out of a position when you didn't want to be.

Quantity Limits. Most orders for commodities are placed in terms of contracts. If you say you wish to "buy 5 September soybean meal" that means you wish to go long 5 contracts of 100 tons each of soybean meal. In the case of the grains, however, orders are placed in terms of 1,000's of bushels. Since a standard contract is for 5,000 bushels, an order to sell one contract of oats would be "sell 5 May oats." That is an order to sell 5,000 bushels of May oats, which is a standard contract.

* Actually the short seller should be viewed as some sort of hero during inflationary times, as his activity does initially have a tendency to temper rising prices. Perhaps the President should consider having his Council of Economic Advisers decorate certain groups of bears with medals. The citation could read: "The Group Bear Award is hereby presented by the People of the United States to all those speculators who sold March copper short. Their valor in the face of determined and prolonged activity on the part of the copper bulls did not go unnoticed by the People, who will pay less for their electrical wire and copper bracelets because of the copper bears' efforts. In a time of generally rising prices they were among the few who stood their ground on the ramparts of price stability."

Time Limits. Many commodity houses treat all commodity orders, unless otherwise specified, as *day orders.* That means that at the end of the trading day the order, if not filled, automatically expires without your doing anything to kill it. An order might not be filled, for example, if the market never traded at the price specified in the order. Commodity traders use day orders a lot because between today's close and tomorrow's opening lots of things can happen which might cause them to revise their judgment of their position.

Open orders or good till cancelled (usually called GTC) are orders which will remain in effect until filled, killed, or changed by you in some way. Some brokers will send you a notice the day after you place an open order giving you the details on the order that you have left open.

You can also give orders to be filled at certain times. One of the most common is an order to buy or sell "on the open" or "on the close." An "on the open" order could instruct your broker to buy, for example, 40,000 pounds of February live cattle as the bell rings to begin trading, no matter what price might be asked for it. With an "on the close" order he would do the same thing except that this order would be filled in the last thirty seconds or so before the bell rings to announce the end of trading. As discussed in the next section, such orders carry more risk than limit or market orders because no one knows at what price trading will open or close.

Price Limits. The most common type of order given is the *market order.* It is an order with no restrictions on it; it is to be executed as soon as received and at the best price available when it hits the trading pit. That means, if you are buying you will pay what the lowest seller is asking, and if you are selling you will get what the highest buyer is bidding. The order is phrased, for example, "Buy 1 February hogs at the market."

The next most common order is a price-limit order, which has several variations. It generally is used to specify a *maximum* buying price or a *minimum* selling price, though it does not have to work that way. Consider the hog example again. "Buy 1 February hogs $22.65 limit" means buy a hog contract only if the price is 22.65 cents *or less.* If it were a sell order it would mean to sell a hog contract at 22.65 cents *or more*. It can only be executed at the *limit price or better*.

Stop-loss, or simply, *stop* orders are a variant of the limit order. They are usually placed above or below the current market. Suppose hogs are trading at 23.25 cents and you have a nice profit at that price. You are willing to hold your position in the hope that the market will move higher. However, in case your judgment is wrong and the market starts to fall, you would like to get out with most of your profit. Thus you place the following order: "Sell 1 February hogs 22.90 stop open." If the market falls to 22.90, your order will become a market order and the floor broker will get as much as he can for you—but it could be below your stop price if the market is falling rapidly. The "open" means the order will remain in effect until filled or unless canceled by you.

It is also possible to use stop orders to establish a long position at a higher price, or a short position at a lower price than the prevailing market price. Suppose that you would like to buy another February hog contract if the market rises to 23.45 cents because you believe that the market would be showing good strength if it was able to reach that price. You could then place a *buy stop* order to add another contract. Thus with hogs now trading at 23.25 cents you would give a buy stop order as follows: "Buy 1 February hogs 23.45 stop." If hogs trade up to 23.45 cents, then your order will become a market order to buy at the best possible price.

Conversely, *sell stop* orders are always written at a price lower than the market price prevailing at the time the order is written. If you believe it would be a bearish sign if hogs traded down to 22.90 cents and you would like to offset your one long position and also go short one contract, then you would give the following order: "Sell 2 February hogs 22.90 stop." As soon as the market traded at 22.90 cents, your floor broker would then sell two contracts for you at the market. One contract would close out your long position and one contract would be a new short position.

If you were not willing to accept a price below 22.90 cents, you could place a *stop-limit* order: "Sell 2 February hogs 22.90 stop limit open." This order cannot be executed at any price below 22.90 cents; therefore if the floor broker cannot get that price or better, once there has been a trade at 22.90 cents your order would go unfilled until the broker could fill it at your limit price; of course, he might not ever be able to fill it at that price if the market continued to fall. You are probably well off to avoid stop-limit orders as the market could move right by your limit leaving you with your contract but little or no profit.

Another order that is sometimes useful is the *on-close stop* order. Suppose you expect hogs to jump around a lot today and you believe they might even dip below 22.90 cents, but you also feel strongly that they will recover to some price above 22.90 cents before the close. You may enter an order that says to the floor broker to take you out only if February hogs look as if they are going to close below 22.90 cents. The order would be written as: "Sell 1 February hogs 22.90 on-close stop." Hogs can sell down below your limit price now, say to 22.80 cents, but you would still hold your position if they recovered before the close to some price *above* 22.90 cents. The risk in this type of order should be obvious—hogs could sell down to 22.50 cents or lower and not recover, and thus you would be taken out at a price far below the price at which you hoped to be out of the market. There is no accurate way to judge at which price you will actually be sold out, and thus there is no way to accurately judge your actual loss or profit.

The last order we will consider is a *one-cancels-the-other,* or OCO, order. This is another contingency order. Say that hogs are trading at 23.25 cents and you are still holding one contract. You have decided that if hogs go up to 23.45 cents this would be a bullish sign, and you would then like to buy another contract, while if hogs drop to 22.90 cents you would sell your one contract and take your profit. You don't care which happens—that is, whether you add to your position or sell out. You can place the following order: "Buy 1 February hogs 23.45 stop or sell 1 February hogs 22.90 stop OCO." If hogs rise to 23.45 cents the broker will buy another contract at the market and cancel the stop loss at 22.90 cents. If hogs fall to 22.90 cents the broker will sell out the one contract you already hold and cancel the order to buy another contract at 23.45 cents.

These are but a few of the orders that can be given to your broker but I believe they cover all of the ones that you are likely to need in your first few years of trading. The most important thing is for you to be certain that you understand exactly what the orders that you give your broker mean.

What Happens to Your Order

Once you have placed an order with your broker, the staff of your brokerage house takes over. One thing is certain: If it is a market order it will be executed within a few minutes of the time you hang up the phone to give the order.

Suppose you are sitting in your office in Atlanta and you decide to buy one contract of February hogs at the market. The order is sent by private-wire teletype to the wire room of your brokerage house; if your firm's main office is in New York it might clear through their wire room, or if a larger firm, through their computer, where it is routed to an office of your firm at the Chicago Mercantile Exchange. It is then telephoned down to a clerk sitting on the edge of the hogs trading pit, where he signals to his broker to buy a February hogs contract at the market. If trading is active, the pit can be noisy and hand signals will be used to complete the trade. A palm turned out means a broker is selling; turned in, he is buying. Your firm's broker, upon receipt of your order, spots the broker who is offering to sell with the lowest selling price. The buyers and sellers nod at each other, make a note of the price and time of the transaction, and each of them signals back to their respective clerks that a trade has taken place.

The Mercantile Exchange employs pit reporters who have a vantage point from where they can see every part of the pit. It is their job to record immediately any price change of 0.025 cents above or below the last price. Suppose you bought your hogs at 22.65 cents and the last reported trade took place at 22.625 cents. The reporter notes this and uses a time stamp to record the hour, minute and fraction of a minute at which the price changed from 22.625 cents to 22.65 cents. This information is then fed by operators onto a ticker system where it would be telegraphed to commodity-trading firms all over the world that a hog contract changed hands at 22.65 cents.

At the same time the telephone operator has now relayed the details of the trade back to his wire room, where it retraces its route back to the branch office where you do business in Atlanta. Your broker would receive a wire confirming your trade and would then phone the details to you. In the next day or two you would receive a confirmation of the trade in the mail.

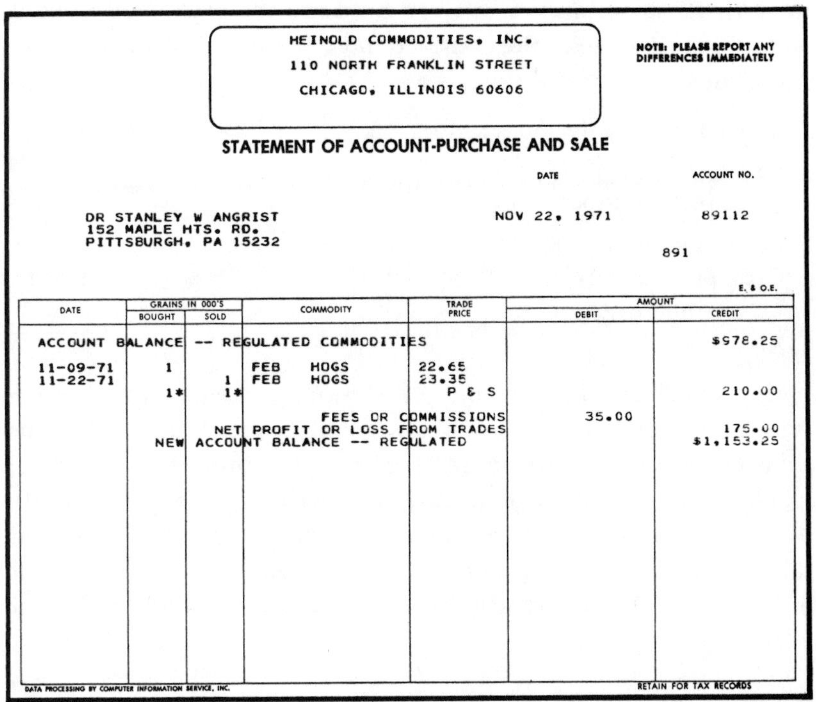

HEINOLD COMMODITIES, INC.
110 NORTH FRANKLIN STREET
CHICAGO, ILLINOIS 60606

NOTE: PLEASE REPORT ANY DIFFERENCES IMMEDIATELY

STATEMENT OF ACCOUNT-PURCHASE AND SALE

DATE: NOV 22, 1971
ACCOUNT NO.: 89112

DR STANLEY W ANGRIST
152 MAPLE HTS. RD.
PITTSBURGH, PA 15232

891

E. & O.E.

DATE	GRAINS IN 000'S BOUGHT	SOLD	COMMODITY	TRADE PRICE	AMOUNT DEBIT	CREDIT
ACCOUNT BALANCE -- REGULATED COMMODITIES						$978.25
11-09-71	1		FEB HOGS	22.65		
11-22-71		1	FEB HOGS	23.35		
	1*	1*		P & S		210.00
			FEES OR COMMISSIONS		35.00	
			NET PROFIT OR LOSS FROM TRADES			175.00
			NEW ACCOUNT BALANCE -- REGULATED			$1,153.25

DATA PROCESSING BY COMPUTER INFORMATION SERVICE, INC.

RETAIN FOR TAX RECORDS

FIGURE 4. A purchase-and-sale statement (generally called a P & S) for a trade is issued when the trade is completed. Such statements show the date and price at which the trade was initiated and closed out, the commission on the trade, the net profit or loss, and the credit balance in the account.

Say a couple of weeks pass and hogs have moved up 80 cents per hundred pounds or so, and you begin to feel uneasy about your position. You decide to put in a stop-loss on your hogs contract at 23.40 cents. Hogs sag down to your stop but because the selling is heavy your floor broker is unable to get you out there and has to accept a price of 23.35 cents. Soon after the transaction is completed your broker calls you and informs you he sold your hogs .05 cents below your stop price. You will then receive shortly a confirmation of the sale and then a "P & S" statement (purchase and sales). The latter shows both sides of your transaction and your final profit and loss on the trade. A typical purchase-and-sales slip for this hog transaction is shown in Figure 4.

Computing profits and losses in commodities is no more difficult than in the stock market. All you need are the prices you bought and sold at, the size of the contract and the amount of the commission. Thus:

Sold 1 February live hogs contract at	23.35 cents
Bought 1 February live hogs contract at	22.65 cents
Gross profit per pound	0.70 cents
But a contract is for 30,000 pounds so	
Gross profit = 0.70 cents/lb × 30,000 lbs =	$210.00
Less a commission of	35.00
Net Profit	$175.00

This profit should be the same as is shown as a credit on your P & S statement; I believe you should always verify the credits and debits shown on any statement you receive from your broker.

Thus $175 was made on a margin of perhaps $400, giving a rate of return of about 43 percent in a few weeks. Of course, if you had taken a loss of 0.70 cents per pound you would have had a loss of $210 plus a $35.00 commission, which would equal a net loss of $245.

Records a Trader Should Keep

Successful traders are almost always aware of how they stand on each position and how their entire account stands at the close of trading each day. That is, they rectify, in at least a rough way, their positions and their account every day. This rectification must include both those positions being held at a profit and those positions being held at a loss. In that way a trader will not fool himself into believing that there is greater equity in the account than there really is. Not being aware of the true account equity is the fastest way for a trader to slip into overtrading, which is an almost certain way to trade right out of the market. Two simple forms are all that are needed to prevent this folly. These forms can be typed up or even hand lettered and then duplicated or copied by any convenient means.

The first form, illustrated in Figure 5, is for keeping track of individual positions. It is filled in for the February hog trade previously discussed. The top of the form gives the details on the position—long or short, margin required, commission, trading hours,

Commodity Position in February Hogs (Long)

Margin $400; Commission $35 in points 12 Trading Hours 9:20 - 12:50

Bot 1 contracts at 22.65 on 11/9/71; Sold 1 contracts at 23.35 on 11/22/71;

Bot ____ contracts at ____ on ____; Sold ____ contracts at ____ on ____;

Bot ____ contracts at ____ on ____; Sold ____ contracts at ____ on ____;

Gross Profit or (Loss) $210; Net Profit or (Loss) $175

Net Profit or (Loss) as a Percent of Margin 43%

Date	Open	High	Low	Close	Stop	Risk		20-day Moving Average			
11/9	22.57	23.00	22.57	22.92	22.15	$230		22.28			
11/10	22.85	23.00	22.80	22.90							
11/11	22.75	23.25	22.75	23.22							
11/12	23.10	23.30	23.07	23.27	22.45	215					
11/15	23.30	23.65	23.30	23.42	22.65	230					
11/16	23.40	23.47	23.15	23.17				22.54			
11/17	23.25	23.20	23.45	23.27				22.61			
11/18	23.30	23.35	23.10	23.15	22.87	81					
11/19	23.05	23.45	23.02	23.42							
11/22	23.25	23.52	23.25	23.50							

FIGURE 5. A commodity-position statement is a convenient way to record each trade entered into. Such a statement may also be used to keep track of daily prices for the commodity being traded. Moving averages or other technical indicators may be recorded in the blank columns.

entry points and exit points, and the like. Some columns are used to record daily prices, stop locations and the like. Other columns can be used to record moving averages or other technical information. At the bottom of the page is recorded the net profit or loss and its percent of the margin supplied.

DAILY OPERATING STATEMENT

	M	Tu	W	Th	F
Date	11/15/71	11/16	11/17	11/18	11/19
1. Capital (includes realized gains and losses)	3200	3200	3000	3000	3000
2. Unrealized Gains & Losses					
Feb Hogs	200	120	150	125	200
Feb Silver (Chi.)	50	20	–	-60	-50
Jan Plywood	–	60	100	75	150
3. Total Unrealized G & L	250	200	250	140	300
4. Total Capital (1 + 3)	3450	3400	3250	3140	3300
5. Margin on Open Trades	1400	1400	1400	1400	1400
6. Gross Buying Power (4 - 5)	2050	2000	1850	1740	1900
7. Risk on Open Trades	500	400	400	300	400
8. Net Buying Power (6 - 7)	1550	1600	1450	1440	1500
9. Additions and (Withdrawals)		(200)			

FIGURE 6. The daily operating statement is filled in after the close each day and shows the gross loss or gain on every position held. It also shows the total capital in the account, the margin on open trades and the buying power left in the account, as well as the risk on open positions.

The second and equally important form, illustrated in Figure 6, is the one that takes into account the cash balance of the account (line 1) and all unrealized profits and losses (line 2). Subtracted from the accounts total capital (line 4) is the margin required on all open trades (line 5) which gives the gross buying power (line 6). Then the risk on all open trades is estimated by taking the difference between the closing prices and stop-loss orders on all trades, and their sum is entered as line 7. This risk is then subtracted from the gross buying power to give net buying power (line 8), which can then be applied against new positions. If additions or withdrawals are made after the close they are entered in line 9 which would be reflected in the next day's capital.

I believe that the daily posting of these two forms will save you more grief and more money in the long run than perhaps any other single step that you can take as a trader, except for the setting of stop-loss orders.

CHAPTER **7**

Two Approaches to Price Forecasting

□

Whether you lose money or make money when speculating in commodities depends almost solely on how well you do in correctly estimating the direction in which prices will move. While you might use the flip of a coin* to determine whether you should go long or short a given commodity, most professional speculators eschew such a capricious system in favor of either a so-called technical method or the fundamental method.

At any rate it will prove useful for a commodity trader to be familiar with both of these approaches for price forecasting. These two methods may be viewed as the working tools of the commodity speculator; and just as a good carpenter knows how to use the hammer and level, a good speculator knows how to use both the technical and the fundamental methods of price forecasting. In order to be good at the business of trading commodities, a successful speculator must follow trading procedures which in the past have been found to be profitable. It is only by consistently using a successful trading plan that the commodity speculator is able to reap the rewards from his risk-taking. At this point you may come to the conclusion that I am overstating the need for having and using a trading plan. Believe me, I am not. I make that statement on the basis of personal experience.

One of the most important functions of a trading plan is that of

* I know of no studies that have been done that categorically rule out the profitable use of this technique.

protecting you from yourself. Recall that even the best professional speculators are wrong six out of ten times. Thus, if you were to begin trading based on the hunch that you should be long all the grains and that strategy resulted in a number of big losses, you might then decide that you should really have been short all the grains. And so you switch all your positions. Then, the market reverses itself and you are again holding the wrong positions. And thus you bounce from one hunch to the next until eventually you run out of capital. Every now and then hunches may pay off, but you don't want to be in the market every now and then—you want to be continually taking sensible risks that will, overall, lead to moderately large profits.

So part of the job of a trading plan is to protect you from wild hunches. But the consistent use of a trading method will do something else. All speculators, whether they be stock, land, or commodity, are driven by two emotions—fear and greed.* Whether you like it or not, these two emotions will try to influence every trading decision you make. Suppose you have taken a short position in iced broilers and now the price is down 2 cents per pound from where you shorted them. You are ahead $500 on your position. It is greed that will tell you to stick with your position in the hope that broilers will continue to fall in price. But it is fear that tells you to take your profit and run. It is these two emotions which will be in constant struggle within you as you try to make up your mind on what to do.† If it is any consolation, thousands of other speculators who are short iced broilers will also be faced with trying to make peace with *their* constant companions. It is precisely under these conditions that the use of a trading method will help you to contain those two struggling little demons. Because with such a plan you are able to come up with a set of ra-

* One long-time observer of Wall Street went so far as to tell a reporter who was in the process of writing a rather long piece on the stock market not to waste his time looking for an overriding philosophy down on the Street; the way he put it was, ". . . down there all they know is fear and greed . . . the rest is just bullshit."

† It is the lot of the speculator who has no trading plan that when he crawls into bed at night, his old buddies, fear and greed, will crawl right in with him. While the speculator may wish to sleep, alas, they *never* sleep—they are indefatigable. Thus it is imperative that the speculator find a way to at least control them—for fear and greed can never be completely banished.

tional arguments for making your trading decisions; such arguments are really the only effective weapon against emotion.

The Fundamental Approach

Fundamental analysis and technical analysis are really two completely different breeds of cat. They are based on different hypotheses about how the market operates. Thus, it is common to find traders who strongly favor either one approach or the other. In general they are inclined to believe that the method they do not favor is all but worthless. There is no good reason that I know of which says that you must adopt one method or the other exclusively. Experience has shown that both methods can produce substantial profits even when applied to the same position. It would seem prudent, then, to try to examine both the technical and fundamental aspects of a position before assuming it and for as long as the position is open in your account.

A trader using fundamental analysis bases his buying and selling decisions on his knowledge of those factors that he believes will most influence the price trend. He studies all the factors he believes to be relevant in detail and then tries to come to a conclusion about whether he believes prices will advance or decline. Some of the factors that are usually taken into account include supply-and-demand statistics, the price level relative to the Government loan rate, seasonal trends in prices, prices in past seasons when similar conditions seemed to prevail, inflationary and deflationary forces at work in the economy, and political developments.

The fundamentalist argues that it will be supply relative to demand that will ultimately determine a commodity's price history. He believes that if supplies are scarce relative to what is required, higher prices must result; likewise if supply appears to be in excess of demand, lower prices must hold in the marketplace. But, as indicated in the preceding paragraph, other factors can alter the supply-demand balance and thus alter prices. Though the supply-demand situation is the most important factor to the fundamentalist, he must also examine the effects of how the other factors will probably influence that balance. After examining all the data and considering the effects of the other factors on the supply-demand situation, he then usually takes a position in the market corresponding to whether or not he believes higher or lower prices will prevail.

Fundamental analysis is necessarily tied in with normal seasonal price tendencies. For example, the crop year for corn begins with the commencement of harvest in October and continues through the following September. Then another crop year begins. If the corn crop is relatively close in size to estimated demand it usually produces a seasonal pattern of prices. Once the harvest has found a "storage home," cash prices as well as future prices usually move higher. Prices during December are frequently higher than those of October and November. Fundamentalists are close students of all seasonal trends of the commodities they are interested in. For example, they know that November soybeans have a tendency to fall from a spring or summertime high to a fall harvest-time low. Or that hog prices are generally higher during the spring and summer months, and lower during the late fall and early winter months.

By being aware of these seasonal patterns and having a good understanding of the factors that influence prices, the fundamentalist market student is able to decide in his own mind whether a particular situation is likely to result in a normal seasonal price pattern or a distorted pattern. In either case he should be able to take advantage of a major price move. Unlike the technical trader, who generally does not take a position until after the market begins its move and his technique has confirmed the move, the fundamentalist is in a better position to capture a bigger portion of the move if it occurs.

The fundamentalist approach to commodity trading appeals to large numbers of commodity traders for a number of reasons. It appeals to those traders who want to know why prices are moving higher or lower, and usually such price action can only be determined by studying those factors that cause price change. Such an approach also allows traders who are interested only in the longer-term price swings to take a position and maintain it with a minimum of attention to day-to-day market activity. Lastly, fundamental analysis appeals to those who get satisfaction from analyzing a situation by taking it apart piece by piece and then drawing a conclusion about the price direction which subsequent events, hopefully, will prove to be correct.

The Technical Approach

Speculators who depend solely upon the technical or price movement approach say, Don't tell us about corn blights, stocks in storage, strikes, seasonal influences or any of the factors mentioned in the previous section. They say, Just tell us the price. They rest their arguments on the fact that all of the factors that the fundamentalist considers are reflected in the current price and price history of the contract, and therefore if one wishes to make money in the commodity markets one simply studies price movements. Technicians believe that past prices are an important guide to future prices. By using a microscope to examine price changes instead of the telescope that the fundamentalist employs, the technician necessarily takes a short range view of the market. It should be obvious that if the technician is going to do better than a person who times his trades on a random basis, then the method that he uses must uncover and utilize some sort of serial dependence of price changes as they occur.

Most "absolute" technicians ignore fundamental considerations because they believe that giving any consideration at all to fundamental factors means giving them double consideration since, presumably, such factors have already been taken into account by price changes that have previously taken place. One of the advantages claimed by technicians is that they can view the market objectively, and thus they are not tempted to stick with any position because of an incorrect appraisal of fundamental factors. That is not to say that technicians are never subject to bad interpretations of their tools; technicians who ply their trade without stop-loss orders can, and do, experience huge losses.* Nevertheless, a technical approach can produce profits in the commodity market. Price-movement analysis can detect a worthwhile trend after it develops and will frequently allow its users to realize substantial returns on risk capital.

Essentially, technical analysis is a method that is concerned with

* The classic explanation frequently proffered by true-believing technicians is: "My charts were right again. . . . I just read them wrong."

timing. The actual price at which a transaction will take place is of no consequence; only the price pattern is of any importance to the technician. Suppose that the December live-hogs contract has been trading just above the season's low price; every time the market attempts a rally, prices meet overhead resistance and they fall back to the level just above the seasonal low. The technician would study this pattern of price movement and come to the conclusion that if prices were to drop below the season's low price it would be a bearish sign and thus he would want to be short December hogs. In this case the level of the seasonal low is important to the price-movement analyst only because it represents a previous resistance level, the penetration of which would have bearish implications. Such a penetration would provide the timing signal to go short. Note that almost without exception technicians use price-movement analysis as a timing method to locate trend-reversal points. The market is invariably entered by buy or sell stop orders *when* a certain price is reached.

By and large, a new trader will do better using a technical approach rather than a fundamental one. However, technical methods can produce sizable losses in markets that lack pronounced up or down trends; that is, they might swing up a few points, causing the technician to go long, and then drop a few points, causing him to close out his long position and take up a short position only to see the market bounce back to its original upside level. Such "whiplash" markets are a bane to the technical trade. I shall describe in subsequent chapters several techniques used by technicians to protect themselves from such debilitating activity.

Unfortunately most traders, especially new ones, expect too much from technical trading techniques. It cannot be overstressed that price-movement analysis is not an exact science, computers, random walk techniques and statistical tests of significance notwithstanding. Allowance must be made for mistakes and false starts. Events which cannot be predicted—weather developments, overnight shifts in Government policy, announcements of a widespread plant disease—are typical of events that can destroy the significance of a chart pattern that a technician might be using. Needless to add, price trends forecast by technical methods, like those forecast by fundamental analysis, frequently fail to take place in the expected direction for reasons that are difficult to explain.

Which Approach Is Best?

I think you will realize by now that there is no perfect price-forecasting method. If someone discovered such a method he would soon wind up with all the chips and the game would be over. It is, of course, also impossible for me to tell you which method is best for you. First, I suggest that you read with an open mind the chapters devoted to both methods before wedding yourself to one or the other. Furthermore, I believe that the really wise trader will not choose one method to the exclusion of the other after studying both, but rather will use them in tandem to help make his trading decisions. This idea will be explored in more detail in subsequent chapters.

CHAPTER **8**

Fundamental Analysis

□

While the market technician states that he needs to know only past prices to predict future prices, the fundamentalist calls only for information about the basic market factors—supply-and-demand statistics, seasonal price tendencies and general price levels. He claims that while drawing pictures (charting prices) might be a pleasant hobby it won't really do you much good when it comes to price forecasting. The student of market fundamentals believes that by doing careful analysis of the economic factors that influence a market he can predict future price levels. It is also important to note that while nearly all technicians take their positions after a price trend has begun, the fundamentalist need not wait for such signals; if his analysis tells him that a commodity will be in short supply, which leads him to believe that its price will rise from present levels, then he will take his position up immediately and wait for the market to prove him right—or wrong.

In order to make some sense out of the basic market factors, you must know what they are and how to use them. That is, you must understand what figures are used to compute supply-and-demand balances, what the seasonal price tendencies are in the commodity you are interested in, and what to look for when comparing current and past price levels. In this chapter I shall discuss those fundamental factors which I consider to be the most important.

BALANCE BETWEEN SUPPLY AND DEMAND

The single most important factor that influences a commodity's price is the supply-demand balance—that is, how much of that commodity is available in relation to how much is needed. The answer to this question is almost always looked for in statistics supplied by the Government. Most of these statistics come from the U.S. Department of Agriculture (USDA) and are generally called "official" estimates. Some commodity brokerage houses also issue crop estimates or utilize the services of private consultants to estimate production and consumption figures. If there is a big difference between the "official" estimates and the privately prepared ones, you have no choice but to "pay your money and take your choice." In actual practice you would have to decide which set of statistics to believe on the basis of the reputation of who was making the estimate.

Supply-and-demand statistics for a given agricultural commodity are always computed on the basis of the crop year. The crop year, of course, is closely related to the growing season of that particular commodity. The crop year for corn and soybeans, for example, begins October 1 and ends September 30. For wheat, oats and rye, the crop year begins July 1. In order to make the statistics as simple as possible it is commonly assumed that a new crop becomes fully available on the first day of the month at the start of the new crop season.

The supply of a given commodity is made up of three components:

(1) the new crop
(2) old crop carryover
(3) probable imports (if any).

Old crop carryover includes all the unused stocks from either the previous or earlier crops that are on hand at the beginning of the crop year.

The first clue to the probable size of the current crop becomes available well in advance of the actual harvest. Around the middle of March the USDA releases the findings of its March 1 Planting Intentions Survey. This indicates the acreage that farmers intend to plant in corn, durum wheat and other spring wheat, oats, barley, flaxseed, sorghum, soybeans and cotton. In the case of some crops, this report is very accurate—corn, for example—in which, in the time period between 1963 and 1969, actual acreage planted has been within one percent of March 1 intentions. Then, beginning in July, and updated each month after that until harvest is completed, the USDA publishes an estimate of the prospective production, based on acreage and probable yields. Just as one would expect, the later-in-the-season estimates tend to be the most accurate.

On the other side of the coin is the demand for a commodity. Two factors cause commodities to disappear—one is domestic utilization and the other is exports. Domestic utilization can be further broken down in the case of a commodity like corn, for example, into the amount fed to livestock and the amount utilized in food such as breakfast cereals, corn oil, and corn snacks. Some corn, of course, is used for seed. In the case of corn, it is interesting to note that approximately nine-tenths of the domestically consumed corn is used for livestock feed.

Naturally people who use a commodity as a raw material, those who produce it, and speculators in it are all extremely interested in the rate at which the commodity is being consumed during the course of the crop year. Is the commodity being consumed at an increased rate this season? Are supplies readily available to meet projected requirements of the commercial market? To help answer these questions the USDA releases a report called the Stocks in All Positions Report* about the twenty-second of January, April, July and October. These reports cover wheat, rye, corn, oats, barley, sorghum grain, soybeans and flaxseed and tell how much of each of the grains remains on farms, off farms, and in all positions as of the first of the month in which the report is released.

After personally gathering the data from reliable sources or using data compiled by an advisory service or brokerage house a supply-demand balance sheet can be drawn up. Table 3 illustrates a crude five-year supply-demand balance sheet for corn. This kind of data is not very useful in predicting future prices but it will give an idea of how the important factors can be tabulated. A more refined treatment will be presented later. In the case of corn, the

* A complete list of USDA reports that are available may be obtained by writing the U.S. Department of Agriculture, Washington, D.C. 20250. A partial list of titles that might be of interest to speculators is given in Appendix B.

Table 3

Balance Sheet—Corn Supply and Demand, 1965-1969
(in millions of bushels)

Item	Crop Year Beginning October				
	1965	1966	1967	1968	1969
Total Carryover October 1	1,147	840	823	1,162	1,113
Corn Production	4,084	4,117	4,760	4,393	4,583
Total Supply	5,232	4,985	5,583	5,555	5,696
Feed Consumption	3,347	3,284	3,421	3,535	3,688
Food and Seed Usage	358	364	368	372	395
Exports	687	487	633	536	616
Total Demand	4,392	4,135	4,422	4,443	4,699
Total Ending Carryover	840	823	1,162	1,113	997

Source: The Feed Situation, U.S. Department of Agriculture.

critical variable is supply. Until 1970 the major influence on corn production was the weather; however, in 1970 Southern leaf blight, a crop fungus, reduced supply and drove prices up sharply. Because corn reserves rarely exceed three months' normal usage, unfavorable weather or crop disease which would cause a significant drop in production can produce sudden and dramatic changes in price. For example, over the weekend of August 15, 1970, the USDA announced the presence of widespread corn blight in the corn-producing states. On Monday, when trading resumed in corn at the Chicago Board of Trade, prices were up the daily limit (for corn that is 8 cents per bushel) in all the grains at the opening bell. It took several days before some semblance of order returned to the market. Figure 7 illustrates the effect that a piece of fundamental (though unpredictable) information can have on futures prices; this price data is for the December 1970 corn contract.

Less than a year later there was again talk of corn blight, and in June 1971 corn prices made a dramatic 20 cents per bushel upward move. Once again, for a few days, corn futures were in great demand in the pit. Then, as one wag put it, the corn-blight rumor machine ran out of scare stories.* Figure 8 illustrates what happens

* One battle-scarred trader expressed it well as the blight scare just started to peak out: "There is more corn blight on the trading floor of the Chicago Board of Trade than in all of the rest of the state of Illinois."

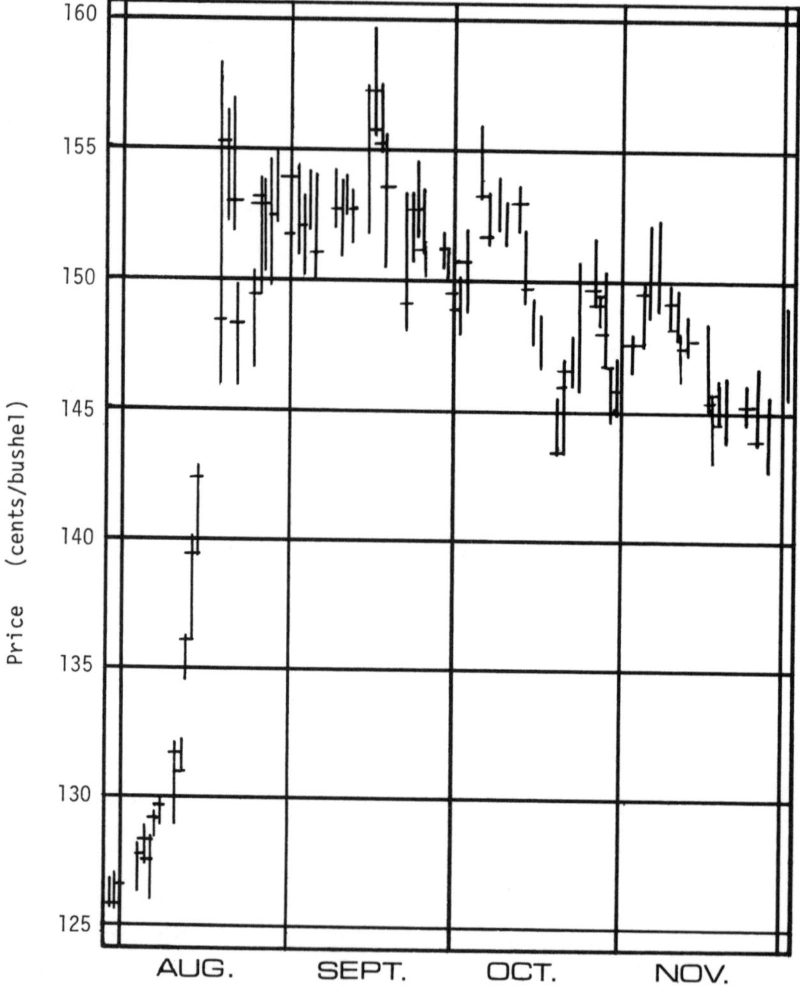

FIGURE 7. This chart illustrates the effect a piece of fundamental—though unpredictable—information can have on futures prices. The announcement of wide-spread corn blight over the weekend of August 15, 1970, caused this sharp rise in the price of the December 1970 corn contract.

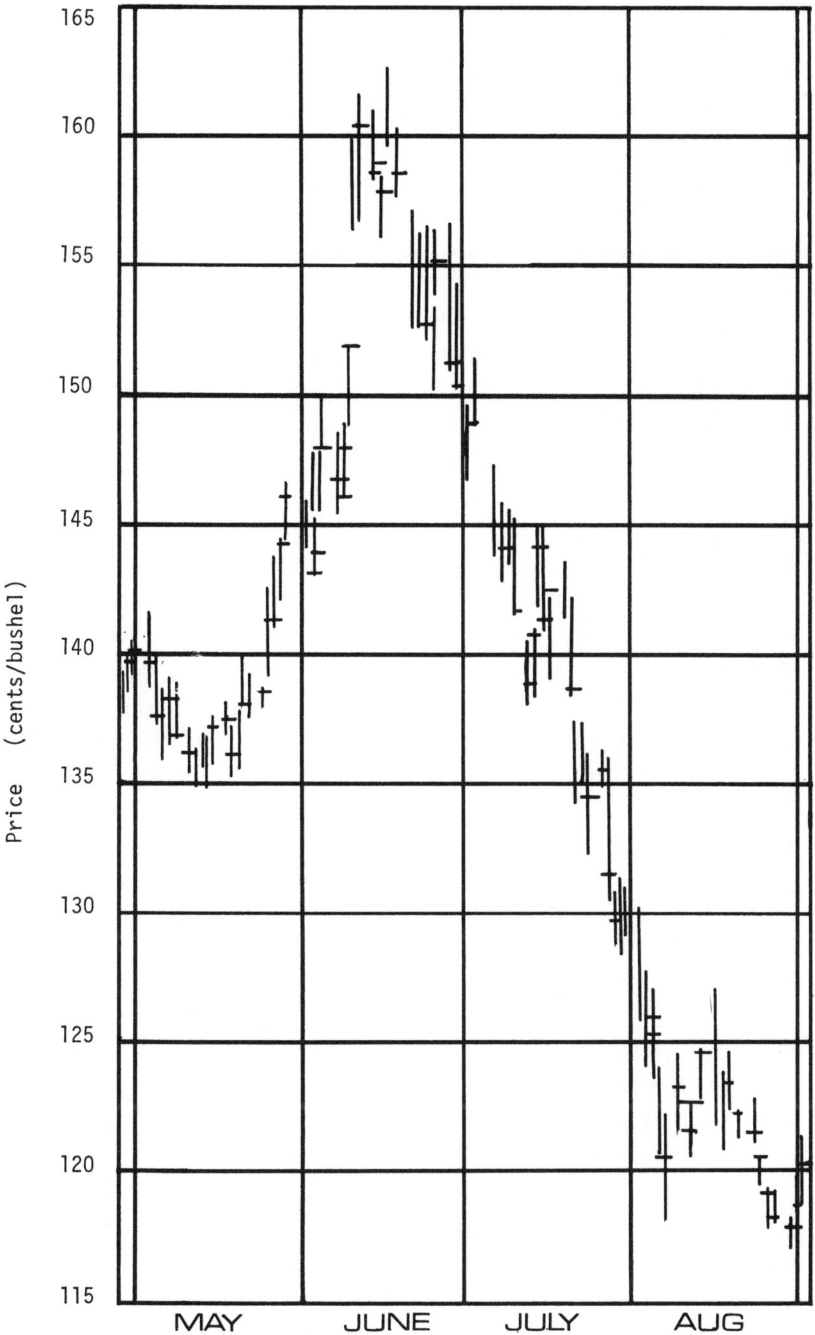

FIGURE 8. The corn blight did not reappear in 1971 as corn bulls hoped, and this chart shows what happened to the price of the December 1971 corn contract between June and September 1971. A short seller of corn could have realized $2,500 per contract in those four months.

to prices when scarcity rumors lose their credence as happened in this case. The 50 cents per bushel drop in price between June and September that December 1971 contracts suffered would represent a profit (or loss, if you were long and stayed long) for a short seller of corn of $2,500 per contract on a margin requirement of about $500 per contract.

Hog-Corn Ratio. Before examining other fundamental factors I will briefly discuss one of the more important terms heard most frequently among grain, pork and pork-product speculators. As I have already indicated, 90 percent of all domestic corn is used as livestock feed, and thus the price of corn is influenced by the value of those things that corn is used to produce. If a farmer finds that the price of livestock is high or if he *expects* livestock prices to be high in the future relative to the price of corn, he is generally encouraged to feed corn to his livestock and enlarge his animal production. Conversely, if livestock prices are low relative to the price of grain, he is not eager to turn expensive corn into cheap hogs.

Thus livestock-feed ratios express the ratio between livestock prices and corn prices. Each month the USDA publishes feed-price ratios for hogs, beef cattle, milk, eggs, broilers and turkeys.

For example, during September 1971 the average price of live hogs was $18.50 per hundredweight while Number 3 yellow corn averaged $1.17 per bushel, thus yielding a hog-corn ratio of 15.80. This ratio can be interpreted as the number of bushels of corn that it would take to buy 100 pounds of live hog. (It *does not* represent the number of bushels of corn it takes to produce 100 pounds of pork.)

When the hog-corn ratio is higher than usual, hog feeding is more profitable and farmers respond by breeding and feeding more hogs. When the ratio is lower than usual, the opposite holds true. A hog-corn ratio of 14 is considered by many farmers to be a break-even point. If the ratio drops below 14, most farmers believe that they can make more money by selling their corn than by feeding it to hogs. This causes a drop in hog production. The effect of this ratio is clearly illustrated in Figure 9. Note that as the hog-corn ratio drops, the number of sows farrowed (delivering pigs) falls correspondingly. Though the hog-corn ratio cannot accurately forecast the direction and extent to which prices will move, it is a

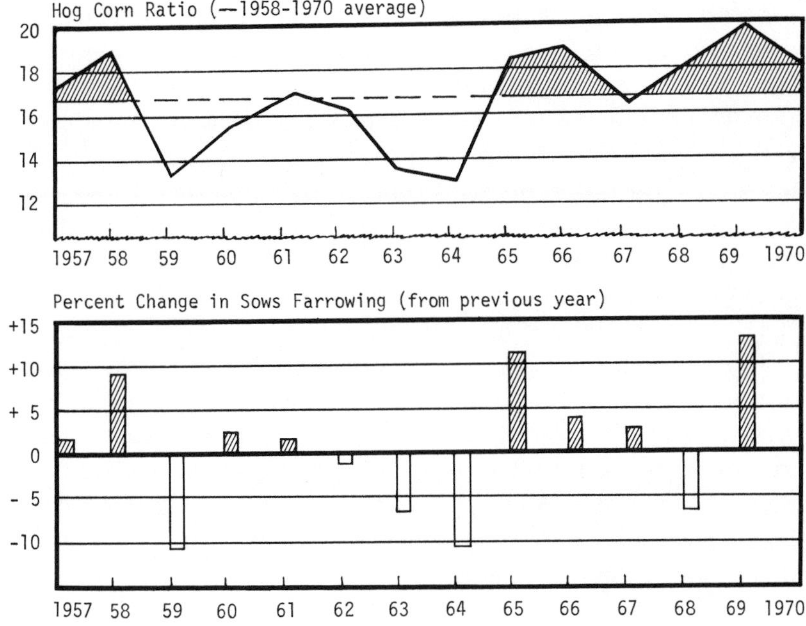

FIGURE 9. The hog-corn ratio may be thought of as the number of bushels of corn that it would take to buy 100 pounds of live hog. Note that as the ratio drops the number of sows delivering pigs falls correspondingly.

useful tool to indicate the direction in which hog production is heading. Keep in mind that an outlook for higher hog prices six months from now can trigger an increase in the demand for corn now.

Government Agricultural Programs

It would be foolish for a speculator in wheat, corn, oats, soybeans, rye or cotton to be unaware of the fact that the Government has the power to enter the market for these commodities in a significant way. Government intervention in the market can have a major impact on futures prices. Two of the numerous Government programs are especially important to the speculator: the loan program and the program to limit acreage planted.

The Loan Program. This program is a price-supporting device that is used to place a floor under certain commodity prices. Farmers who cooperate in limiting acreage are eligible to place their crop under loan. The loan rate for each of the six commodities mentioned earlier is generally adjusted each year. The adjustment usually prompts speculators and hedgers to reappraise the new acreage allotments and the crop that can be expected from those acres. The loans that the Government makes on the pledged crops are non-recourse loans. That is, the crop is pledged as collateral and can be redeemed at any time by payment of the loan plus accrued interest. Interest rates on such loans are usually well below the prevailing commercial rates.

In the event that market prices during the crop season continue at a relatively low level, that is, not much higher than loan rates, farmers who have placed their corn under loan can elect to default at the termination date by forfeiting the crop used as collateral. In that event the loan does not have to be repaid, the interest charge is canceled and the corn becomes the property of the Government, that is, the Commodity Credit Corporation (CCC).

Farmers can also continue their loans on farm-stored loan crops at the conclusion of the crop year. This program is referred to as the "reseal" program. The loan is extended with the Government paying storage charges for farmers who are willing and able to store their crops.

The Government, then, can have three separate categories of Government-controlled crops: crops under loan from the current year; crops under loan from previous years and resealed; and crops owned outright by the Government.

The Acreage Control Program. Though farmers are not compelled to participate, many of them do choose to curtail planting of their crops. Farmers who do sign up for the program receive special payments and in addition gain the right to place their crop under loan.

The technical details of both of these programs have not been described because the actual administration and the amount of money actually received by farmers who participate vary from year to year.

Effects of Government Programs. Government loan programs without a doubt act to place a floor under market prices. However, the Government's possession of certain commodities can also act to exert a ceiling on the prices of those same commodities. This can come about because the Government is authorized by law to begin selling stockpiled commodities when market prices exceed Government accumulation prices by a designated amount or an established percentage. Furthermore, the Government may sell stockpiled commodities in the marketplace at any time when, in the judgment of the appropriate Federal agency, they have stocks that are in danger of going out of salable condition for any reason.

Thus, most, but not all, fundamentalists recognize that total supply and demand of a commodity is not really the controlling variable for a given commodity's price in the market—the important thing is the "free supply and demand." Arriving at an estimate of the free supply-and-demand balance is not a difficult task. One method frequently used is to add together the new crop, estimated imports, free stocks in the carryover at the start of the season and an estimated total CCC sales for the season. From this figure the total estimated disappearance (consumption) is subtracted. The difference is the *free supply margin* or *free surplus.*

The free supply-and-demand balance must be given greater weight when forecasting price levels if large stocks of that commodity are owned by the Government than for those commodities for which Government stocks and loan impoundings are small.

Supply and Demand in Action. As noted in the previous section, the key factor in the price of any commodity is the balance between the available free supply and the market requirements. As this relationship changes, so do prices. It is for this reason that many speculators and hedgers make a monthly estimate of this balance. In order to demonstrate in detail how such a balance can and does influence prices I shall present an outlook analysis for corn as prepared by the Chicago Board of Trade. It should be clear that such analyses might be prepared for almost any of the widely traded commodities. In general, however, such analyses are easier to prepare for agricultural commodities because the USDA makes such a tremendous amount of statistical information so readily available. Sources for this information for various commodities is given in Appendix B.

Let us first consider the economics involved. Obviously, at any

Table 4

Corn Supply and Demand:
Quarterly Outlook for 1968-69 Crop Year
(in millions of bushels)

Item	Outlook October 1	Outlook January 1	Outlook April 1	Outlook July 1
1. Carryover, October 1	1,162			
2. Corn Production in 1968	4,393			
3. Stocks-in-all-Positions (or total supply)	5,555	4,204	3,040	2,053
4. Government Program				
5. Under Loan (current crop)	401	180	368	295
6. Reseal Loans (previous crops)	532	448	445	392
7. Owned by Government	182	261	257	270
8. Total Under Government	1,115	889	1,070	957
9. Free Commercial Supply	4,440	3,315	1,970	1,096
10. Demand-Balance of Season	4,442	3,091	1,927	940
11. Free Carryover	- 2	+224	+ 43	+156
12. Pipeline Requirements	250	250	250	250
13. NET SURPLUS OR DEFICIT FOR COMMERCIAL MARKET	-252	- 26	-207	- 94
Quarterly Demand*	1,351	1,164	987	940

*The quarterly corn demand is listed separately to indicate the usual trend in corn disappearance. The "Demand-Balance of Season" (Line 10) is reduced each quarter according to the amount of the Quarterly Demand.

instant of time, there is only so much of a commodity (corn, in this case) available. Part of this corn is available immediately to the market and part is held by the Government under one of its programs. If the free commercial supply is insufficient with respect to market requirements, prices must be bid up to levels above the net loan rate at which the required supplies from Government programs will become available. Thus prospects for higher or lower prices will depend in large measure on whether there is going to be a supply surplus or a supply deficit.

Table 4 gives the surplus versus deficit arithmetic on a quarterly basis (such tables can be prepared monthly) for the 1968–69 crop year. In this table a figure of 250 million bushels is used as the pipeline requirements for corn needed for continuous operation by feed mills, food processors, distillers and the like. This figure is believed to be conservative.

Obviously, if one is preparing such a table on a current basis, estimates must be used; for example, in Table 4, the amount of corn that will be placed under loan (line 5) and the probable demand (line 10) for corn are estimated. The best guide to such estimates is usually marketing statistics for previous crop years.

The October 1 data in the table show the supply of corn as the sum of corn production for 1968 (4,393 million bushels) plus the "carryover" (1,162 million bushels) at the beginning of the new crop year, which yields a stocks-in-all-positions total supply of 5,555 million bushels.

The supply must now be reduced by the effects of Government programs, which in this case comes to a total of 1,115 million bushels. The available free commercial supply is then 4,440 million bushels. The free supply is now compared with the demand for the balance of season, thus revealing that for the first quarter of the new crop year, free carryover supply is found to fall short of demand by 2 million bushels. When pipeline considerations are included, the outlook shows that supply will fall short of demand by 252 million bushels in the first quarter (line 13).

If supplies are in deficit, then corn may have to be obtained from stocks held under Government programs. Note that it is customary to assume that all corn not in the Government program will be marketed at some time during the crop year.

In those years when a deficit in supplies has occurred, prices have generally risen to levels that would attract corn out from under loan. In recent years a cash price of from $1.30 to $1.35 or a July futures price of from $1.30 to $1.32 has been able to attract sufficient supplies from under loan to meet commercial requirements.

The key line in Table 4 is the one that indicates a net surplus or deficit for the commercial market (line 13). Table 5 gives this figure by quarter for the five years between 1965 and 1969. It is interesting to compare these figures with the price of July corn futures.

Table 5

Net Surplus or Deficit Corn Stocks Based on Quarterly Outlook of Supply and Demand, 1965-1969 (in millions of bushels)

Crop Year Beginning October	Outlook October 1	Outlook January 1	Outlook April 1	Outlook July 1
1965-66	-559	-398	-391	-149
1966-67	-117	+ 63	+ 39	+159
1967-68	+ 84	+356	+152	+177
1968-69	-252	- 25	-207	- 94
1969-70	-438	-171	-340	-245

Figure 10 gives the price trend of the July futures contract for the 1966–67 and 1967–68 crop years—years which for the most part ran a surplus of supplies. Figure 11 shows the price trends for the three crop years (1965–66, 1968–69 and 1969–70) which generally ran a deficit in supplies.

The fundamentalist who carefully assembled an outlook for corn could have used his work to gather a profit each year. However, as you will note from Figures 10 and 11 the prices generally did not move in a straight line and such a trader might have had to close out positions a number of times with small losses before latching onto a substantial price move.

Seasonal Price Tendencies

The seasonal price patterns that most agricultural commodities display rank next in importance to the supply-demand balance as a fundamental influence on commodity prices. To enter the market unaware of the seasonal tendency in prices is both foolhardy and not necessary. Seasonal tendencies exist primarily because of the growing characteristics of agricultural commodities, and while exceptions happen frequently, the patterns occur with enough regularity so that experienced traders who use the fundamental approach take up positions counter to the seasonal tendencies only

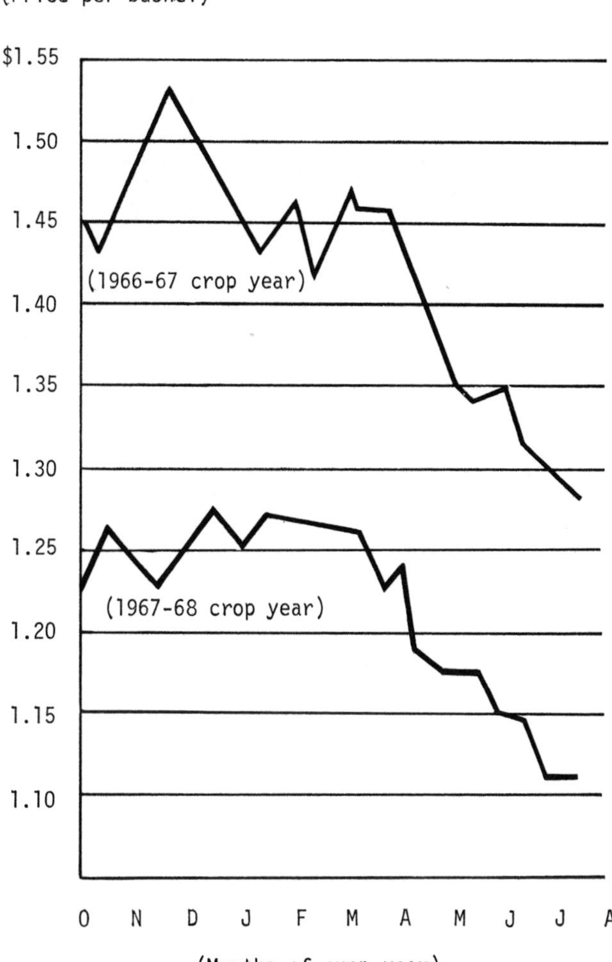

FIGURE 10. This chart illustrates the price trend of the July corn futures contract when there are sufficient supplies available to the commercial market. (These prices are as of the first and fifteenth of each month.)

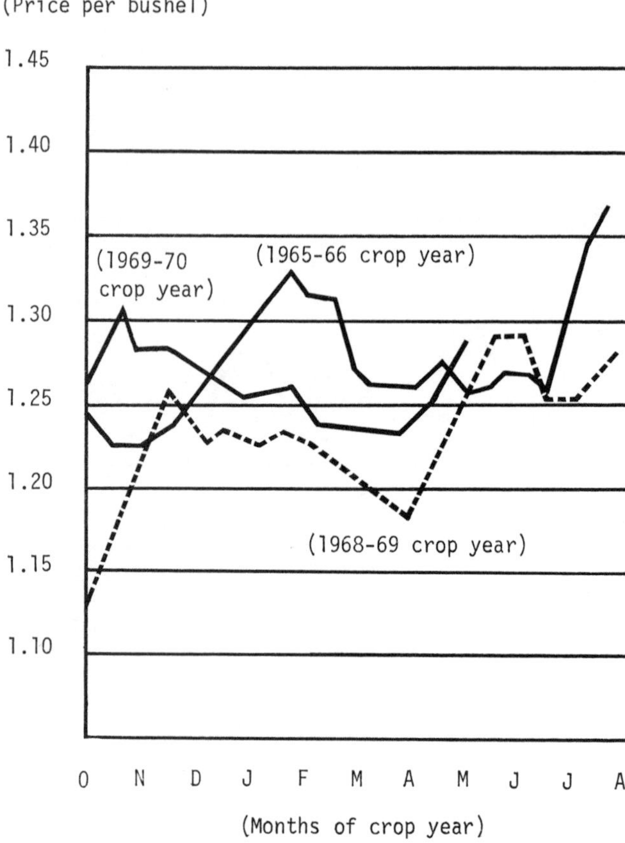

FIGURE 11. The July corn futures price responds quite differently when there is a deficit of supplies available to the commercial market. (Prices are as of the first and fifteenth of the month.)

when they have excellent justification. It is impossible for me to begin a discussion of seasonal price tendencies without repeating an oft-told tale about such a set of patterns. This story, like so many of the legends that persist about commodity trading, lends a further air of mystery to those peculiar people called speculators who risk money on crops they neither raise nor want. The story (which just might be true) even has an appropriately sepulchral name—it is called "The Voice from the Tomb."

As legend has it, a wealthy speculator lay on his deathbed. As the end drew near, he called his loved ones to him and told them that his most valuable possession would be found in the strongbox in his study. Shortly after he had passed on to the Great Board of Trade above, they made a beeline for the strongbox. In it they found a scrap of paper with the following cryptic (no pun intended) notation on it:

Buy Wheat	*Sell Wheat*	*Buy Corn*	*Sell Corn*
	January 10	March 1	
February 22			May 20
	May 10	June 25	
July 1			August 10
	September 10		
November 28			

Unfortunately the story does not tell us what the family did with this information and how it influenced their memory of the deceased. It is interesting to note that there are still traders around who consider these dates to be significant ones in the wheat and corn market. History has revealed the sad, but true, result that a blind following of this trading pattern will not produce great wealth for those who take their guidance from the tomb. But the dates do conform well enough to the seasonal price tendencies of wheat and corn so that they cannot be dismissed as completely lacking in merit.

In Table 6 I have listed the usual seasonal trends for spot prices for a number of agricultural commodities that might be of interest to new traders. Notice that commodities such as the metals are not listed; they have no seasonal tendencies because they are not related on either the production or consumption end to any season. It should also be noted that a couple of commodities show double highs and double bottoms, meaning that they execute two full cycles in a crop year.

Very few speculators try to trade on the basis of seasonal trends alone, but, as stated earlier, these should be kept in mind. Some market students feel that while seasonal trends are insufficiently reliable to be used as a trading vehicle, seasonal spreads are more

Table 6

Seasonal Price* Tendencies[†]

Commodity	High	Low
Cattle	May	June
Cocoa	December-January May-March	September
Corn	August	November-December
Cotton	July	October-December
Eggs	November	March-April
Live Hogs	June	November
Oats	January*** and May	August
Pork Bellies	July	November
Potatoes	June-July	October
Soybeans	January*** and April	June and October
Soybean Oil	July	October
**Soybean Meal	April	December
**Sugar (World)	September	March
Wheat	January*** and May	August-September

*Spot prices.

**Numerous exceptions to the seasonal trends.

***These commodities are frequently subject to a February break after which a significant rally sometimes occurs.

[†]This table has been abbreviated from a more complete one in Modern Commodity Futures Trading by Gerald Gold, Commodity Research Bureau, Inc., New York, 1968.

useful. That is, these students believe that price differences between certain contract months, for example July and November soybeans, change in a more highly predictable way than prices alone. The possibility of using seasonal spreads will be discussed in greater detail in Chapter 12, which is devoted to spreads.

In order for you to appreciate what is meant by a seasonal price movement, here are a couple of samples for you to examine. The first one we will consider is soybeans. Cash prices for soybeans have a tendency to advance from a harvest low in October to a peak in the spring. This comes about because supplies are heaviest shortly after the harvest and farmers tend to market most of their crop between harvest time and the end of the calendar year. Later in the season crushers and exporters begin to compete for remaining supplies, thus firming up cash prices. But we are not really interested in cash prices—we are concerned with futures prices.

Figures 12a, 12b, and 12c are the daily high, low and close charts for the May soybeans contract from 1961 through the year 1971. Your first reaction on studying these charts might be: "What seasonal price pattern?" Indeed, on first inspection one perceives no seasonality, and, in fact, there is not one price pattern on these charts that repeats itself *every year*. But I never claimed that such perfect patterns exist.

Now let us examine these charts from a trader's point of view. Suppose you went long May soybeans on October 1 (or the nearest trading day to it) and you closed out your long position on the last trading day in January. How would you have fared? In eight of the eleven years whose price data is presented here you would have had at least a small profit. Your profit never would have been less than 7 cents per bushel and in three (1961, 1965, and 1966) of those eight years you would have had a profit of 30 or more cents per bushel ($1,500 per contract). I assumed that you were a prudent trader not given to pigheadedness, and thus you set your stop-loss order 5 cents below where you got in so that in the four years (1960, 1962, 1964 and 1967) when you didn't have a profit you would have lost a total of about 20 cents per bushel.* If you had traded this seasonal for all twelve years you would have accumulated a total profit of about 160 cents per bushel ($8,000) and a total loss of $1,000 giving you a net profit of $7,000 over the twelve-year period. Margin on a single contract probably never exceeded $1,000.

Keep in mind that I told you many traders are happy to be right 40 percent of the time; and I have just demonstrated a seasonal price pattern that has worked profitably 66 percent of the time in a twelve-year period. It is rare to find a straight seasonal specula-

* The chart for May 1964 soybeans is worth a little study. In my calculations I assumed that in 1964 we were stopped out with a 5 cents per bushel loss. In fact, between October and January this contract made no less than six moves up or down of more than 20 cents per bushel. In my opinion such price swings are an internist's dream and a trader's nightmare. While the internist treats the trader's ulcer collecting sufficient fees to pay for his winter vacation, the trader is staying up nights drinking warm milk and trying to figure out how he ever got into May soybeans. If you ever find yourself in such a market, cut your losses and get some sleep. There will be May soybeans to trade next year.

FIGURE 12. Daily prices for May soybeans for the 1961 futures contract through the 1971 contract.

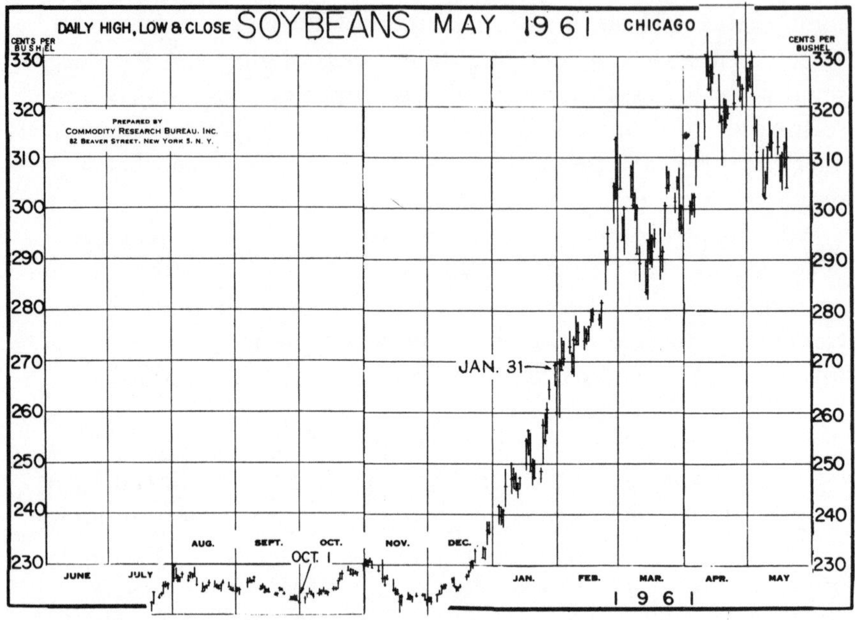

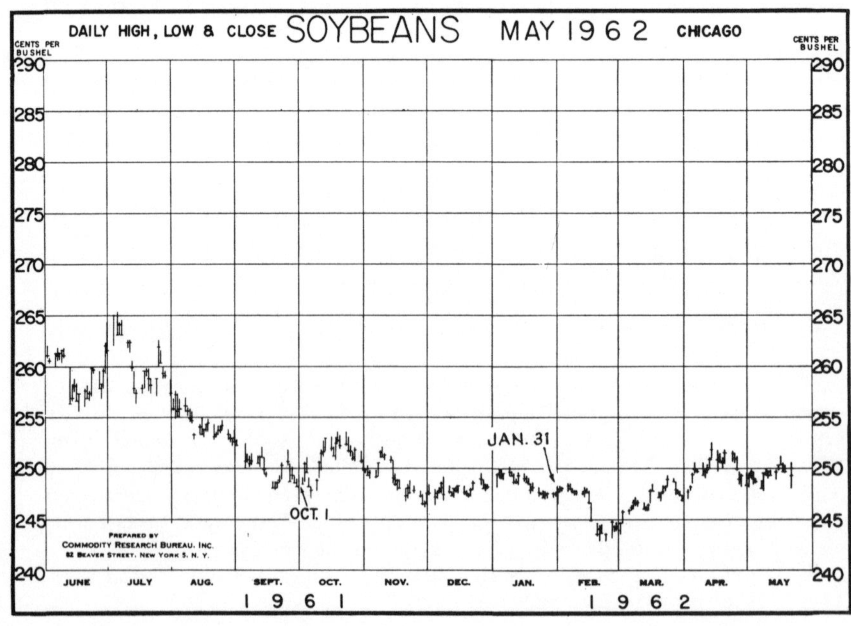

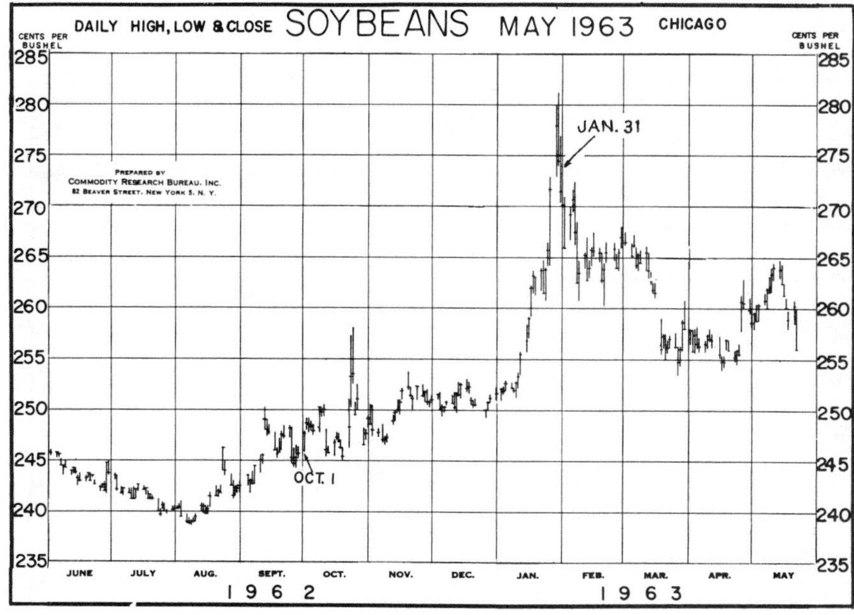
DAILY HIGH, LOW & CLOSE SOYBEANS MAY 1963 CHICAGO
CENTS PER BUSHEL
PREPARED BY
COMMODITY RESEARCH BUREAU, INC.
82 BEAVER STREET, NEW YORK 5, N. Y.
JAN. 31
OCT. 1
285
280
275
270
265
260
255
250
245
240
235
JUNE
JULY
AUG.
SEPT.
OCT.
NOV.
DEC.
JAN.
FEB.
MAR.
APR.
MAY
1962
1963

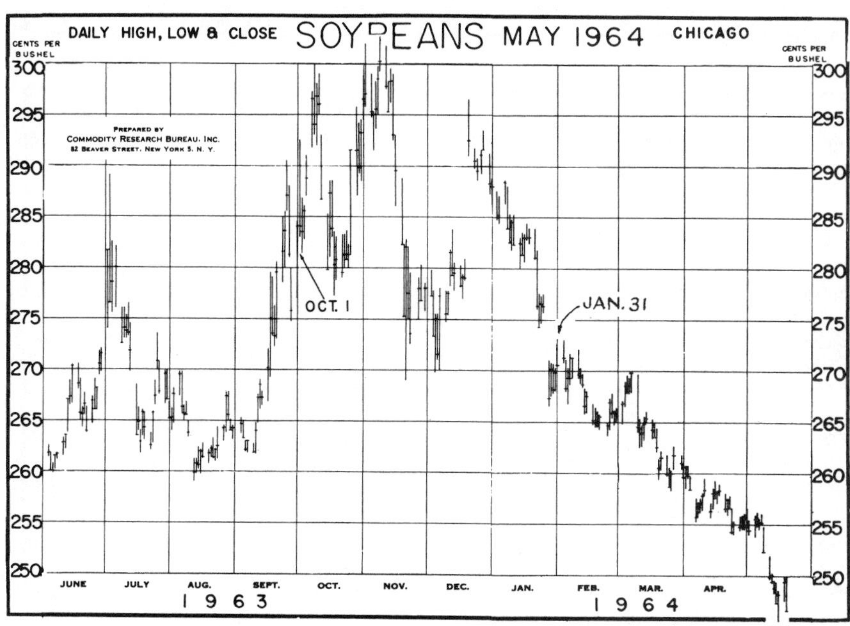
DAILY HIGH, LOW & CLOSE SOYBEANS MAY 1964 CHICAGO
CENTS PER BUSHEL
PREPARED BY
COMMODITY RESEARCH BUREAU, INC.
82 BEAVER STREET, NEW YORK 5, N. Y.
OCT. 1
JAN. 31
300
295
290
285
280
275
270
265
260
255
250
JUNE
JULY
AUG.
SEPT.
OCT.
NOV.
DEC.
JAN.
FEB.
MAR.
APR.
1963
1964

FIGURE 12. Daily prices for May soybeans for the 1961 futures contract through the 1971 contract.

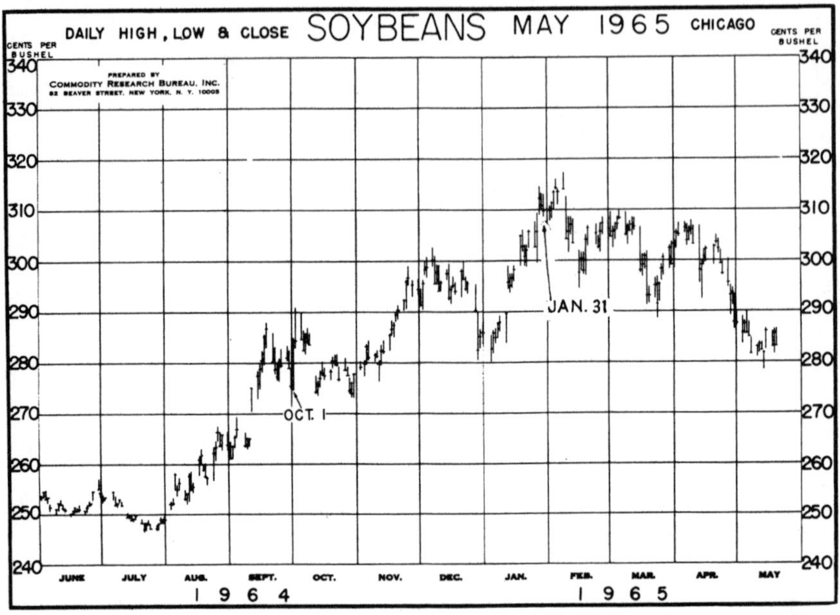

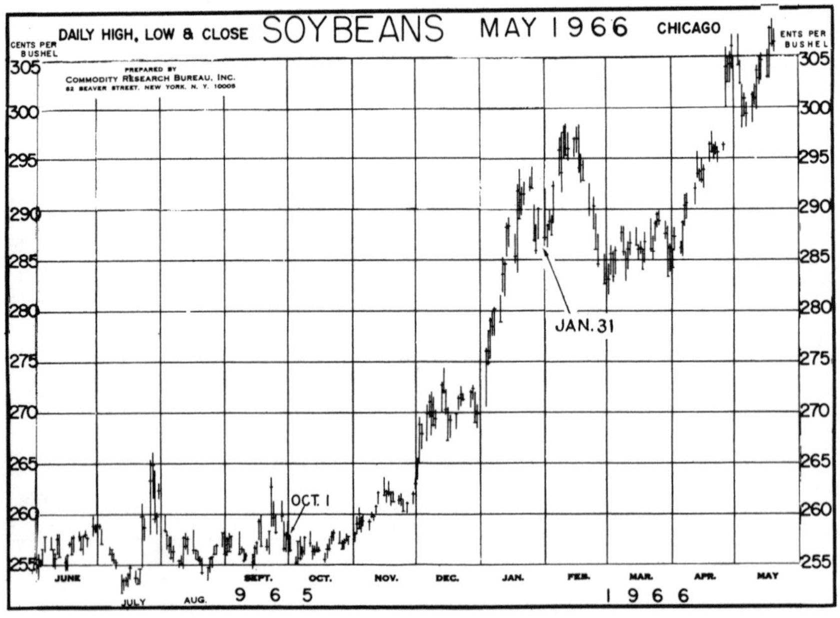

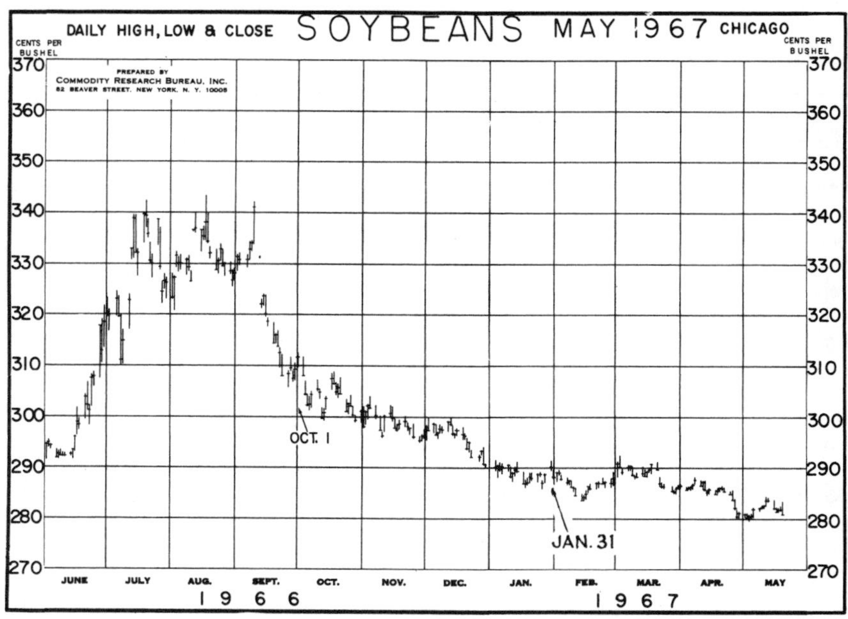
DAILY HIGH, LOW & CLOSE SOYBEANS MAY 1967 CHICAGO
CENTS PER BUSHEL
PREPARED BY COMMODITY RESEARCH BUREAU, INC. 82 BEAVER STREET, NEW YORK, N. Y. 10005
370
360
350
340
330
320
310
300
290
280
270
OCT. 1
JAN. 31
JUNE JULY AUG. SEPT. OCT. NOV. DEC. JAN. FEB. MAR. APR. MAY
1966
1967

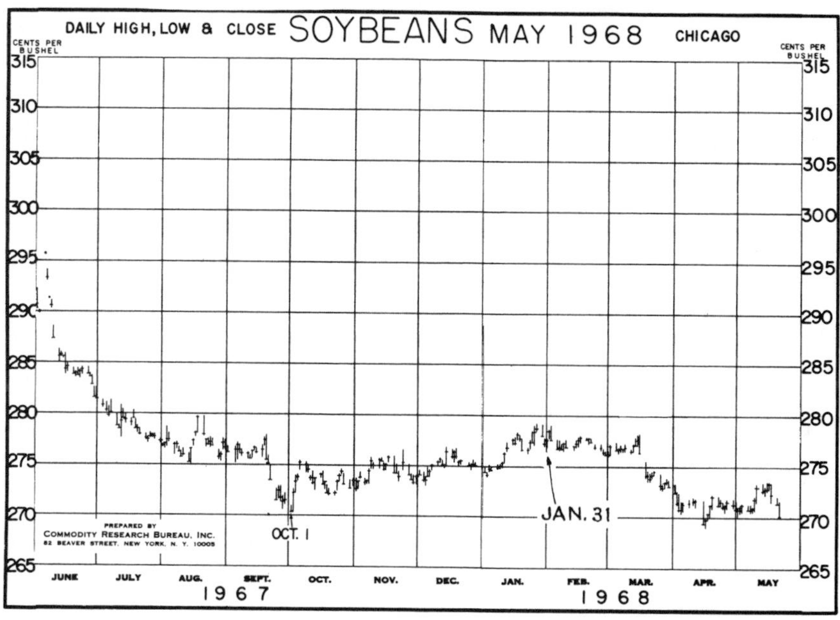
DAILY HIGH, LOW & CLOSE SOYBEANS MAY 1968 CHICAGO
CENTS PER BUSHEL
315
310
305
300
295
290
285
280
275
270
265
PREPARED BY COMMODITY RESEARCH BUREAU, INC. 82 BEAVER STREET, NEW YORK, N. Y. 10005
OCT. 1
JAN. 31
JUNE JULY AUG. SEPT. OCT. NOV. DEC. JAN. FEB. MAR. APR. MAY
1967
1968

FIGURE 12. Daily prices for May soybeans for the 1961 futures contract through the 1971 contract.

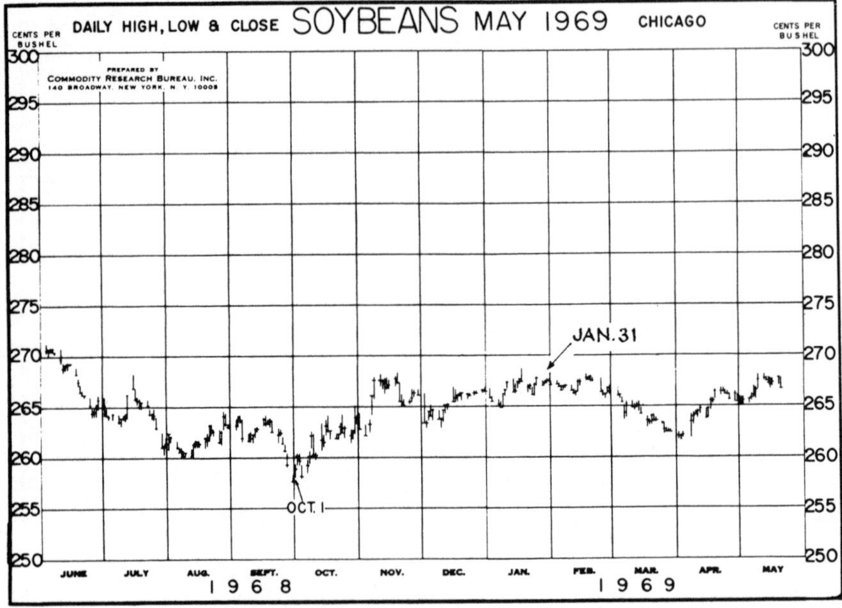

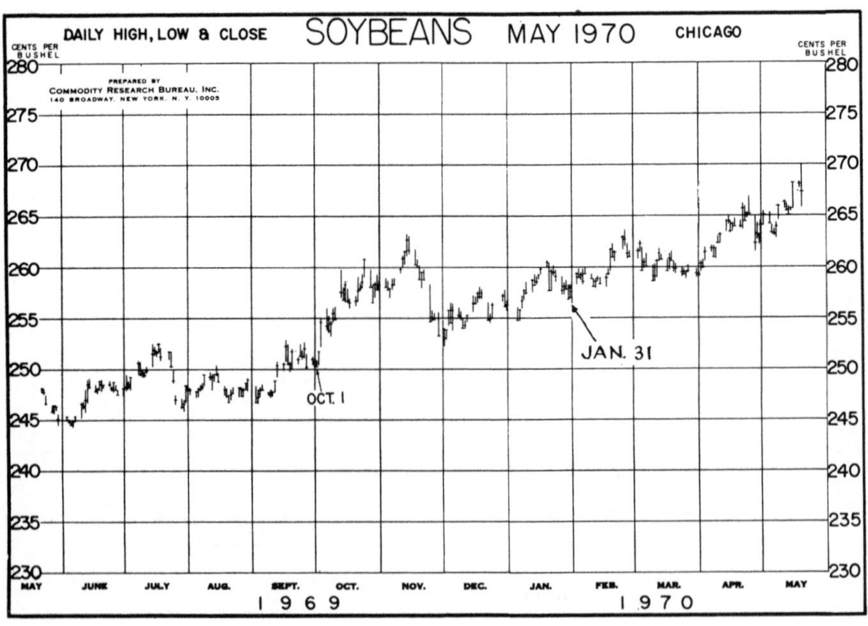

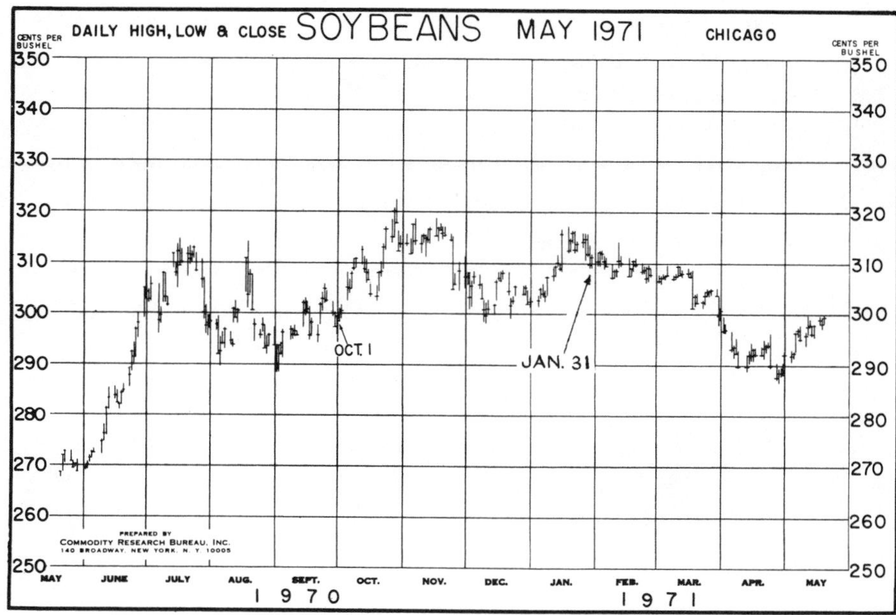

tive position that works with more frequency than this. Other seasonals may be found by studying price charts and articles in the back issues of the annual publication entitled *The Commodity Year Book,* published by Commodity Research Bureau, Inc., New York.

General Price Level

Price level is also an important factor that the thorough fundamentalist must give careful consideration to before taking up a position. Most analysts believe that it is the price level at which a commodity is selling that will usually be the determining factor as to whether a bullish or bearish stand is warranted.

The three types of price comparisons that are usually made to determine whether a commodity is selling too high or too low are as follows:

1) At what price is the commodity selling in relation to the current or anticipated government loan rate? Obviously, if the Gov-

ernment loan price is above the commercial market price for a given commodity it will induce farmers to pledge their crops and accept a Government loan. Such loans, when effective, create an artificial scarcity which cause prices in the free market to move higher—hopefully, above the loan price.

2) Speculators should observe at what price the commodity is selling compared to prices in past seasons when similar conditions have prevailed. An example of such a consideration can be found by examining the seasonal price movement of July soybean meal. This futures contract has a tendency to advance from about May 1 to July 1, as the market has a tendency to speculatively underestimate demand. Table 7 gives the closing prices on May 1 and July 1 for the July contract for the past twelve years. It should be noted that when a sizable price break occurred in 1961, it was the aftermath of a major bull market, prices having advanced from a low of $50 per ton in November 1960 to a May high of $78. At that

Table 7

July Soybean Meal
Net Change From May 1 to July 1

	Price (dollars/ton)		
Year	May 1	July 1	Net Change
1971	80.35	85.90	+ 5.55
1970	73.45	79.70	+ 6.25
1969	76.40	77.30	+ 0.90
1968	75.60	80.40	+ 4.80
1967	70.60	76.00	+ 5.40
1966	74.80	97.75	+22.95
1965	66.20	71.80	+ 5.60
1964	62.95	62.80	- 0.15
1963	65.75	71.80	+ 6.05
1962	57.25	64.60	+ 7.35
1961	74.50	61.90	-12.60
1960	57.20	54.15	- 3.05

price all the factors contributing to price strength had been fully discounted. Moral: Do not bet on a seasonal move, no matter how regularly it seems to occur, if the market has already had a major price move in the direction of the seasonal prior to the time the seasonal usually occurs. Note, however, that this seasonal is a pretty regular one which would have produced a fairly substantial profit if traded consistently over the twelve years examined. It worked in nine of the twelve years examined.

3) Thirdly, the speculator should note whether the price is too high or too low in relation to the price of other commodities. For example, Russian sunflower-seed oil, African peanut oil and domestic cottonseed oil can be substituted for soybean oil. If soybean oil prices rise substantially above the prices of these other oils, the price advance will be hard to hold, as consumers of soybean oil begin to make substitutions for it.

Scare Situations

The threat of damage to a growing crop or the spread of a disease that could be harmful to livestock frequently has a very strong bullish influence on price. The effect is most pronounced when the supply of a commodity is in fairly close balance with expected demand; a sizable reduction in supply can further tighten the supply-demand balance in the current season or the new season.

Almost without exception the scare takes prices far beyond those that are justified economically. One reason for this is that crop scares are usually given wide publicity and damage reports frequently exaggerated. Crop scares can and do make it onto the network-television news programs as well as onto the front pages of newspapers all over the country. The widespread publicity frequently attracts into the market new, amateur speculators who have just become aware of both the commodity market and the scare at the same time. Almost invariably these speculators arrive at the party late, but they are always welcome guests. For generally it is to these speculative virgins, who are long their first commodity contracts, that the old hands unload their contracts. Once the process of unloading begins, an unusually swift and sharp descent generally follows.

One need look no further than the corn futures market in 1970 and 1971. As mentioned earlier, one weekend during August 1970 Southern leaf-blight fungus was reported to be widespread in the main corn belt of the U.S. It actually reduced the corn crop by 10 percent, but there was talk of much greater damage. Corn ran up 30 cents per bushel in a few days, and as television put the blight into every living room in the nation, it prepared thousands of sheep for a giant shearing operation to be administered by hedgers and experienced traders. Many a small investor who had lost his pants in the stock market in the first half of 1970 felt certain that he would not only get new pants but a coat to match at the Chicago Board of Trade. There was much talk of $2-a-bushel corn, and thus the new speculators should have been a little bit surprised when they found the hedgers and more experienced speculators willing to sell corn contracts to them for $1.60 per bushel. Corn never went much higher than $1.60, and, in fact, it started to drift lower by October. Though prices periodically rallied, they never made it over their late-August highs. The whole scene was replayed again in June 1971, when corn blight appeared on the commodity wire services' teletypes in heavy concentration but failed somehow to make it into the cornfields. In this case the shearing operation was completed in a matter of weeks as corn dropped more than 50 cents per bushel by the middle of September (see Figure 8).

It is well to keep in mind that during the growing season concern over crop progress can become the dominant market influence. During the spring and summer most agricultural commodities are termed "weather markets." That is, weather forecasts for the growing areas can influence futures prices in very dramatic ways. Experienced traders view the price excursions caused by drought, too much rain, heat, frost and the like with a certain amount of skepticism. They claim that if you added up the dire warnings issued during the growing season you would find that most crops are usually lost two or three times before they are harvested. It has been well established that price fluctuations due to weather are greatly magnified beyond any real effect that the weather can actually have on the crop production. These fluctuations in price are usually short-lived because ultimately the only crop damage that is really important is that which changes the actual balance between supply and demand. In general, it is a risky business to carry a short position early in a crop's growing season before the supply-demand picture is fairly well established. Crop scares probably do more damage to the restful nights of bears than whatever force that actually produced the scare—whether it be a drought, flood, etc.—ever does to the crop.

General Inflation and Deflation

During inflationary periods commodities will generally increase in price to a level higher than that warranted on the basis of supply-

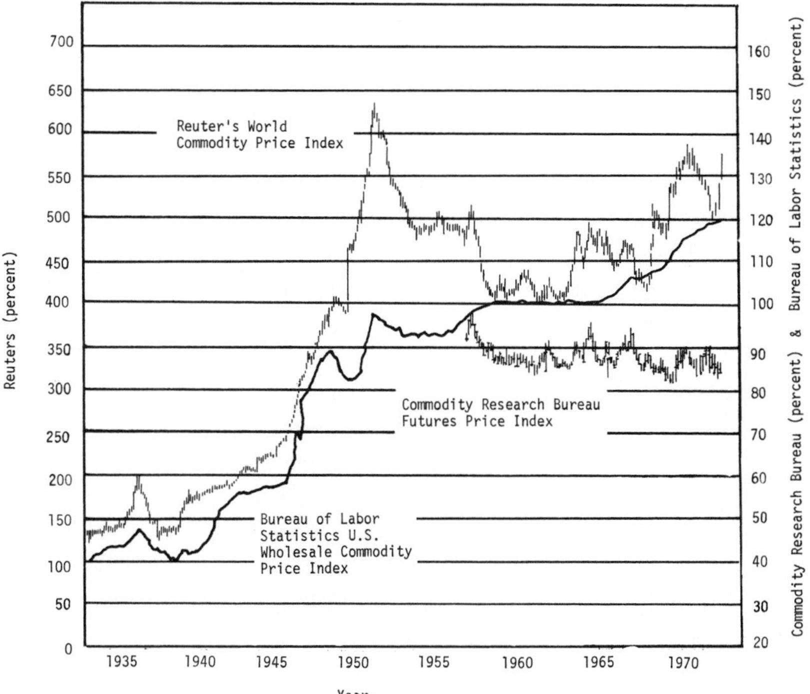

FIGURE 13. The long-term trend in commodity prices as measured by three widely followed indices. This chart courtesy of the Commodity Research Bureau, Inc., New York, New York.

and-demand statistics; of course, during extreme deflation the opposite will hold true. The pattern of these price movements can be observed for a number of years in Figure 13. Some weight, then, should be given to the state of the economy in general before assuming a speculative position.

Fear of inflation can produce price movements that are even more exaggerated than those caused by crop scares. An excellent example of such fears at work took place in the silver market with awesome results. Shortly after the U.S. Treasury quit selling silver at $1.29 per ounce in April 1967, silver started to move up sharply in price. In the first two quarters of 1968, price movements became more pronounced and dramatic. By midyear thousands of new commodity speculators had been attracted to the market as silver futures posted prices in excess of $2.50 per ounce. The amateurs were lured to the market by wild rumors of $5- and $10-per-ounce silver that were being spread by a group that was apparently a perfect match for the silver futures market.

This group, which we can call the "silver bulls," had long distrusted paper currency and deficit financing by governments; its members believed that the world was on the road to an inflation akin to that which swept Germany in the 1920s. They further believed that the only things of value that could be trusted were the precious metals; and since Americans cannot legally own gold, the hard-money people turned to silver. They buttressed their arguments for going long silver by pointing out that both the photographic industry (the single largest consumer of silver) and the electronics industry (the next largest consumer) were bound to expand their use of silver in the coming months. They were persuasive and persistent, and their following grew each day. In July, 1968 the silver bulls—or better yet, the silver sheep—were locked into the shearing pen, where they were given very close crewcuts by those who didn't believe: (1) that the world was facing a giant runaway inflation; and (2) that the world was about to run out of silver altogether. Some observers of the silver market believe that the silver bulls did not take into account that as soon as silver prices rose substantially above $2 per ounce, hundreds of thousands of ounces of silver would be attracted to the market from India. There, a family's collection of silver is its savings account, and as prices climbed, more and more Indians were willing to turn their silver into currency. This savings-account silver was smuggled out of India, eventually making its way to the London futures market where it proceeded to wreak havoc. By February 1969, silver was down to $1.90 and thousands of new commodity speculators had vowed that they would never enter the market again. Sylvia Porter, the financial columnist, estimated that more than a half billion dollars was lost in the silver shake-out.

Does this story mean that nobody made any money in the great silver run of 1968? No, it doesn't mean that at all. The one lesson to be learned from markets that attract the public interest in a grand swoosh is: *If you come to the party late you must be prepared to leave in a great hurry. It is foolish to hang around once the band has quit playing—and the band almost always quits just after those couples who have just learned to dance arrive.* The new silver speculators were mostly people who had dealt in stocks and had never faced a margin call in their lives. Many of them, much to their sorrow, put up additional margin after the market had turned against them by 10 cents an ounce or so because they couldn't believe that silver consumers were not anxious to buy silver at $2.50 per ounce, or that people would rather keep their money in a savings account drawing 5 percent interest, instead of tied up in silver bars or futures contracts that paid no interest in cash but held out the promise of $10 per ounce *sometime soon.*

Summary

The successful application of the fundamental method of price forecasting requires careful attention to a number of different factors. You must consider the estimated balance between supply and demand, and the role of the Government in the commodity you propose to trade—that is, loan rates and acreage controls. You must also examine seasonal price tendencies, the relative price level of that commodity to the price in previous years, and competing commodities. Furthermore, you should be aware of the general trend of the economy and alert to news that could cause panic buying or selling in the commodities you might be trading.

You may complain that you have no time to make such analyses. Fortunately there are a few advisory services who do concentrate on fundamental analysis, and for not very much money you can let them keep track of these items for you. More about that in Chapter 13 and Appendix C, which are devoted to advisory services.

CHAPTER **9**

Technical Trading I: Basic Chart Reading

□

As pointed out in Chapter 7, a true technical trader has nothing but disdain for compilations of supply-demand statistics, seasonal trends and Government-support programs. As far as he is concerned, price is the only relevant bit of data. (Some technicians extend their charts to include volume and open interest—a move that I hope to convince you in Chapter 10 is a wise one.) Their reasoning for this method of trading is that almost all the data that the fundamentalist uses are subject to interpretation, and, as has happened time and again, the same set of data can lead different traders to diametrically opposed positions. They argue further that much of the fundamental data available is not current but reflects conditions that held in the past. Of course, all the data projected for consumption or disappearance of a given commodity must of necessity be an estimate.

Technicians make these same objections to the evaluation of news events as they influence prices. They say, and many speculators agree, that it is extremely difficult to trade on news. The difficulty comes about because there are always those who know about the news even before it appears on the commodity wire services, and when it does appear, floor traders and board watchers will be able to act on the news long before the average trader even hears it. Therefore, part or most of the price effect will have been felt in the marketplace before the average trader can act. Thus trading on the news almost always means entering the market after some price adjustment has already occurred. Also, the trader must come up with the correct interpretation of the news, which might not be obviously bullish or bearish. This opens the possibility of taking the wrong position even though the news may be acted on promptly.

Chartists also argue that the trading public frequently fails to act on specific news events in what would appear to be a rational manner. They note that sometimes clearly bearish news is incapable of turning a strong upward-moving market down. In these cases, apparently, the trading public's confidence can be so strong that it chooses to ignore the news or else dismisses it as unimportant. The same kind of thing can happen when markets are in a bearish trend; in this case traders dismiss bullish news and choose to keep pressure on already falling prices. It does seem that at times the trading public is just not going to be influenced by rationality.

Lastly the technician notes that fundamental data are of no practical use unless they lead to buying and selling. The technicians argue, and rightly so, that it is price changes, volume, and open interest that tell us about buying and selling. In the final analysis no market influence is important unless it is reflected in changes in volume or open interest. There can be myriad arguments for buying and selling, but all arguments are meaningless unless they actually cause buying and selling.

Limitations of Technical Methods of Price Forecasting

No one knows for certain how long technical trading methods have been used, but presumably they have been around about as long as there has been organized markets. Traders have sought, in vain, of course, the perfect trading system—that is, a system that permits one to remove large profits from the market automatically and consistently. The idea is as intriguing as it is elusive. Perfect trading systems fall into the same class of chimera as perpetual-motion machines—the latter forbidden by the laws of thermodynamics, the former by the very nature of a free market. Hundreds, perhaps thousands, of technical trading systems have been proposed down through the years. Most of the systems that have been suggested are worthless, or nearly so. But a few have merit, and a knowledge of the principles on which they are based should be an essential part of every trader's bag of tricks.

Why are so many technical systems all but worthless? One of the most common reasons is that the originator of the system took a very limited amount of data and carefully developed a system that would produce a profit using that data and that data alone. The chances of that exact price pattern coming up again is so remote that the system turns out to fit that commodity contract (now expired) and none other. That is, as a description of past price events it is just fine—but as a predictor of future price action, you might as well use a Ouija board.

Sometimes originators of technical trading systems phrase their trading rules in such vague terms that there is really no way of knowing what you are really supposed to do in an actual trading situation. When confronted with the fact that the system failed to perform adequately the originator can then claim that the user misinterpreted the rules.

Nearly all technical trading systems attempt to go with a price trend. The worth of any such system should be judged by two things:

(1) How well it has performed in past markets.
(2) The extent to which it is based on sound principles.

A system that works well for a month or two with a March wheat contract really has not proven itself. If a system is able to demonstrate profitable results with ten years of wheat contracts, then it should become an item worthy of your study.

Technical trading systems perform well in markets that fluctuate over broad price ranges and in markets where, once a price movement gets under way, it continues relatively uninterrupted. Almost all technical systems do poorly in markets that are moving sideways. It is this kind of market that the technician fears the most, because it causes him to go long one day and short the next, meanwhile running up a number of small losses. If a trader believes in a system implicitly and it begins to whipsaw him, it can wipe out his trading capital in a matter of weeks. It is for this reason that few experienced traders will switch from a long position to a short position on the same day—rather, they prefer to wait a few days or so to ensure that a new price trend has really started, even if this means that they miss part of the action. This method of trading is best explained by saying that when utilizing a technical trading method one waits for the first show of strength following a weak market before taking up a long position, and one waits for a show of weakness following a strong market before establishing a short position. One way to do this in a market you believe is turning bullish is to place a stop order to buy above the market; in a market you believe to be turning bearish you place a stop order to sell below the market. It should be pointed out, though, that every trader will fall into a "bear trap" or a "bull trap" on occasions, and that the best he can hope for is that his method will stop this from happening too often. I shall point out in Chapter 11 several methods that are sometimes used to reduce the probability of being whipsawed.

Because of space limitations I shall discuss only four different types of technical trading systems in Chapters 9, 10 and 11: bar charts, with and without volume and open-interest data, moving-average systems, and a price-difference method. Though there are numerous other systems, I believe that these four are typical of the most important ones widely used today. I have excluded one method—point-and-figure trading—which is used to some extent in both stock-market and commodity-market trading. My exclusion is based on the personal bias that it makes no sense to me; but it does have its advocates, and for those persons who want to know more about this method I suggest that they take out a trial subscription to one of the point-and-figure services listed in Appendix C. In the balance of this chapter the bar chart is discussed, while the next chapter deals with the use of the bar chart with open-interest and volume data.

Basic Bar Chart Patterns

Bar charts are probably the simplest of all charts to make and interpret and take but a few minutes a day to keep current. They give a very clear picture of price movements from one day to the next, and even the most confirmed fundamentalists keep bar charts of those commodities that they are trading.

Along the vertical side of a piece of graph paper is marked a price scale that covers the region in which you believe the commodity you are studying is going to be trading. Along the horizontal scale are marked the trading dates, omitting weekends and holidays. Now for each trading day a vertical line is drawn from the high price for the day to the low price for the day. A short horizontal bar is then drawn across this line at the closing price for the day. If there is a split closing with two closing prices, then two horizontal lines can be drawn across the vertical line. Each day a new line and bar are drawn, resulting in a picture like that shown in Figure 14.

Trend Lines. The easiest pattern to recognize on a bar chart is a trend line. This is a recurring phenomenon seen again and again on bar charts for nearly every commodity. It has been frequently found that once a price trend gets under way, price fluctuations tend to remain along a straight line. More exactly, in an uptrend, the lower price limits of the daily price fluctuations tend to remain above a straight line, and in a downtrend the upper price limits have a tendency not to exceed a line connecting the daily highs. Figure 14 is a bar chart for the December 1971 copper contract. Suppose that it is now mid-February 1971 and suppose you had been keeping an eye on this copper contract ever since it made its lows in December. You decide to draw a trend line, noted as A–A′ on this chart, by connecting the low made the last week in January with the low made February 8. This is now your first trend line, and you go long December copper at 48 cents. You would want to protect yourself with a stop loss just below the trend line, say, at 46.80 cents. Since each penny's move on a copper contract is equal to $250, you have risked $300 of your capital on this position. (Assuming that the broker required margin of $1,000 on your copper contract, then you risked about 30 percent of your capital—which seems to me to be about the right amount.)

Things work out very well and after a week or so copper starts to move up smartly, reaching 52 cents by the middle of March. Prices have pulled sharply above your first trend line, and so you draw a second line (B–B′). You now use this line to help you set

FIGURE 14. A bar chart for the December 1971 copper contract. Trend lines in a rising market are made by connecting lows (line A-A′), and in a falling market by connecting highs (line D-D′). Stops to protect long positions are normally set just below a rising trend line and just above a declining trend line to protect a short position. This chart courtesy of Commodity Research Bureau, Inc., New York, New York.

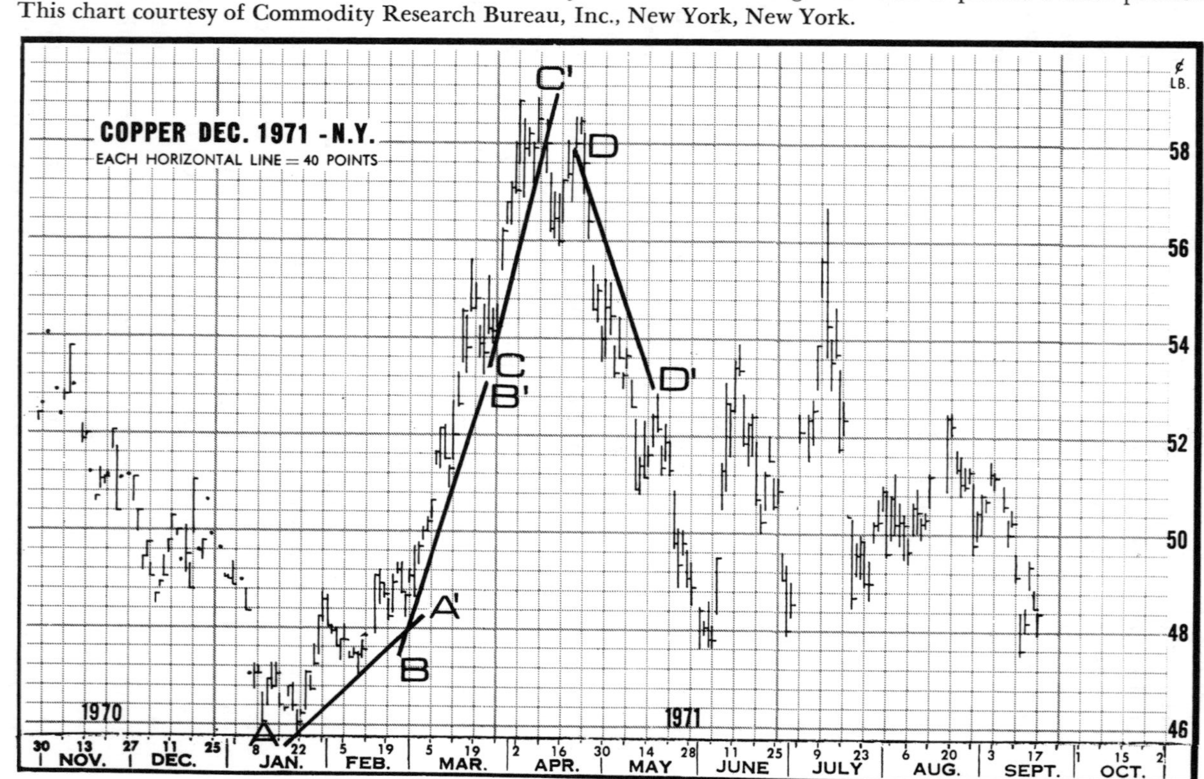

your stops; in each case you would place the stop just below the trend line. Toward the end of March prices have reached 54 cents, and you probably would want to draw another trend line (C–C′). This last line is penetrated in mid-April at about 57 cents, at which time you are stopped out of your position with a 9 cents per pound, or $2,250 per contract, gross profit. Prices idled around the 58-cent level for a week or so before breaking sharply, reaching 48 cents again by mid-June. By May 1 a clear downtrend line (D–D′) was evident and you could have gone short then catching at least part of the downside move. Note that downtrend lines are always drawn above the daily highs. Stop-loss buy orders would have been placed just above the downtrend line.

The prudent chartist never, never tries to guess the top or bottom of a trend—he always lets the chart tell him when to get in and when to get out. The chart tells him when to close out one trade and when to begin a new one. By necessity he can only enter the market after a trend is under way because unlike the fundamentalist he has no basic reasons for buying or selling copper at any time other than when "the picture looks good." The chartist, like all technicians, trades *with the trend and never against it.* Superimposed on the basic trends are moderate upside moves and downside reactions that might appear to be potentially profitable. You would be well advised to avoid trying to trade these short, sharp moves. To trade them successfully requires the nimblest of feet—like those of a tap dancer rather than of a ballroom type. And the tune always seems to change just after you get on the dance floor.

Double Tops and Double Bottoms. Besides just trend lines, chartists profess to see numerous patterns that indicate to them the future direction of prices. And indeed some patterns are clearly visible from time to time. Two of the most looked-for patterns are the double top and the double bottom. Let us look again at the December 1971 copper contract, but now let us concentrate on the time period between the middle of March and the middle of May in Figure 15. The market is in an established uptrend—remember we have been successfully drawing uptrend lines since February—and about April 9 a reaction begins that carries prices from a high of almost 59 cents down to 56 cents. However, the bulls appear to be in command and another rally ensues, carrying prices again to

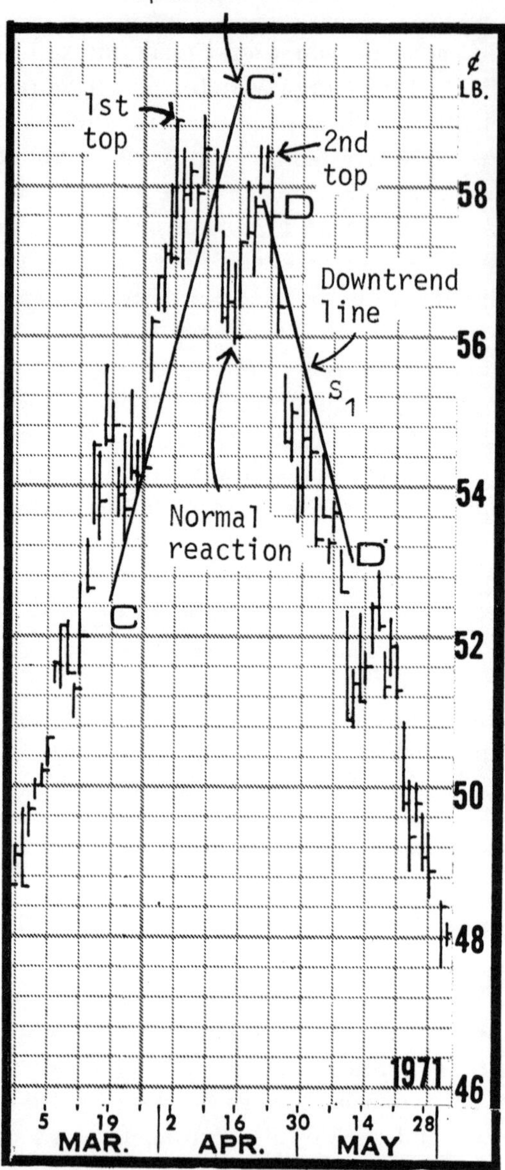

FIGURE 15. The formation of a double top by the December 1971 copper contract. After a substantial run-up in prices the market suffers a normal reaction before resuming its upward move. The market being unable to top its previous high, a sustained downward move ensues, bounded by the downtrend line.

just about 58.45 cents, but the market fails to break through its old high of 59 cents. Prices then sag, and before the end of April prices have broken the previous reaction low of 56 cents. Chartists leap to the fore, point to their pictures, and tell one and all that a *double top* has been formed and that a downtrend will now begin. And sure enough it does. The prudent chartist would have waited a few days for the complete scenario to be played out, not going short until the price had dropped below 56 cents—say, to point S_1 (see Figure 15) at about 55.5 cents. Stop-loss buy orders would be set above the downtrend line as indicated earlier.

The inverse of the double-top formation, not surprisingly, is called the double bottom, and it is frequently used to indicate when a price decline has ceased and an upturn has begun. Figure 16 illustrates such a formation for the December 1971 cotton contract. Traders, fearing a small crop due to a drought, and large export demands, sent cotton prices on a swift rise in the spring of 1971. In the two-month period from the beginning of April until the end of May, cotton went up more than 6 cents per pound ($3,000 per contract). Then an unusually sharp reaction set in, and cotton fell more than 5 cents in five days.* Over the next six weeks cotton prices formed a double bottom. Observe that on two successive days early in July cotton touched 29 cents but failed to penetrate the low of 28.60 cents that was hit the last week in May; following that successful test of the May low, cotton rallied strongly, going up the daily limit as technicians became convinced that a double bottom had been formed. Many technicians obviously did not wait for prices to rise above the midpoint level of the double bottom, which was at 31.30 cents, before jumping on the bandwagon. It should be pointed out that some traders believe that double tops and double bottoms are not very useful in pinpointing the beginning of a new price trend. But I have opted to put them near the beginning of this discussion because they are easy to recognize and they do seem to work sometimes.

Head-and-Shoulders Formations. The one formation that most chartists believe has more forecasting value than any other

* Note that this reaction occurred without forming a double top. Which means that while chart formations can help sometimes, they are far from infallible as indexes to the next price move.

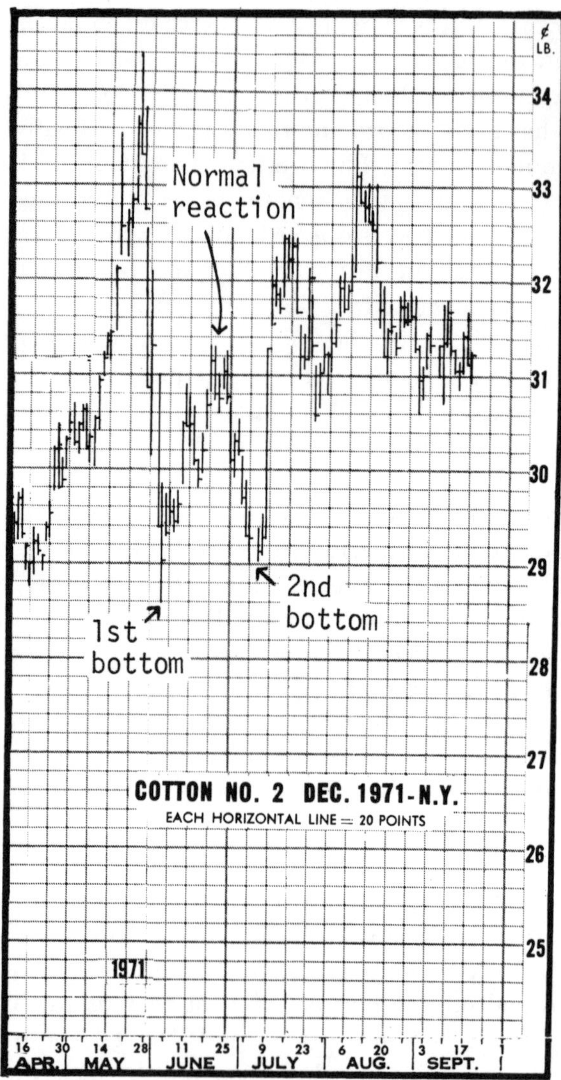

FIGURE 16. Traders sometimes look for double bottoms to mark the bottom of a price decline. Once again, after the first bottom is made, a normal upside reaction takes place before a second bottom is made, which signals higher prices are on the way. This chart courtesy of the Commodity Research Bureau, Inc., New York, New York.

for signaling the beginning of a new price trend is the "head-and-shoulders formation." While not every bull market ends with a head-and-shoulders top, probably a majority of them do. Such formations generally appear after an uptrend has been under way for some time; frequently the uptrend is then followed by a moderate reaction. Such a reaction is normal, and some traders use such reactions to establish new long positions. In Figure 17, note that this type of reaction occurred in late February in the Novem-

FIGURE 17. The head-and-shoulders formation is considered by many chartists to be the surest signal of the beginning of a new price trend. The first reaction creates the left shoulder, the new high that follows represents the head, the second reaction precedes the right shoulder. Once the right shoulder has formed, a downtrend line may be drawn against which short sales may be made. This chart courtesy of the Commodity Research Bureau, Inc., New York, New York.

ber 1971 contract of plywood; this reaction forms the left shoulder. The market rallies again after a week or so and goes on to a new high. The reaction to this next rally is severe enough to carry it through the upward trend line. Presumably at this point chartists who were long would have been stopped out of their positions. Stop-loss orders and shorts establishing new positions force prices lower until a resistance area is encountered. This completes the formation of the head. Then, some traders who are not convinced that the uptrend is over, and shorts who are covering their positions for a quick profit, create upward pressure on the market again, causing it to rally once more, but prices fail to make a new high. Then heavy selling develops, completing the formation of the right shoulder. The chart is now complete, and almost all technicians would agree that prices are headed lower, as the last rally created both a lower high and a lower low than the previous rally. A prudent chartist probably would not take up his short position until the right shoulder was nearly completely formed. More adventuresome speculators might start to go short somewhere around the right ear.* Stops would be set just above the top of the shoulder initially. Later, as the downtrend line became clearer, stop-loss buy orders could be set just above that line. This formation, inverted, of course, is seen less frequently at the bottom of a downtrend, where it would signify the beginning of a new uptrend.

Rounded Tops or Bottoms. The last formation that I am going to discuss is the rounded, saucer top (or bottom) or scallop top (or bottom). It frequently occurs in commodities that do not enjoy big daily price swings. The rounded shape is generally modified by a scalloping effect which is clearly visible in Figure 18 for December 1971 milo. The pattern generally becomes obvious before it is completely developed. Long positions could be closed out and new shorts established in this type of commodity by means of a moving-average stop—a subject that will be discussed in some detail in Chapter 11.

Other Formations. In addition to the patterns discussed here you will hear traders and some advisory services discuss numerous

* And they might wind up taking it there too; on the other hand, they might be rewarded with substantially higher profits for their daring.

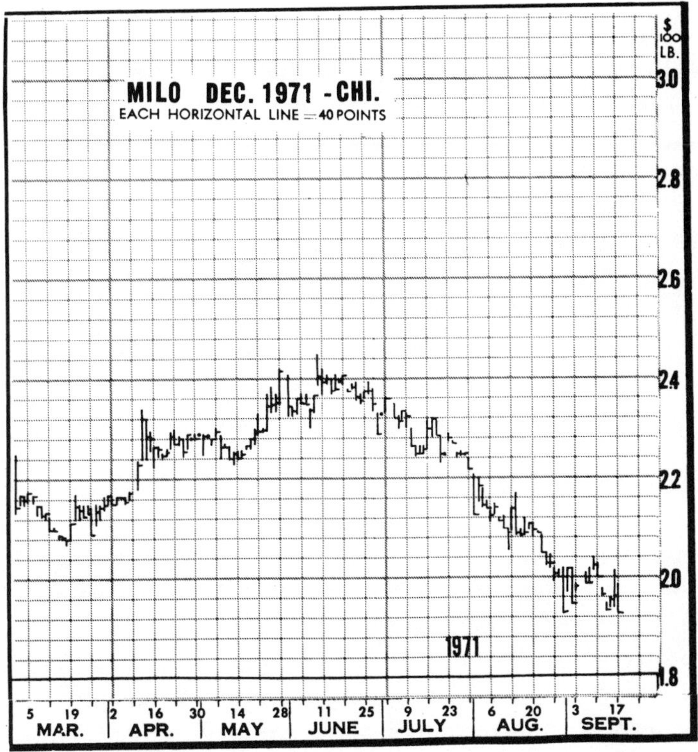

FIGURE 18. The rounded-top formation as illustrated by the December 1971 milo contract. This pattern is most commonly illustrated by commodities that do not have big daily price swings. This chart courtesy of the Commodity Research Bureau, Inc., New York, New York.

other chart pictures with such colorful names as coil (sometimes called ascending or descending triangles), symmetrical triangle and pennant or flag (sometimes called "pennant on a pole"). These patterns can be found on just about every price chart—the question is, What, if anything, do they mean? I am not sure, but you should understand that a lot of people think they mean a great deal. One of the problems of looking for them and trying to use them is that where one trader sees a descending triangle another sees a flag. And since a descending triangle is generally thought to be a precursor of lower prices, while a flag is generally thought to indicate higher prices, it stands to reason that it is important that a trader know which pattern he is looking at.

It is only fair to point out that there are some charts that display no meaningful trends at all. No matter how good your imagination, or how skilled you are at drawing trend lines and picking out double tops or head-and-shoulder formations, you simply will fail to find a direction other than sideways exhibited by some contracts. The chart for November 1971 Maine potatoes shown in Figure 19 is such a contract. Prices never went lower than 2.5 cents per pound nor higher than 2.83 cents per pound, giving a maximum contract fluctuation of $165. How do you trade such a contract? That is easy—you don't. In Chapter 10 you will find some clues that will tell you when a contract is likely to be a dull one.

What Charts Can Do

Charts are widely used by both speculators and hedgers for they are probably the single fastest way to see what the price tendency and pattern have been. They *may* be very helpful in providing some *tentative* conclusions about the direction of future price moves. It is important to realize that if enough traders are using the usual chart interpretations to trade a given commodity *it will influence the price of that commodity in the direction the chartists expect prices to move.* For example, if prices have just made a double bottom, then that is a bullish sign, and so the chartists will begin to go long and thus drive prices up just as expected. In this way the chart followers can prove their own theory right. While sometimes this works out very well it can also lead to some uncomfortable situations. Consider this case: A commodity's open interest is low and the only people who are interested in a given commodity contract are the chartists, who are now long; their charts tell them that the party is over and they all decide to run for the exit at the same time—but by then there may be no one to sell to. Did you ever see several hundred people try to get out a single door at a movie house? Under these circumstances you might see prices drop the daily limit two or three days in a row.

While a *pure chartist* does not wish to know anything about fundamentals, a *wise trader* will try to combine features from both

FIGURE 19. Sometimes a commodity contract exhibits a completely featureless trading characteristic. Technical or any other methods are of very little use for trading such contracts. This chart courtesy of the Commodity Research Bureau, Inc., New York, New York.

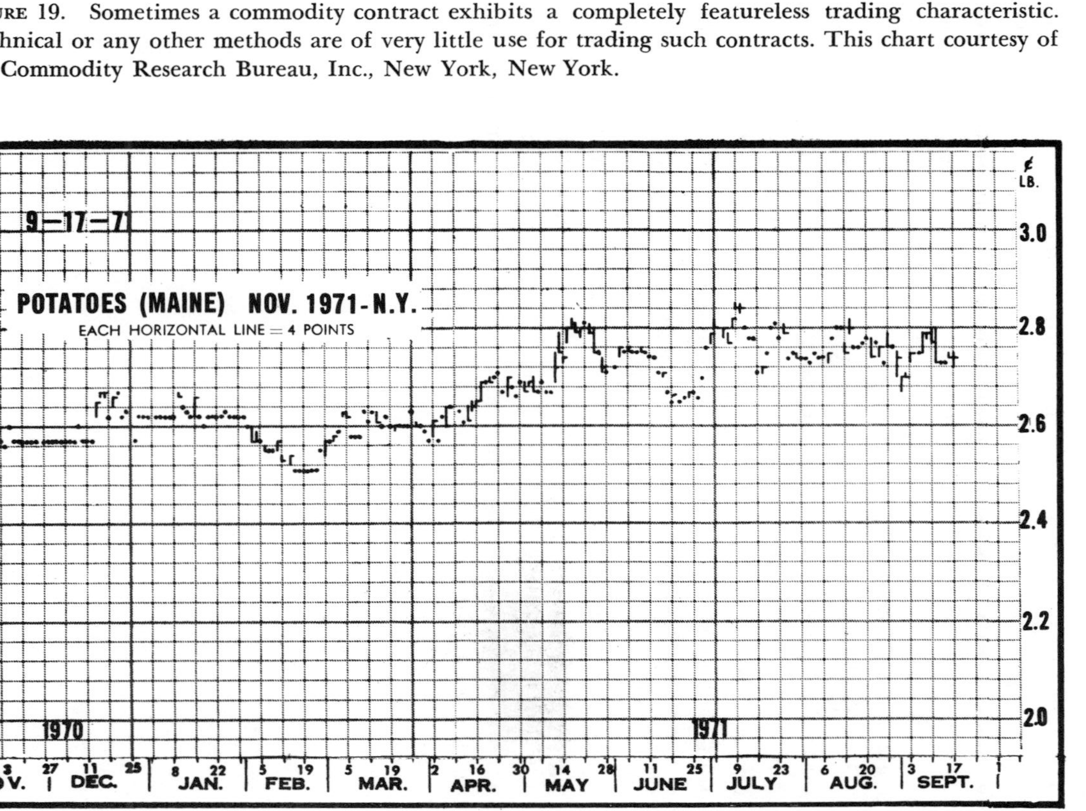

strategies. He will first determine as best he can what the fundamental situation looks like: How does the supply-demand balance stand? Are Government's actions likely to influence prices, and if so in which direction? And are there pronounced seasonals that argue for a price move one way or the other? After putting together as much of this information as he can, he will then turn to the charts to help set a price at which a position should be taken. Once a position has been assumed, charts can be used to help establish stop-loss points by use of trend lines.

The point cannot be overstated too much that chart reading should be tempered by fundamental information as much as possible, and with a little common sense thrown in to boot. Charts used in this way are surely better than working without any charts at all or depending on fundamentals alone. Charts will allow you to trade with the trend, and that is indeed the name of the game when it comes to profitable speculating.

But we have not exhausted all the information that is available to us from charts. A wise trader also charts open interest and volume. For we shall see in Chapter 10 that these two bits of information, when teamed together with price data, can increase the usefulness of a simple price chart by several times.

CHAPTER **10**

Technical Trading II: Charts with Open Interest and Volume Data

□

As was demonstrated in the previous chapter, price charts can be very useful in helping a trader to make market decisions. But, as was noted, "picking out the pictures" does not automatically lead to profits, because sometimes not even two experienced chartists will agree on what the pictures mean for future prices. A downturn in prices *can* be signaled by a double top, head and shoulders, saucer top, descending triangle, or none of the above. Therefore it would seem that additional guides would be welcome.

Fortunately the technical trader does have a couple of additional tools that will improve his chances of success significantly. These are open interest and volume data. To review briefly, let me remind you that open interest is simply the number of contracts that remain to be settled in a futures market.

Suppose you decide to go long May wheat. Whom you bought your wheat contract from will determine whether or not there is a change in open interest. If you bought your wheat contract from another long ("an old long"), then the open interest has not changed, because you will simply take over one of his wheat positions. However, if you bought your wheat contract from a new short in the market—a speculator who believes prices of May wheat will fall—then between your new long position and his new short position you have created 5,000 bushels of additional open interest. A new long and a new short are now in the market that were not there before. If when you finally liquidate your wheat position you sell your contract to a short seller who is covering his short position, the open interest will drop by 5,000 bushels. But if you sell your wheat contract to a newcomer to the market, the open interest will not change, as the newcomer simply takes over your old long position. At some point this wheat contract must be settled, either by a sale of it to a covering short or by someone who accepts delivery of the wheat upon expiration of the contract. Because the open interest is the number of contracts remaining to be settled, it represents the number of long positions in the commodity and, of course, the number of short positions. Suppose you read in the newspaper that the open interest in May wheat is 2,020,000 bushels—that means 404 contracts (2,020,000 bushels at 5,000 bushels per contract) are held by speculators and hedgers who are long, and 404 contracts are held by speculators and hedgers who are short. That is, 404 contracts are open and remain to be settled.

The volume of trading in a commodity is the total amount of that commodity that changes hands during a specified period of time. Volume data are given in the newspaper on a daily basis. When the data on volume of trading are published, only one side of the trades is shown, as purchases must equal sales at all times.

The Trading Mix

Many traders believe that *who* it is that makes up the open-interest data is just as important as the open-interest data themselves. That is, they remind themselves that markets are not really democratic institutions, for they take money from the many and distribute it to the few. Experienced traders characterize this effect by saying that the money goes from "weak hands" to "strong hands." The public is always characterized as weak hands, while the hedgers and professional speculators are thought to be strong hands.

Why should the public be stigmatized by the epithet "weak hands"? The answer to that question lies in the public's trading habits and resources. First, public speculators are usually thought of as small traders of limited resources who have a tendency to overtrade. At the first sign of a trouble, they frequently must liquidate their positions. That is, they rarely have the resources to withstand even a moderately adverse price reaction. Public speculators frequently are also poor students of the commodities they are trading and have only recently begun commodity trading. Unfortunately, much of their information is based on "hot market tips." rumors and hunches. Because they know their positions are based on shaky grounds, they close them out quickly as a way of finding protection against unanticipated price developments. It is also sad but true that many public speculators are out to make a "quick killing" in the commodities market—that is, they are *plungers.* It is precisely this type of person who is so easily outmaneuvered by the strong hands. For the strong hands are not interested in the quick killing today, as they know the commodity market will be here tomorrow; this attitude allows them to choose their risks carefully, and then, by using cautious trading practices, they are able to shear the plungers with remarkable regularity.

Strong hands possess all the characteristics that weak hands lack: adequate financial resources and patience; and they generally ignore rumors and other hot tips but give careful attention to sound fundamental and technical information. Strong hands are usually commercial interests, that is, producers or consumers of the commodity they are trading, who use the market for hedging purposes, or they are well-financed professional speculators. Because of their resources they can absorb reasonably sized paper losses while waiting for their expectations to be proved right. Thus they are far more difficult to shake loose from a good position. Taking losses does not bother them because they know they will be in the market this time next year and thus they look forward to all the gains that they will be taking over the next twelve months.*

For the most part, strong hands are careful students of the market, making it their business to know as much as possible about each of the commodities in which they trade; they know who pro-

* Surely one of the major reasons why weak hands remain weak or, what is more likely, leave the market altogether, is that they would rather look back and brood over what they should have done than look ahead to what must be done. Such backward-looking activity is incapable of producing profits; that is not to say that one should not consider what mistakes were made on a losing trade—but one should certainly not spend weeks replaying every trade before going to sleep at night. Not only will you be sleepy the next day, but such thinking is counterproductive in terms of helping to make the next trades profitable ones.

duces the commodity, what are the methods used to process it, what are the trade channels through which it flows, and what can be substituted for it. They generally have a pretty good idea of what they can expect as a profit on their position before they get into it and what they feel is a tolerable loss at any given time. They do not mind being out of the market for a while; they realize that the opportunities that they seek are not necessarily available in the market all of the time. They do their homework and weigh profit opportunities against potential loss with great care before establishing new positions.

That is not to say that the public trader is always wrong—because, in fact, he is not. But it is to say that he frequently lacks discipline in handling his trades. He also usually lacks a trading program and is far more given to getting in and getting out on an emotional whim.

The question of how well or how poorly strong hands and weak hands actually do in the market has been quantitatively answered, at least partially, by H. S. Houthakker.* Houthakker took the data collected by the Commodity Exchange Authority, which places traders in three categories: large hedgers, large speculators, and small traders. Houthakker studied three commodities—corn, wheat and cotton—for the period from 1937 through 1952; because of wartime restrictions, corn and wheat were omitted for the years 1940 through 1946. He then developed a crude measure of the profits achieved in the market by the various classes of traders. This was done by assuming that the commitments of a group of traders that existed at the end of a month were opened at the average price during that month and closed out at the average price during the following month. The profit or loss of that group was then found by multiplying the end-of-month position by the change in the average price. For example, if small speculators were long 2,000,000 bushels of May wheat on February 28 and the average price of May wheat was $1.40 per bushel during February and 1.47 during March, then their gain on that position was estimated to be $140,000 ($.07 × 2,000,000 = $140,000). Commissions were ignored in the study. This method of estimation has serious limitations but it is better than nothing. Because the data were available

* H. S. Houthakker, "Can Speculators Forecast Prices?," *The Review of Economics and Statistics*, May 1957, pp. 143-151.

Table 8

Net Profits (+) or Losses (-) of Three Categories of Traders in Commodity Futures[a]

(millions of dollars)

Crop Year[d]	Corn[b] Large Hedgers	Corn[b] Large Spec's.	Corn[b] Small Traders	Wheat[b] Large Hedgers	Wheat[b] Large Spec's.	Wheat[b] Small Traders	Cotton[c] Large Hedgers	Cotton[c] Large Spec's.	Cotton[c] Small Traders
1937-38	+ .46	+ .22	- .68	+21.93	+ .36	-22.30	- 3.43[e]	+ .44[e]	+ 2.99[e]
1938-39	+1.68	- .81	- .88	+ 5.91	- .45	- 5.46	- 3.80	+ .58	+ 3.22
1939-40	-1.67	+ .56	+1.11	- 2.59	+ 1.70	+ .90	- 8.04	+ 1.59	+ 6.45
Sub-total	+ .47	- .02	- .45	+25.26	+ 1.61	-26.87	- 15.27	+ 2.61	+ 12.65
1940-41	---	---	---	---	---	---	- 20.98	+ 2.04	+ 18.95
1941-42	---	---	---	---	---	---	- 9.39	+ 1.80	+ 7.59
1942-43	---	---	---	---	---	---	- 7.14	+ .82	+ 6.33
1943-44	---	---	---	---	---	---	- 1.84	+ 1.12	+ .72
1944-45	---	---	---	---	---	---	- 3.59	+ 1.41	+ 2.19
1945-46	---	---	---	---	---	---	- 79.77	+15.06	+ 64.71
Sub-total	---	---	---	---	---	---	-122.72	+22.24	+100.48
1946-47	- .20	+ 6.12	-5.92	+ 6.77[f]	+ 1.43[f]	- 8.20[f]	+ 11.00	+ 1.87	- 12.86
1947-48	- .36	+ 1.28	- .92	-22.86	+13.39	+ 9.46	- 12.80	+ 3.35	+ 9.46
1948-49	+3.58	- .55	-3.03	- .34	+ 1.56	- 1.22	+ 2.18	+ 1.85	- 4.02
1949-50	-6.06	+ 2.56	+3.50	- 5.44	+ 5.10	+ .34	- 12.93	+ 7.28	+ 5.65
1950-51	-5.52	+ 2.50	+3.02	- .47	- .19	+ .66	- 34.11	+ 9.25	+ 24.86
1951-52	+2.00	- .27	-1.73	- 9.19	+ 4.24	+ 4.95	+ 1.20	+ 4.13	- 5.33
Sub-total	-6.56	+11.65	-5.08	-31.53	+25.54	+ 5.99	- 45.47	+27.73	+ 17.75
GRAND TOTAL	-6.09	+11.62	-5.53	- 6.28	+27.16	-20.88	-183.45	+52.58	+130.88

[a] Figures may not check downward or across because of rounding.

[b] Computed by Method A (see text). Prewar years Chicago Board of Trade only; postwar years all markets combined.

[c] Computed by Method B (see text). Until August 1, 1945 New York and New Orleans only; thereafter all markets combined.

[d] Crop years start October 1 for corn, July 1 for wheat, August 1 for cotton.

[e] Excluding first two months.

[f] Excluding first six months.

in different form, a variation on this method was used to make the estimate for cotton.

Table 8 is a summary of Houthakker's work. Though there is considerable variability in the results, certain broad conclusions can be drawn. Small traders lost in the grains but did quite well in cotton. It should be noted that of the small trader's total computed profit of $130.9 million in cotton, no less than $100.5 million was made during the period 1940–1946, which was excluded in the grains because of lack of data. The data for hedgers shows only their profits and losses on futures commitments, which must be offset against profits and losses in the cash market. Most notable is the consistent profitability of the large speculators' transactions. In cotton they made a net profit in each year studied, and although they lost a few years in the corn and wheat markets, they never lost very much. One other interesting result that came from this study was to give the lie to the idea that small speculators are incurable bulls. Houthakker found that small traders do not appear to be less inclined toward the short side of the market than large speculators, although they are less successful on the short side than are large speculators.

Houthakker also found that, in general, large speculators tend to do better in the nearby futures, while small traders have a tendency to do better in the more distant ones. Furthermore, Houthakker asserts that since prices tend, in general, to rise as maturity of the contract approaches, small speculators who simply go long and have sufficient capital to take care of interim market reversals will, in the long run, show a profit.

Houthakker finally concludes that "Yes" must be the answer to the question posed in the title of his article, though he admits that by and large the big speculators do better than the small ones. He notes that since large speculators are professionals whose existence depends on their forecasting skill, this finding is hardly revolutionary, edifying though it is to see virtue rewarded.

Since, in general, the strong hands of the large speculator do better than the weak hands of the small speculator, it might be prudent to trade with the strong hands and not against them, unless you have excellent reasons to believe they are on the wrong side of the market. But how does one determine what the strong hands are doing? The only authoritative way that I know is to look

Table 9

Open Interest—Large and Small Traders

	Large Traders August 31, 1971		Net Change From July 31, 1971		Small Traders August 31, 1971		Net Change From July 31, 1971	
	% Long	% Short	Long	Short	% Long	% Short	Long	Short
Wheat (Chi)	64.9	57.7	- 1.6	-15.3	35.1	42.3	+ 1.6	+15.3
Wheat (K.C.)	89.4	92.4	+ 4.2	- 2.2	10.6	7.6	- 4.2	+ 2.2
Wheat (Minn.)	80.0	84.2	-13.0	+ 4.2	20.0	15.8	+13.0	- 4.2
Corn	68.9	63.2	+ 6.8	- 1.6	31.1	36.8	- 6.8	+ 1.6
Oats	24.7	63.2	- 5.9	- 1.3	75.3	36.8	+ 5.9	+ 1.3
Soybeans	76.7	65.1	+ 1.5	- 3.0	23.3	34.9	- 1.5	+ 3.0
Soybean Meal	78.8	83.7	+ 4.2	+ 1.8	21.2	16.3	- 4.2	- 1.8
Soybean Oil	81.5	80.7	- 1.7	- 1.3	18.5	19.3	+ 1.7	+ 1.3
Eggs (Shell)	14.7	35.0	- 5.8	+18.8	85.3	65.0	+ 5.8	-18.8
Cattle (Live)	36.6	37.5	- 5.3	+ 1.5	63.4	62.5	+ 5.3	- 1.5
Hogs	21.4	22.5	+ 8.1	- 5.0	78.6	77.5	- 8.1	+ 5.0
Pork Bellies	46.5	44.8	+12.9	+ 3.3	53.5	55.2	-12.9	- 3.3
Orange Juice	52.6	56.9	- 6.2	+13.6	47.4	43.1	+ 6.2	-13.6
Potatoes, Maine	28.1	40.8	-18.4	+ 1.8	71.9	59.2	+18.4	- 1.8
Cotton #2	41.1	67.8	+ 1.9	- 7.9	58.9	32.2	- 1.9	+ 7.9
Wool (Gr.)				NO LONGER REPORTED				

at the data reported monthly by the Commodity Exchange Authority. Some advisory services report this data regularly.* Table 9 reproduces a typical compilation of such data. The statistics cover only those commodities regulated by the Authority. There are some limitations on the use and interpretation of this data; for example, there are seasonal positions taken by hedgers which can cause large shifts in positions. Also, it should be noted that some markets are traditionally large-trader or small-trader markets.

Open Interest and Price Correlations

Now let us examine the role that open interest plays in forecasting price movements. The fact that open interest can be a useful addition in technical price forecasting has been established by a number of people. One group, Connor, Heiser and Smith, seeking a correlation between price and open interest, reported† the results

* The Commodity Chart Service, which is published by Commodity Research Bureau, Inc., in New York (see Appendix C for the address), is one of those services that do.

† G. E. Connor, R. A. Heiser, W. Smith, "Open Interest and Commodity Prices," *Journal of Commodity Trading,* Vol. 4 (1969), No. 2, pp. 8-15.

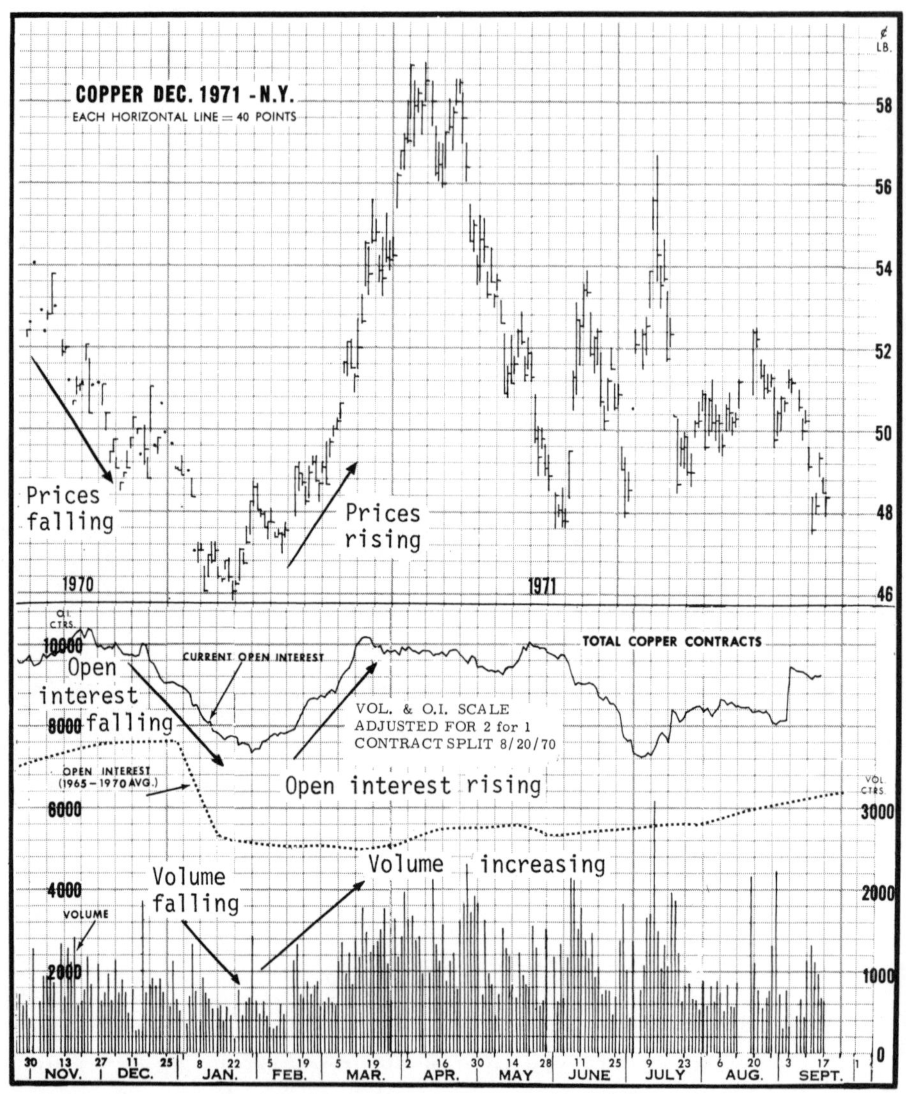

FIGURE 20. In February both open interest and prices began to rise for copper contracts—a characteristic of a bull market, according to many technicians. As prices began to rise, volume of trading also picked up, lending weight to the price idea of the copper bulls. The stage for a strong bull market was forecast by the decline in prices and open interest that took place in the months just preceding the February rally. Figure 23 also illustrates the pattern of falling open interest and falling prices setting the stage for a bull market.

of surveying over 2,000 chart patterns. They found that certain chart patterns were followed by certain price actions in as many as 93 percent of the cases studied. These results will be given in greater detail as they are presented.

Open Interest Increasing and Prices Rising. Indicates that the market is technically strong. New positions are being established, with some traders going long and some going short, but the buyers are more aggressive than the sellers because they are willing to pay higher prices to establish their positions. The report previously cited indicates that there is an 82 percent probability that prices will rise under these circumstances. Let us examine the December 1971 copper contract again in Figure 20. At the bottom of the chart you will find the open interest plotted as a continuous line, with the number of remaining contracts open given on the left-hand scale. The daily volume is plotted as a vertical bar on the bottom of the drawing, with its scale on the right. In all open-interest and volume studies, both the total open interest and the volume are plotted for all contracts that are being traded at the time the chart is prepared. Once again, let us suppose it is early February and we believe that an uptrend is starting but we would like more evidence before establishing a position. We examine the open interest line for early February in Figure 20, and sure enough it has started up. With both prices and open interest rising, we can feel fairly confident about establishing a long position.

Open Interest Decreasing and Prices Rising. The market is technically weak. The shorts have realized that they are on the wrong side of the market and thus they are buying back their contracts at higher prices, temporarily sending prices up. Their closing out their short positions by making purchases reduces open interest. No new buyers are being attracted to the market at these higher prices, and some longs might be closing out their profitable positions. There is about a 78 percent probability that prices will decline under these conditions. As an example of this pattern, we turn to the February 1972 silver contract as shown in Figure 21. In mid-January 1971 this silver contract was selling at $1.70 per ounce and there were 35,000 silver contracts remaining to be settled. By the first week in April the open interest has dropped to

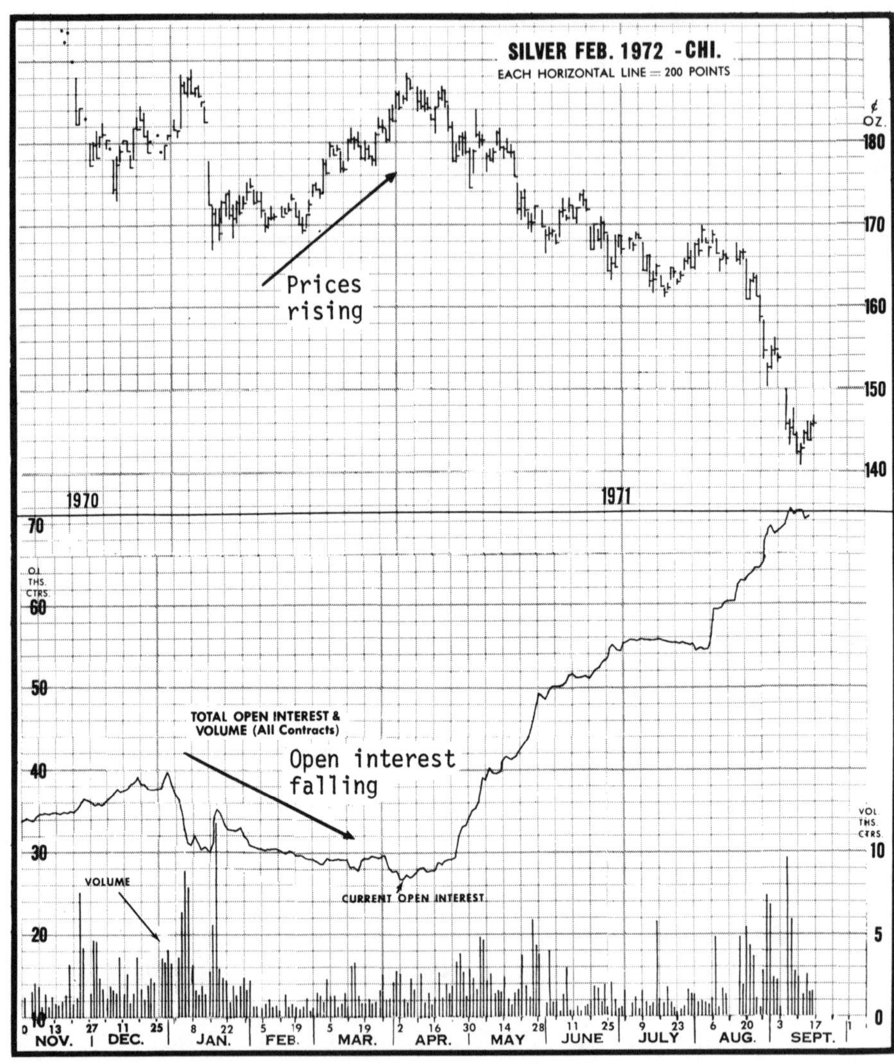

FIGURE 21. When open interest falls as prices rise, the market is technically weak. The shorts have realized the errors of their ways and are buying in their short positions, temporarily sending prices up and reducing open interest. Without new buyers some of the longs begin to close out their profitable positions, thus setting the stage for a sell-off. This chart courtesy of Commodity Research Bureau, Inc., New York, New York.

27,000 contracts while the price of silver has risen to $1.85. This pattern flashes a bear signal to all chartists, and just as expected, a sell-off begins, eventually dropping prices to the $1.30 range by November 1971.

Open Interest Increasing and Prices Falling. The market is technically weak. The bears are in charge and they are selling aggressively, while the bulls are not strong enough to offset additional short positions being created by the bears. Under these circumstances there is a 93 percent probability that prices will decline. This pattern is especially prevalent at the top of bull markets. Examine Figure 22, which is a bar chart for the November 1971 plywood contract with open interest and volume data added. Now we note that on March 5 open interest stands at about 5,000 contracts while prices closed at $110 per 1,000 square feet. By mid-April, open interest has risen to 5,900 contracts but prices are down to $100. We take the hint and decide to bail out, believing that the market has topped out. Subsequent events prove us correct.

Open Interest Decreasing and Prices Falling. The market is technically strong. The bulls are taking their profits, or else they are being forced from their positions by margin calls. The bears are reluctant to make additional sales at these lower prices, and older bears who are holding profitable positions have decided to take profits by buying in because they do not believe that the market will go down much further. Their covering action also reduces open interest. All these signs indicate that a downward trend in prices is coming to an end. If this pattern holds during the last phase of a bear market, you can expect the formation of a double bottom or V-type bottom 88 percent of the time. Figure 23 is the chart for the December 1971 live hogs contract. At the end of May, prices for December hogs were at about 24.8 cents per pound, while the total open interest was at 9,600 contracts. By mid-August, open interest was down to 5,200 contracts, while prices stood at 19 cents. This was a pretty strong signal that the bear market was over and a recovery would soon begin.

The rules then are easy to summarize for these four cases:

(1) When open interest and prices are moving in the same direction, up or down, market strength can be predicted.

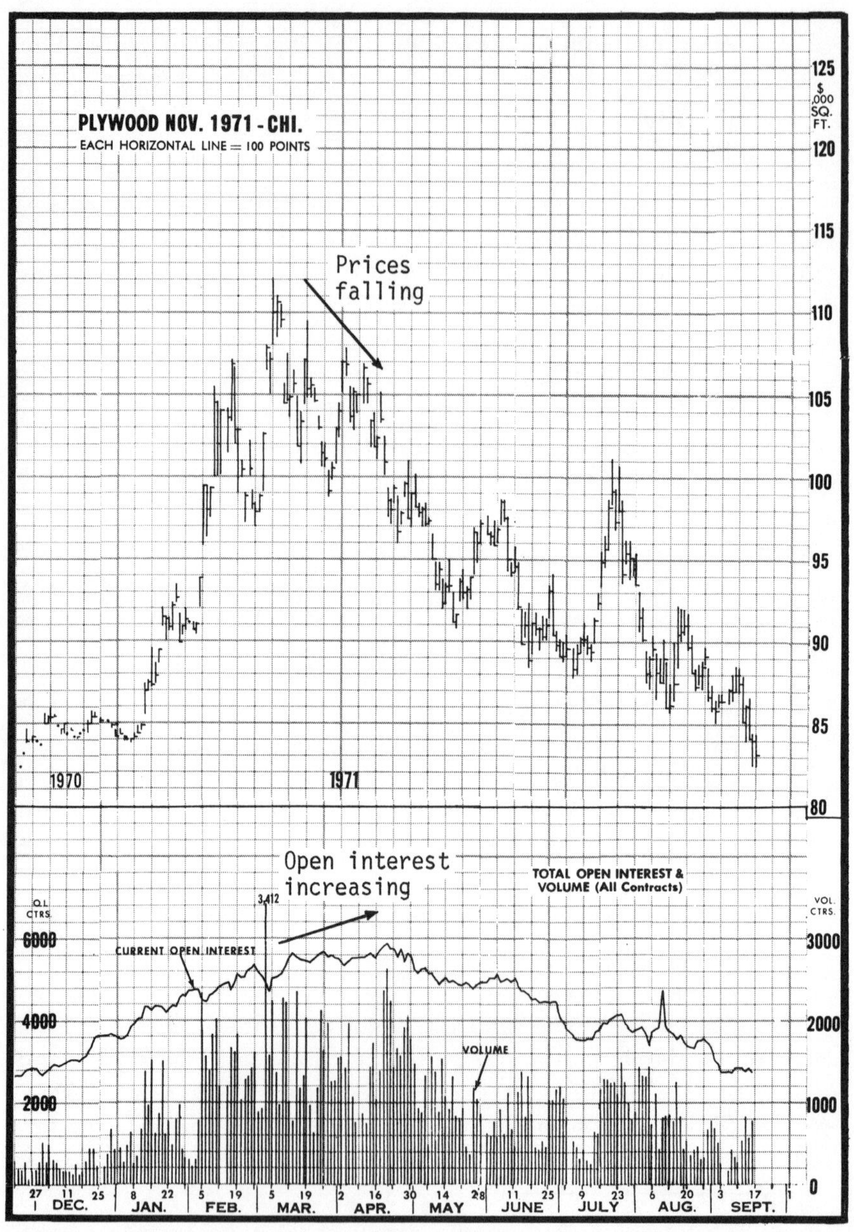

FIGURE 22. When open interest increases as prices fall the market again is signaling that it is technically weak. The bears are again in charge as the bulls are not strong enough to offset the increased selling by the bears which is causing the expansion in open interest. This signal is frequently given at the top of a bull market.

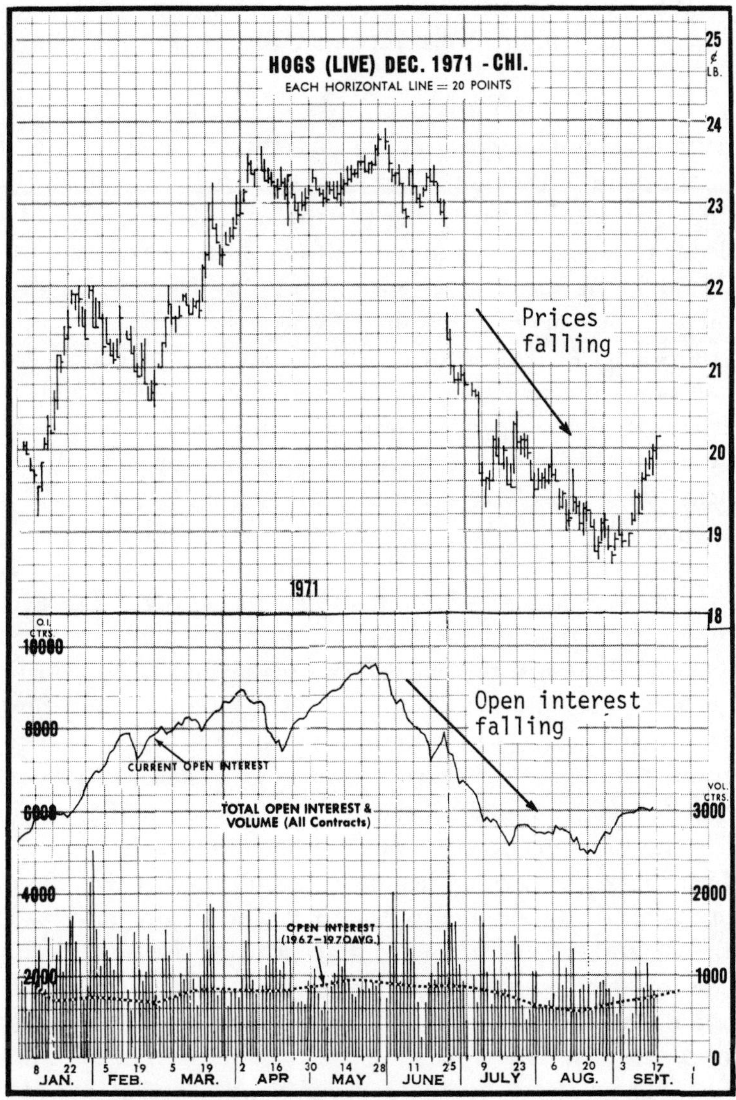

FIGURE 23. When open interest falls dramatically as prices plummet, the market indicates that it is becoming technically strong. After several months of shrinking open interest and falling prices, the December 1971 live hog contract experienced a rally that carried it from a price of 19 cents per pound to nearly 24 cents per pound by the time the contract expired. This chart courtesy of the Commodity Research Bureau, Inc., New York, New York.

(2) When open interest and prices are moving in opposite directions, there is a high probability that the market is technically weak.

Little Change in Open Interest and Prices Rising. This situation is generally thought to mean that both bulls and bears are buying. The bears are covering their short positions, which has a tendency to reduce open interest, but new bulls are coming to the market and thus open interest stays about the same. The only thing useful that you can deduce in this situation is that everyone is bullish, and sooner or later a correction will set in. The end of a bull market (and, of course, the beginning of a bear market) ends with great activity, large open interest and considerable volume. Generally the quality of this open interest will be poor and will reside in weak hands who have come into the market late and will run at the first sign of trouble.

Little Change in Open Interest and Prices Falling. The declining prices are due to the fact that both bulls and bears are selling. The bears are new in the market, causing an increase in open interest, while the bulls are closing out their long positions thus reducing open interest, which means that there is no net change in open interest. Once again this pattern is of limited usefulness, except that it will eventually lead to an oversold condition. Some help in this case can also be obtained from volume data.

A bear market generally begins (or a bull market will top out) on pretty good volume. Let us examine again Figure 20, the chart for the December 1971 copper contract. During the time when the double top was being formed, roughly from the end of March to the middle of April, volume frequently reached over 2,000 copper contracts per day. This tipped the chartists off that a top was in the making. Then prices began to decline, while open interest remained almost constant during all of April and May. The old longs were able to close out their profitable positions by selling (at a price concession) to some bears who were taking quick profits and covering their earlier short positions, while some new longs were attracted by the now apparently "cheap" copper, and thus open interest held constant.

Bear markets end in dullness—the daily price range becomes

small, open interest declines, and volume is at a low level. Once again the December 1971 copper contract in Figure 20 illustrates this point well. The end of the decline of copper prices, which began in September 1970, was clearly signaled in late January as price ranges narrowed, open interest shrank by almost 2,000 contracts from the November level of 10,000 contracts, and daily volume averaged only 500 contracts or so per day. Open interest at the end of this bear move and at the beginning of the bull move is normally considered to be in strong hands and of high quality. They have come early because they are pretty sure the show will begin soon and that it will be a good one.

There are several advisory services listed in Appendix C that have developed indicators that integrate price, open interest and volume; the use of such services can save a technical trader considerable time in making his trading decisions.

In both the case where the open interest changes little and prices rise and the case where open interest changes little and prices fall, "contrary-opinion theory" may sometimes be profitably employed along with these major technical indicators. The reasoning behind this theory is simple enough: A bull market cannot continue unless new bulls can be attracted to the market at higher and higher prices. Likewise a bear market cannot continue unless new bears can be attracted to the market at lower and lower prices. At some point during a bull market there will be no more new bulls to be found, or at some point during a falling market there will be no more new bears around. It is at these points that a bull market will end and prices will begin to fall or a bear market will bottom and prices will begin to rise. So a contrary-opinion theorist simply wants to find out how many people are bullish and how many are bearish.

Since most commodity speculators use advisory services to help them with their market decisions one need only find out what the services are recommending in order to judge the extent to which the market is bullish or bearish—at least, that is what most followers of the contrary-opinion theory believe. Thus, shortly after 90 percent of the professional advisers have turned bullish on July wheat, a contrary-opinion speculator would want to short it because all the people who are bullish on July wheat would now be long this contract and there would be no one else left to turn into a bull to send prices up further. Conversely, this theory holds that when only 20 percent of the professional advisory services are bullish on a given commodity, and 80 percent are bearish, that commodity is primed for a rally. (The reason why you can have a rally with a 20 percent bullish factor, but it takes a 90 percent bullish factor to get a decline, is that the public normally has a bullish cast to it at all times anyway.) Contrary-opinion speculators, then, are followers of the overbought and oversold theory of markets. When the consensus of the professional advisers is in the neighborhood of 55 percent, anything can happen and contrary opinion will not help. Advocates of this theory claim that it has been remarkably successful in calling market turns, but the theory must generally be used in connection with other technical tools as it lacks a certain precision in timing moves; this, no doubt, is due to the fact that there is a certain lag between when an advisory service makes a recommendation and when its clients actually act on that recommendation. You will find several advisory services listed in Appendix C that use contrary-opinion theory in making their recommendations.

Conclusions

I hope I have been able to convince you that while the price movement of a commodity is important, it is not nearly as good a predictive method as the simultaneous studying of price movement, open interest, and volume. Technicians who do not use all three of these tools are penalizing their price-forecasting efforts unnecessarily.

CHAPTER **11**

Technical Trading III: Moving Averages

□

Commodity prices sometimes do strange things. One day they go up the daily limit and then the next day they may go down the same amount. A new trader is frequently bewildered by these apparently wild gyrations. After a while he may convince himself that he can make money on these short swings, and more often than not he is soon wiped out. The trend reverses just as he gets in. A fact that is usually expensive to learn is that money is made consistently in the commodities market by riding with a reasonable-length trend and ignoring the short swings. If a wrong position is taken, losses are taken while they are small, and a new trend is sought. One way to find reasonable-length trends is to use a moving average.

What Is a Moving Average?

A moving average is just what the name implies—an average of a quantity, in this case, prices, adjusted to reflect the latest information. Sometimes charts used by stock-market analysts use a 200-day average to give them a graphic estimate of the long-term trend of a particular stock's price.

The Standard Average. The standard moving average is obtained by adding a certain number of days of representative prices (usually closing prices) and then dividing that sum by the number of days used to compute the sum. For example, to compute the five-day moving average, one would add the five most recent closing prices for the contract of interest and then divide that sum by five. That would be the current five-day moving average. The next day, one would add in the new close and delete the closing price from six days ago. An example should make this process clear. The five-day moving average for the December 1971 soybean oil contract for October 8, 1971, will be computed thus:

Date	*Closing Price*	*5-Day Sum*		*5-Day Moving Average*
October 4, 1971	12.08 cents/pound			
October 5	12.04			
October 6	12.15			
October 7	12.40			
October 8	12.54	61.21 ÷ 5	=	12.24

The moving average for the next day is found by adding in the closing price for October 11 and deleting the price for October 4 and so on, in each case adding in the close and deleting the first price of those that made up the previous sum. Thus the moving averages for the week of October 11 through October 15 for the December 1971 soybean oil contract are:

October 11	12.71	61.84	12.37
October 12	12.70	62.50	12.50
October 13	12.97	63.32	12.66
October 14	13.13	64.05	12.81
October 15	13.22	64.73	12.95

The moving average can tell a number of things, but its most important use is as a smoothing device. It always has a tendency to move slower than actual prices; in fact, the more days included in the average, the more sluggish the average will be. For example, the ten-day moving average for the December 1971 soybean oil contract for October 15 is 12.59, which is considerably less than the five-day average of 12.95 computed for that date.

The standard moving average has several attractive features as well as some drawbacks. Its chief advantage is that it is simple to compute and readily interpreted. While the use of a calculator can save considerable time in making the necessary calculations, if necessary all the calculating actually required can be carried out fairly quickly by hand. The chief disadvantage, according to critics of the standard average, is that each day's contribution to the result remains unchanged from day to day until suddenly that contribution disappears altogether. Thus the portion of the average that is about to disappear has just as much effect on the change in the average as the most recently added portion to the average—that is, today's closing price. The critics claim that surely the most recent price is a far more important index to where *prices might go* than is the closing price of five or ten days ago (or for whatever length of time the moving average is calculated).

The Linearly Weighted Average. The obvious solution to the problem of giving the same weight to today's contribution as is given to the closing price of three, five or ten days ago is to weight prices according to when they occurred. That is, to consider the newer prices to be more important than older prices. In this way a price's contribution to the average diminishes each day until finally a contribution disappears completely. P. C. Kettler and R. Heiser* have pointed out that a particularly simple weighting average to calculate is the linearly weighted four-day average. The procedure to calculate this average is as follows:

1. Multiply today's closing price by four.
2. Multiply yesterday's closing price by three.
3. Multiply the day before yesterday's closing price by two.
4. The closing price of four days ago remains the same.
5. Add the four resulting figures and divide by ten.

The sum is divided by ten because, in effect, there are really ten prices in this average. This can be demonstrated by simply writing down today's price four times, yesterday's price three times, the day before yesterday's price two times, and the price on the day previous to that once. The term "linearly weighted" comes from the fact that each day's contribution diminishes by one digit

* P. C. Kettler and R. Heiser, "Standard, Linearly-Weighted and Exponentially-Weighted Moving Averages," *The Journal of Commodity Trading,* Vol. 1 (1966), No. 12.

each day. This method can be applied to find the weighted average for the December 1971 soybean oil contract for October 15.

Date	*Closing Price*	*Weighted Closing Price*
October 15	13.22 cents/pound	13.22 × 4 = 52.88
October 14	13.13	13.13 × 3 = 39.39
October 13	12.97	12.97 × 2 = 25.94
October 12	12.70	12.70 × 1 = 12.70
	Sum of Weighted Closing Prices = 130.91	

Dividing this sum by 10 gives a linearly weighted four-day average for October 15 of 13.09 cents per pound.

Compare this figure with the ten-day standard average calculated earlier of 12.59 cents per pound and the five-day standard average of 12.95 cents per pound. Notice that the weighted-average figure is only 0.13 cents per pound beneath the closing price for October 15. Clearly this average is much more sensitive to the recent prices (and events) than is a standard average. A price does not simply disappear from this kind of average but sort of linearly fades away. However, it should be pointed out that a moving average that covers only four days is a very short period of time on which to base trading decisions. If one wanted to reflect the past ten days' prices in a linearly weighted moving average it would be necessary to divide the sum created by 55, which is an awkward division to carry out without a calculator. This sum is arrived at by multiplying today's price by ten, yesterday's price by nine, the day before yesterday's by eight, and so on. For comparison purposes it is interesting to note that the October 15 ten-day linearly weighted moving average for December 1971 soybean oil is 12.80, which is substantially less than the four-day linearly weighted average or the five-day standard average. I believe that this average gives a good balance to today's prices without overemphasizing them.

Exponentially Weighted Averages. Obviously there are many ways to compute weighted averages. Some technicians prefer an average that diminishes each day's contribution by a *constant multiple,* instead of a *constant amount* as is done in the linearly weighted average.* I believe that it is not necessary to consider in

* For example, one could assign to yesterday's closing price eight-tenths of the importance of today's close. Then the day before yesterday would have a weighting of eight-tenths times eight-tenths, or sixty-four hundredths, and so on.

detail such techniques in this book because the calculation of such averages without a computer becomes a chore, and I believe that many traders just might have an attitude about such calculations similar to one that Mark Twain expressed in *Huckleberry Finn.* "I had been to school . . . and could say the multiplication table up to 6 × 7 = 35, and I don't reckon I could get any further than that if I was to live forever. I don't take no stock in mathematics, anyway." However, for those readers who do place some stock in mathematics and would like to examine the exponentially weighted average, I refer them to Kettler and Heiser's work.*

Do Moving Averages Work?

Knowing how to compute a moving average is not nearly so important as knowing whether or not they work. Fortunately, some rather careful studies have been done on their efficacy. The use of a moving average as a trading tool is supposed to assist traders in "buying strength" and "selling weakness." Many speculators want to trade this way because they believe that a given price structure has a tendency to perpetuate itself. In order to verify this, Smidt† tested two rules using May soybeans data over the ten-year period from 1952 through 1961. The study is designed so that the trader is always in the market—long or short one contract. The trader can be in cash only before he makes his initial commitment.

Smidt computed an N-day moving average where N could take on values of 1, 2, 3, 5 or 10. In the test described below, the rule of action specified that the trader must buy (sell) soybeans if the N-day moving average should move up (down) by K cents or more in *any given day.* For example, if the trader was using a five-day moving average (N = 5) and K was equal to 1 cent, then his decision rule for either buying or selling would have been: *Buy (sell) one contract of May soybeans whenever the five-day moving aver-*

* They give a rather complete discussion of moving averages in the article previously cited and in two subsequent articles in *The Journal of Commodity Trading* entitled "Standard, Linearly-Weighted and Exponentially-Weighted Moving Averages—Part II," Vol. 2 (1966) No. 1, and "Part III" in Vol. 2 (1967), No. 2.

† Seymour Smidt, "A Test of the Serial Independence of Price Changes in Soybean Futures," *Food Research Institute Studies,* Stanford University, Stanford, California, Vol. V (1965), No. 2.

age advances (declines) by one cent or more on any one day. The prices at which executions took place were statistically determined by use of a random price variable that could take on any value between the high and low price on the day following the signal. Table 10 gives the results of Smidt's work for moving averages of one, two, three, five and ten days while K could take on values between 0.5 cents and 4.0 cents.

An examination of Table 10 reveals, in the example just cited of N = 5 days and K = 1.0 cent, that during the ten years from 1952 through 1961 the trader netted a profit of 110 cents per bushel after commissions. In his best year he netted 72 cents per bushel and in his worst year he suffered a loss of 54 cents per bushel. The rule was profitable, at least a little, in seven out of ten years, it produced losses in two years, and it was a standoff in one year. This combination produced 57 trades in the ten years and generated 21 cents of commission per bushel in that time. Table 11 summarizes the results by year.

Table 11 reveals that the combination of a ten-day moving average with a 1 cent change in price would have produced the highest total net profit of all the combinations investigated; it yielded 197 cents per bushel while causing a loss of not more than 14 cents in any one year. Note that this profit of nearly $2 per bushel was produced from only seventeen trades. Further examination of Table 11 reveals that soybean trading is profitable only if one is able to catch the years in which big moves are made. Even the N = 10, K = 1 rule showed outstanding results because it was able to place the trader on the right side of the market in the major bull-market years of 1954, 1955 and 1956. The sensitivity of such a trading rule is easy to examine by considering what happens to profits as K, the change required to initiate a trade, is varied. If K is dropped to 0.5 cents while the trader is still using a ten-day moving average, profits on 61 trades after commissions drop to 25 cents per bushel over ten years of trading. This rule obviously produces considerable whipsawing, responding far too frequently to short-term market moves while generating a large number of small losses. On the other hand, if K is changed to 2.0 cents while the trade is utilizing a ten-day moving average, only five trades are made in ten years, but those five produce 58 cents of net profit; however, in most years no trades at all are instituted. Tables 10 and 11 tell a very

Table 10

Results of Soybean Rules Testing the Use of Different Moving Average Lengths and Action Signals

Summary—Total profits or losses,* cents per bushel

Action Signals		1952-1961		After Commission, in year with		After Commission, number of years†			
Length of Moving Average N, days	Change required, K, cents per bushel	After commission	Before commission	Best profits	Worst losses	With profits	With losses	Commission, cents per bushel	Total number of moves
1	1.0	-476	-338	1	-112	1	9	138	384
1	2.0	-176	-112	18	-108	3	7	64	117
1	3.0	- 59	- 29	100	- 66	4	5	30	83
1	4.0	146	163	91	- 19	7	2	17	46
2	1.0	- 12	52	104	- 40	4	6	64	178
2	2.0	3	28	83	- 46	4	5	25	69
2	3.0	71	84	93	- 44	5	3	13	37
2	4.0	36	44	51	- 19	3	4	8	21
3	1.0	112	154	142	- 27	4	5	42	116
3	2.0	75	89	108	- 50	7	3	14	40
3	3.0	67	73	61	- 42	4	3	6	18
3	4.0	20	23	41	- 16	1	2	3	9
5	0.5	9	57	52	- 53	3	7	48	133
5	1.0	110	131	72	- 54	7	2	21	57
5	1.5	102	112	43	- 20	6	2	10	28
5	2.0	149	155	77	- 22	6	1	6	18
10	0.5	25	47	65	- 50	5	5	22	61
10	1.0	197	203	100	- 14	7	1	6	17
10	1.5	124	127	113	- 45	3	2	3	7
10	2.0	58	60	54	- 29	2	1	2	5

*Profits and losses rounded to the nearest cent.

†Total does not always equal 10 because of years in which profits or losses were less than half a cent per bushel, or in which no trading occurred.

Table 11

Results of Soybean Rules Testing the Use of Action Signals by Year

Annual profits and losses* after commissions, cents per bushel

Action Signals N	K	1951-1952	1952-1953	1953-1954	1954-1955	1955-1956	1956-1957	1957-1958	1958-1959	1959-1960	1960-1961	Total
1	1.0	-86	-60	- 42	-110	- 1	-29	-16	1	-21	-112	-476
1	2.0	-41	-15	18	- 48	- 1	11	- 5	- 4	17	-108	-176
1	3.0	-35	-24	100	8	-39	3	-14	0	8	- 66	- 59
1	4.0	4	-19	91	- 17	25	12	20	0	1	29	146
2	1.0	-17	-37	104	2	46	-26	-25	-21	2	- 40	- 12
2	2.0	-46	-31	83	7	-10	12	18	0	- 2	- 28	3
2	3.0	-20	-44	93	- 3	19	6	18	0	2	0	71
2	4.0	- 9	-19	28	- 16	51	13	0	0	0	- 12	36
3	1.0	-22	5	142	0	53	-27	5	- 6	-21	- 17	112
3	2.0	-11	4	108	14	- 4	1	11	0	2	- 50	75
3	3.0	-19	19	45	- 42	61	13	0	0	0	28	67
3	4.0	0	0	- 16	0	- 5	0	0	0	0	41	20
5	0.5	-18	-11	46	- 53	52	-14	-13	- 4	- 3	27	9
5	1.0	-26	-54	61	5	15	12	17	0	8	72	110
5	1.5	-20	12	43	- 15	35	9	0	0	3	35	102
5	2.0	-22	2	77	16	35	14	0	0	0	27	149
10	0.5	-50	10	55	- 37	65	-31	-10	- 4	7	20	25
10	1.0	-14	1	100	34	35	16	0	0	1	24	197
10	1.5	-10	0	113	- 45	37	0	0	0	0	29	124
10	2.0	0	0	54	0	33	0	0	0	0	- 29	58
Average per year		-23	-15	65	- 15	25	0	0	- 2	0	- 6	29

*Profits and losses rounded to the nearest cent.

clear story: Use a trading system that will allow you to catch a substantial number of the big moves, but one that is not so sensitive that it causes you to be whipsawed by random price movements. In the next section we shall examine several methods that claim to do just that.

Ways to Use Moving Averages

There are a number of methods to use moving averages in a trading program. All of them require some calculation but none so much that the calculation time would become burdensome.

The Two-Moving-Averages Method. In this technique two moving averages are utilized. One of the two averages is used to identify a longer-term trend while the other is utilized as a timing device to put a trader on the right side of that trend. For example, the ten-day moving average can be used to look for longer term trends while a three-day moving average is used to initiate the buy and sell orders.

The simplest way to use this method is to calculate the averages and then graph the results. Graph paper that has ten squares to the inch may be used for commodities that trade in tenths and hundredths of a cent (or dollars) while paper divided eight squares to the inch is easier to use for commodities like the grains, which trade in eighths of a cent. On the vertical scale mark off the price range around which the commodity is trading, while on the horizontal scale indicate the days of the month on which trading will take place—that is, leave no spaces for weekends or holidays.

To begin, all you need is ten days of price data. Figure 24 illustrates this method as applied to the December 1971 soybean oil contract. Plotting of the data began with Monday, September 20, 1971. That means that first the closing prices for the preceding ten trading days that began on September 7 and ended on September 20 were recorded on a columnar bookkeeping pad. Then the average price based on those ten days—12.46 cents per pound—was plotted on the line marked September 20. Next the three-day moving average was computed by taking the closing prices for the three trading days of September 16, 17 and 20 and that price—12.09 cents

FIGURE 24. The three-day and ten-day moving average method applied to the December 1971 soybean oil contract. When the three-day moving average (dashed line) crosses the ten-day moving average (solid line) going up, this is a buy signal; when it crosses it going down, this is a sell signal.

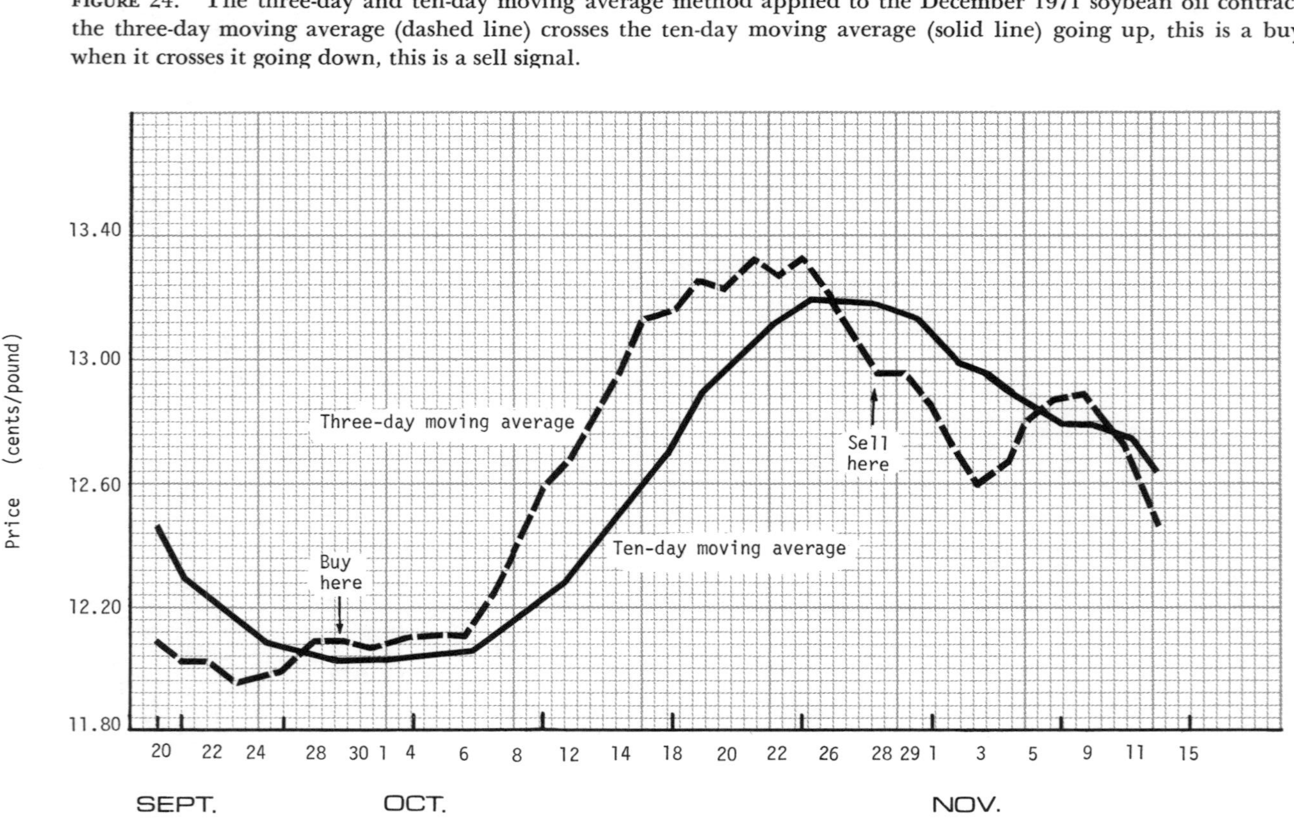

per pound—was plotted also on the September 20 line. This process was continued for a few days and then the ten-day-average figures were connected with a green (or solid) line and the points representing the three-day average were connected with a red (or dashed) line. Some technicians like to plot prices as is done on a bar chart, in addition to using the red and green moving-average lines.

Keep in mind that the three-day moving average will be much more volatile and will jump around considerably more than will the ten-day line. Note that on September 24, after five days of plotting these two averages, that the ten-day line is still falling but that the three-day line seems to be trying to flatten out. The plot (or maybe it's the soybean oil) thickens. After completing the calculations, it is observed on September 28 that the three-day moving average has a value of 12.07 cents per pound while the ten-day moving average has a value of 12.05 cents per pound. *The three-day average has crossed the ten-day average on the upside.* That is a buy signal and is an indication that the market is trying to bottom out. A moving-average trader would call his broker and tell him to buy one December 1971 soybean oil contract at the market on the opening the next day. Soybean oil opens at 12.05 cents per pound, and the trader is in the market long at that price.

The trader continues to compute a three-day and a ten-day moving average and to plot the results on the graph. If the three-day average should close below the ten-day average, that would be a sell signal and he would call his broker and tell him to sell him out on the opening the next day. On September 30 and October 6, the three-day average came within 0.03 cents of the ten-day average but it did not cross it. By October 8, however, soybean oil is showing considerable strength, and the three-day average is starting to move rapidly away from the ten-day average. The trader knows that this will be a profitable position. On October 18, four weeks after the trader has initiated the position, the three-day average stands at 13.14 cents per pound and the ten-day is at 12.69 cents per pound, thus assuring the trader of a gross profit of around 0.64 cents per pound ($384 per contract).

The three-day average did not cross the ten-day average going down until October 27, 1971, at a price of 13.17 cents per pound. The next day the trader calls his broker and sells *two* contracts at the opening. This order is executed at 12.85 cents per pound. One contract offsets his long position with a $447 net profit. The other contract represents a new short position in soybean oil, which will be maintained until the three-day average crosses the ten-day average on the upside. The rule that summarizes the procedure for this method is, then: *Go long and cover shorts when the three-day moving average closes above the ten-day moving average; go short and offset long positions when the three-day moving average closes below the ten-day moving average.*

This rule will not work every time. Less than two weeks later, the three-day moving average crossed the ten-day moving average on an upside move. The trader would have closed out his short position on the opening on November 9, 1971, at 12.87 cents per pound, thereby suffering a loss of $12 plus $33 in commissions for a net loss of $45 on the short sale. Three days later, on November 12, the new long position would have been closed out on the opening at 12.37 cents per pound, incurring a net loss of $333 on this trade. The loss from whipsawing could have been partially reduced by using stops based on an adjusted ten-day moving average. It should be made clear, however, that there is no way to avoid being whipsawed when using a completely technical method to follow the market. But this method will put you on the right side of a major trend shortly after it develops and it will keep you there for a substantial part of the move.

A sensible way to use this method would be to track five or six commodities at once and then take up positions in these commodities as they are called for. That will improve chances of catching a couple of good moves. Losses should be small in most cases, but as was pointed out earlier, a whipsawing market could generate a series of small losses over a period of time. By applying common sense, it should be possible to avoid markets that are going nowhere and thus reduce the losses in commodities that are not showing a definite price trend. No one forces you to be in the market all the time.

This system has been tested and the results have been reported.* Of six commodities chosen at random and "paper traded" by this method during 1968, five of the six showed some profit. Two of the profitable commodities (frozen orange juice and cotton) showed

* W. L. Principe, R. A. Heiser, and S. Gitomer, "A Plea for Simplicity," *The Journal of Commodity Trading*, Vol. 3 (1968), No. 5.

profits in excess of $2,500; pork bellies showed a net loss of $1.

I believe this to be an excellent method for a beginner to use to initiate his trading. If followed rigorously, it will not allow you to stay with a losing position long after you should have closed it out. Once you have had some experience with this method you might wish to try some variations on it. For example, you might want to try replacing the three-day moving average with a four-day linearly weighted average, which will make the method more sensitive to the most recent prices. This increased sensitivity could lead to the catching of a bigger part of a price move; it might also aggravate the whipsawing tendency of this method in certain kinds of markets.

The Seven-Week Moving-Average Method. Another technique that employs a moving average to initiate and close out trades is one developed by Dennis D. Dunn and Edwin F. Hargitt.* This method is, if anything, simpler than the two-moving-averages method described on page 143. The originators of this method have found that a seven-week moving average is a good index to long-range trends. Furthermore they note that it is not necessary to include every one of the thirty-five closing prices in a seven-week period, but that the Thursday closing is a fairly reliable index to long-range price trends. (Friday closings are not very significant because a number of traders like to even out their positions before the weekend so that they hold no open trades on Saturday and Sunday.) Thus, the seven-week moving average is calculated by adding up the closing prices for the past seven Thursdays and, of course, dividing that sum by seven. (If a Thursday close is not available, because of a holiday, for example, the Wednesday close is used.)

This moving average is then plotted two weeks ahead of the actual data for which it is calculated. That is, the moving average calculated for September 16 is plotted for September 30. In this way a trader will always have a moving-average line to trade against and it will not be necessary to wait for the next Thursday's close in order to make a trading decision. Thus the moving-average line will always have a one- to two-week lead ahead of current

* D. D. Dunn and E. F. Hargitt, "7-Week Moving Average Trading Method," *The Journal of Commodity Trading,* Vol. 4 (1969), No. 4.

prices. Daily prices are plotted as is done on a bar chart, with the length of the line indicating the range for the day and a short horizontal bar denoting the closing price for the day. The trading rule is extremely simple: *Go long or cover short positions if the daily price closes above the seven-week-moving-average line; conversely, sell short or offset longs if the daily price closes below the seven-week moving-average line.*

Orders to do this can be "on-the-close" orders, which will automatically set your position, since you will always have a moving-average line to trade against. In Figure 25 the seven-week average line for December 1971 soybean oil is plotted along with a bar chart of prices. Note that the first close above the moving-average line took place on October 11. An on-the-close order would have put a speculator long at 12.71 cents per pound. Recall that the three- and ten-day moving-average method would have put a trader long September 29 at 12.05 cents per pound. Thus it is obvious that the seven-week moving-average is less sensitive to changes in price trends. It was not until November 12 that prices *closed* below the seven-week moving-average line at 12.14 cents per pound, which would have produced a loss of $375 if a trader were using it to initiate and close out his positions. Obviously this method works best in markets with trends that build up over several months rather than several weeks. As in the two-moving-averages method, a short position would be taken up at the same time the long position is offset. This, of course, requires the sale of two contracts.

Dunn and Hargitt used the seven-week moving-average method to trade 14 different commodities for the period 1963 through 1968. This involved more than 1,000 "paper trades." They found that this technique worked best with copper, wheat, cattle, sugar and soybean oil. And of those commodities, December copper was the most profitable, averaging more than $1,000 per trade.

Price-Difference Method. Some technical methods do not depend upon price levels from which to derive buying and selling signals but instead depend upon price changes. Teweles, Harlow and Stone* have pointed out in a rather complete discussion of this method that if the price of a commodity continues up, but at

* R. J. Teweles, C. V. Harlow, H. L. Stone, *The Commodity Futures Trading Guide* (New York: McGraw-Hill Book Company, 1969).

FIGURE 25. The seven-week moving average method applied to the December 1971 soybean oil contract. When prices close above the seven-week moving average line, this is a buy signal; when prices close below the seven-week moving average line this is a sell signal.

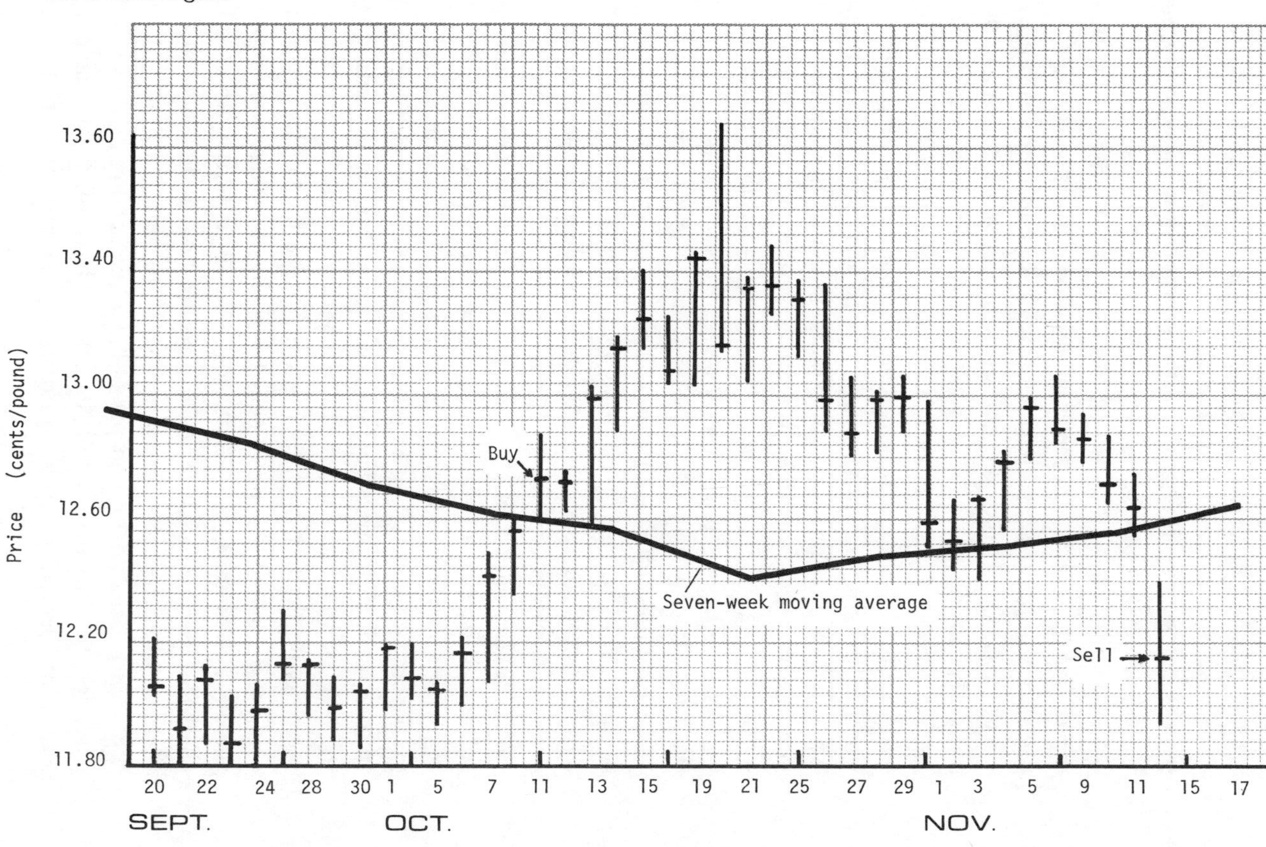

a slower rate, a trader might get the idea that the market is tiring and thus would hesitate to initiate any new long positions. They have termed indicators that use price change "oscillators." Unfortunately this method has not received widespread publicity in the literature. The oscillator method will be applied to the same contract that has been the subject of the other moving-average methods demonstrated in this chapter.

In fact this method could be conveniently used along with the three- and ten-day moving-average method illustrated earlier, since it utilizes, in part, the same calculations. The first step is simply to calculate the three-day moving average. This, of course, smooths the daily closing prices. The next step is to find the daily change in the three-day moving-average price. This number will either have a plus sign or a minus sign in front of it, depending on whether or not the moving average is increasing or decreasing. The next step is simply to add up algebraically the changes in the moving averages for the previous seven days. This figure—the seven-day change in the three-day average—is called the *seven-day oscillator*. The seven-day oscillator can also be found by finding the difference between two moving averages seven days apart.

An example will make this technique clear. Consider the December 1971 soybean oil contract again. Let us calculate the seven-day oscillator for this contract for September 27, 1971. Table 12 presents the data needed. Column 1 gives the date, column 2 the closing price, which in this case was 12.12 cents per pound, and column 3 the sum of the closing prices for September 23, 24 and 27, which totals to 35.96 on September 27. Dividing 35.96 by 3 gives a moving average of 11.99 cents per pound, which is recorded in column 4. The three-day moving average for the preceding trading day, September 24, was 11.97 cents per pound, therefore the increase in the three-day moving average was 0.02 cents per pound; column 5 records the daily change in the three-day moving average in hundredths of a cent, so a +2 is entered there. These changes for the preceding seven days are now added algebraically, that is: $+2 + 2 - 7 - 1 - 6 - 4 - 10$ to obtain a figure of −24. This figure tells how much prices have been changing and in what direction. In this case it tells us that soybean-oil prices have been weak, but that they had been much weaker, for, in fact, the seven-

Table 12

7-Day Oscillator Method Applied to the December, 1971 Soybean Oil Contract

(1) Date	(2) Closing Daily Price	(3) 3-Day Total of Closing Prices	(4) 3-Day Moving Average	(5) Daily Change of 3-Day Moving Average	(6) 7-Day Change in 100th's of 3-Day M.A.	Buy or (Sell) at
September 13, 1971	12.34	37.67	12.56	-13	- 6	
14	12.41	37.40	12.47	- 9	- 36	
15	12.17	36.92	12.31	-16	- 69	
16	12.11	36.69	12.23	- 8	- 86	
17	12.11	36.39	12.13	-10	- 85	
20	12.06	36.28	12.09	- 4	- 78	12.17
21	11.92	36.09	12.03	- 6	- 66	
22	12.07	36.05	12.02	- 1	- 54	
23	11.87	35.86	11.95	- 7	- 52	
24	11.97	35.91	11.97	+ 2	- 34	
27	12.12	35.96	11.99	+ 2	- 24	
28	12.13	36.22	12.07	+ 8	- 6	
29	11.98	36.23	12.08	+ 1	- 1	
30	12.05	36.16	12.05	- 3	+ 2	
October 1	12.17	36.20	12.07	+ 2	+ 5	
4	12.08	36.30	12.10	+ 3	+ 15	
5	12.04	36.29	12.10	0	+ 13	
6	12.15	36.27	12.09	- 1	+ 10	
7	12.40	36.59	12.20	+11	+ 13	
8	12.54	37.09	12.36	+16	+ 28	
11	12.71	37.65	12.55	+19	+ 50	
12	12.70	37.95	12.65	+10	+ 58	
13	12.97	38.38	12.79	+14	+ 69	
14	13.13	38.80	12.93	+14	+ 83	
15	13.22	39.32	13.11	+18	+102	
18	13.06	39.41	13.14	+ 3	+ 94	
19	13.42	39.70	13.23	+ 9	+ 87	(13.02)
20	13.14	39.62	13.21	- 2	+ 66	
21	13.32	39.88	13.29	+ 8	+ 64	
22	13.33	39.79	13.26	- 3	+ 47	

day oscillator had on September 16 recorded a low of —86 before it turned around and started to increase.

Assume that the trader has observed the soybean-oil market for some time and that he notes that changes in the seven-day oscillator within plus or minus 60 hundredths of the base line don't seem to mean much. However, changes that take place outside this band seem to indicate some divergence from a norm. He decides to pay close attention to soybean-oil prices when the seven-day oscillator is more than 0.60 cents from the base line in either direction. At the very least he could use this method to warn him away from taking long positions when the oscillator had a value of more than +60, or taking short positions when it had values of —60 or less. The seven-day oscillator is plotted in Figure 26.

There are any number of more positive trading rules that can be formulated. One of them might be: *Buy (or sell) December soybean oil when the seven-day oscillator first changes direction after having been less (or greater than) —60 (or +60).*

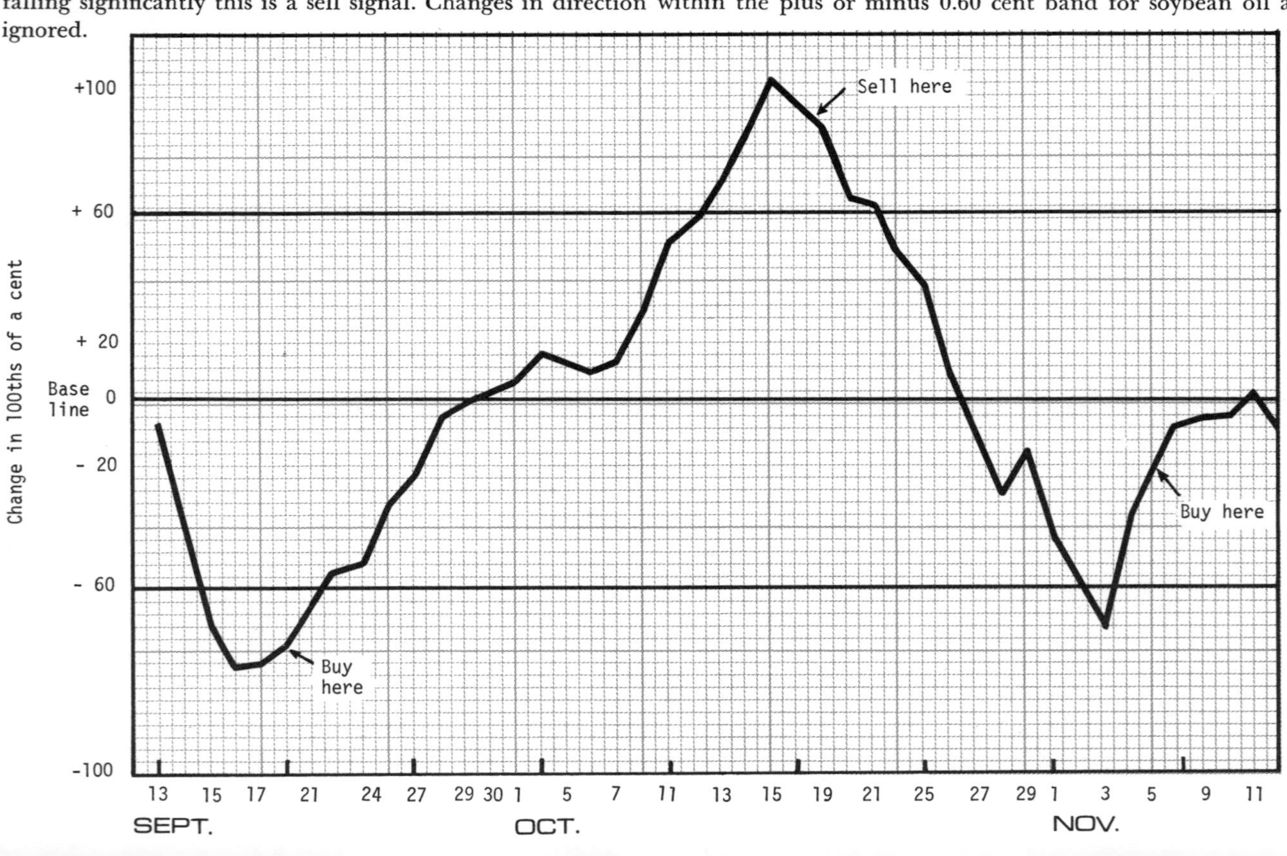

FIGURE 26. The seven-day oscillator method applied to the December 1971 soybean oil contract. When the oscillator quantity changes its sign above or below a certain cutoff band it signals a change in the direction of prices. If the oscillator starts to decrease in value after it has increased significantly, this is a sell signal, while if it starts to increase in value after falling significantly this is a sell signal. Changes in direction within the plus or minus 0.60 cent band for soybean oil are ignored.

Note that this rule would have put a speculator long December soybean oil on September 20 at the opening at a price of 12.17 cents per pound because the day before the seven-day oscillator changed from —86 to —85. He would have closed out his long position on the opening at 13.02 cents per pound on October 19, the day after he had observed that the oscillator fell from +102 to +94. This trade would have given a profit of 0.85 cents per pound, or $477 per contract, net after commissions. The short position taken up on October 19 at 13.02 cents per pound would have been closed out on the opening on November 5, 1971, at 12.77 cents per pound because the value of the oscillator increased from —73 on November 3 to —55 on November 4. This would have produced a net profit on the short sale of $117.

Teweles and his colleagues also present another price-difference method which uses the rate of price change as an indicator to future price movements. However, the marginal increase in effectiveness of this rate of price change method does not appear to justify the additional calculations required. Price-difference methods appear to be most useful in helping to pick out when positions should be taken in trading markets. These methods are not considered very helpful in major bull or bear markets that may pause on their way up or down while prices consolidate for a few days. The price-difference techniques could give a false buy or sell signal during one of these pauses, resulting in great financial loss to the trader. In markets that have steep trends in prices, straight moving-average techniques such as three- and ten-day methods might appear to be more useful.

Conclusions

Moving averages can be used profitably in trading commodities. This statement has been proved in empirical studies by a number of different researchers and by countless traders. It is interesting to summarize the results that each of the three methods presented in this chapter would have given had they been used to trade the December 1971 soybean oil contract in the fall of 1971. Table 13 makes this comparison. The seven-week method was slow to pick up the fact that a rally had started in soybean oil. If that rally had

Table 13

Comparison of Three Moving Average Trading Techniques for December, 1971 Soybean Oil Contract

	3-Day & 10-Day Moving Average Method	7-Week Moving Average Method	7-Day Oscillator Method
Date Bought	9/29/71	10/11/71	9/20/71
Price Paid (cents/pound)	12.05	12.71	12.17
Date Sold	10/28/71	11/12/71	10/19/71
Price Received (cents/pound)	12.85	12.14	13.02
Gross Profit or (Loss) (cents/pound)	0.80	0.57	0.85
Net Profit or (Loss) (dollars/contract)	447	(375)	477
Trading Days in the Market	21	24	21

persisted, the seven-week technique probably would have produced the biggest profits. The seven-day oscillator method and the three- and ten-day moving-average method both called the turn very nicely and produced handsome profits in only 21 trading days, but the three- and ten-day moving-average method was badly whipsawed twice on a short-term market rally.

Will moving-average techniques produce a profit every time? They most assuredly will not. But if used consistently they will allow a trader to catch his share of the big moves that take place in the commodity market each year—and it is precisely those moves that will produce the profits that caused him to begin to trade commodities in the first place.

CHAPTER **12**

Spreads

□

From time to time a broker seeking new traders will send out a brochure or market letter implying that, while trading commodities is indeed a risky business, there is a way to do it with almost no risk at all. He then goes on to explain that the secret of this "new" method is to spread commodities—that is, for example, to buy one delivery month and sell another delivery month of the same commodity. He points out that prices cannot go too far against you because if you are long July wheat and it starts to fall, the December wheat which you are short will also fall, and thus whatever you lose on the long side will be made up for by profits on the short side. If this statement were true, of course, one could also not make any money by buying one month and selling another—for surely sauce for the goose is also sauce for the gander. Thus it should be made crystal clear at the outset that while some spreads do offer a degree of limited risk, many do not, and thus capital can be lost with a speed almost equal to that with which it can be lost in outright speculative purchases or sales. There will always be traders around who will be glad to take your money no matter which way you want to give it to them.

Spreaders in commodities attempt to do the same thing that arbitrageurs do in the stock market—that is, they seek to make a profit on a change in relative prices rather than in a change in absolute prices. The arbitrageur frequently plies his trade after announcement of the details of a proposed merger. He buys the stock of the company being bought up and sells short the stock of the company doing the buying. He hopes that others will do the same after he has taken his position, thus causing the stock of the company he is long to rise and the stock of the company he is short to fall. Sometimes it works and sometimes it doesn't. Frequently the merger is called off, or it is blocked by the courts or something else happens causing the arbitrage to produce little or no profit. In many respects, arbitraging in commodities is much simpler.

The words "spread" and "straddle," which today are used interchangeably, imply one thing—a difference in price between two commodity options or a price difference between the cash commodity and the future price of that same commodity.

Spreads have appeal to traders for two reasons. The first is the one mentioned at the beginning of this chapter—that is, there is less risk in certain spread positions. The second is also due to the supposedly reduced risk, so that brokers generally require significantly less margin on a spread position. For example, if the margin on an outright position in cattle is $600, a broker might require only $300 to carry a spread position in cattle. For this reason spreads frequently seem like a bargain to a small trader with limited trading capital. And sometimes they are. But sometimes they are not, and the spread trader with little capital can become the trader with no capital in an amazingly short time. An example will help to make this important point clearer.

Suppose that a trader in the early spring is bullish on July soybeans. He can go long one contract of July beans with a margin of, say, $750. He believes that a move of 10 cents in this contract is not unreasonable. This would give him a gross profit of $500, less a commission of $30, for a net profit of $470 on his $750 margin. He is willing to risk 4 cents per bushel, or $200 per contract on this position, and thus the reward to risk ratio is about 2 to 1. A more experienced trader overhears his plan to buy July beans and tells him to consider another alternative. He says that in some years July beans gain dramatically with respect to September beans and what he should really do is go long July beans and short September beans. He also points out that while the broker wants $750 to carry the speculative long position, he will only ask $150 to carry the long July, short September spread. (Some brokers might ask $350 or so to carry this spread position—it really depends on your broker's estimation of the risk involved in the spread.) This normally cautious trader leaps at this golden opportunity and eagerly takes up five spread positions with his $750 margin. Suppose that July soybeans are selling at 15 cents per bushel premium over September when the trade is instituted. And suppose that the spread does indeed widen, and by early summer it is up to 20 cents and the trader closes it out. His gross profit of 5 cents per bushel yields him $1,250 less $36 commission on each of the five spreads, which gives a net profit of $1,070 on the original $750 margin. But it is well known that commodity prices don't always do what they are supposed to do; so suppose that this year every crusher wants to hedge his next year's supply of soybeans, and thus they all eagerly buy September soybeans and the spread narrows to 12 cents per bushel. The trader is now faced with a margin call of $500, as the broker would like at least $100 equity on each spread; and if the trader is unable or unwilling to meet the margin call he is liquidated, taking a loss of $750 (his total initial capital) plus $180 in commissions, giving him a total loss of $930. Even if the trader had only taken three spreads and they moved against him by 3 cents per bushel, and he was forced to liquidate, his net loss would have been $558, or more than 70 percent of his initial capital. This is clearly a bigger loss than he was willing to suffer on the single speculative position that he was contemplating taking.

This example is not presented to scare off traders from taking spread positions. It is presented as a precautionary measure so that traders will not be lulled into a false sense of security that arises when one starts to believe that no great financial loss can come from spreads. The one clear disadvantage of spreads is that they tempt traders into overtrading because of their low margin requirements. And there is no faster way to become a non-commodity trader than by overtrading.

Why Price Differences Occur

Hedgers, who normally are in the commodity market because they either produce or actually use a given commodity, pay close attention to the difference between the *cash price*—that is, the price for immediate delivery—and the nearby-futures price. This price difference is called the "basis." In a so-called "normal" market, futures prices are higher than current cash prices by part or all of the costs of holding the merchandise from the present date to the futures' delivery date. Thus in a normal market the more distant the contract is from delivery, the higher will be its price, because it will cost more to hold it the longer it is held. But it must always be kept in mind that markets are not always "normal"—that sometimes the near months sell at a premium or can move to a premium over the distant months. It is the relative scarcity of the commodity that will determine what price differences will prevail. But first let us examine what economic forces produce a normal market.

The storing of a commodity for future delivery involves three costs to its owner: (1) the actual storage cost; (2) the cost of insurance for the commodity (which greatly depends on how susceptible the commodity is to deterioration and on the nature of the storage facility); and (3) the interest on the capital tied up in the commodity—for if the owner decided to sell it today he could then invest the cash received to give him an income. Or the owner of the commodity might have borrowed money to pay for the commodity, which means that by holding it he is incurring an interest charge.

Thus in a market where supply is fairly well in balance with demand, the market will reward the owner of a commodity with a premium on the products he holds for future delivery. This premium, called the "carrying charge," is what the owner demands for storing the commodity. For example, the carrying charges on grains might be around 3 cents per bushel per month. Unfortunately, commodity trading—like life—is not nearly this simple. Futures do not have to show a carrying charge, and, in fact, the distant contracts sometimes sell at a discount to the nearbys.

Discounts on distant contracts occur when there is a relative shortage of the cash commodity and demand is good. The market pays close attention to its immediate needs and "discounts the future." In the face of a serious shortage, nearby supplies will rise much more than the distant contracts, giving rise to "negative carrying charges."

The exact opposite occurs when excessive supplies are available. This situation usually prevails right after harvest time, when the market might be overwhelmed with grain, for example. This forces cash prices and nearby futures contract prices down and offers to reward holders of the commodity with a carrying charge. Figure 27 illustrates the relation between cash and nearby prices and futures prices in three different kinds of markets.

Different Types of Spreads

Keep in mind that the commodity spreader has no interest in absolute price level but only in the difference between two prices. He believes that the difference will either widen or narrow, and he takes up his position accordingly. The market offers him several different ways to exploit these differences.

Intracommodity Spreads. This is probably the most common type of spread assumed by traders. The July-September soybean spread described on page 156 is an example of an intracommodity spread. In that example the trader was speculating that July will gain with respect to September and thus he went long July and short September. In this case the market was inverted because July

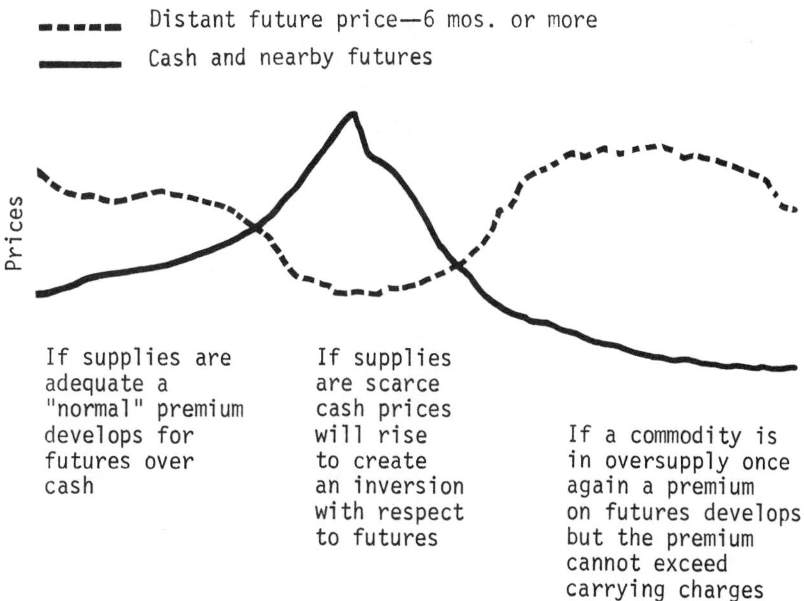

FIGURE 27. The relationship that exists between distant futures prices and cash prices and nearby futures.

was selling at a 15 cent premium over September, and the trader believed that the inversion would widen rather than narrow and revert to a so-called "normal" price relationship. This could occur if the demand for soybeans coming out of the present crop should slacken while projected demand for beans from next year's crop remained strong, causing September to move to a premium over July. If the carrying charges on soybeans is 3 cents per bushel per month, then September beans will not sell for more than 6 cents per bushel over July in the two months between July and September. If the spread were to widen to more than 6 cents per bushel, then a speculator might simply buy the cheaper July contract and sell September immediately, thereby guaranteeing himself a profit. Suppose July is selling for $3 per bushel while September is selling for $3.08. A trader buys July and sells September and then takes delivery when the contract expires in July. He then pays his 6 cents per bushel carrying charges for August and September, thus raising the cost of his beans to $3.06, but he has already sold the beans for September delivery for $3.08 on the same day he bought his July beans; thus he has guaranteed himself a 2 cents per bushel profit on the transaction without risk.

Why doesn't everybody do this kind of transaction and become immensely wealthy? Because not only do more distant futures sell below their carrying charges relative to the nearbys, but they rarely even sell at the carrying-charge limit. Since professional traders are very knowledgeable about how to wring a profit out of a spread, they would institute enough positions to stop any price moves that would permit a distant contract to sell above its carrying charges relative to the nearby. If you should ever witness a situation in which a distant contract sells for a premium greater than its carrying charges, investigate it very carefully before sinking all your trading capital into it.*

* This point cannot be emphasized too strongly. In the spring of 1971 cotton was undergoing a great rally, partly as a result of a drought in the cotton belt and partly due to large exports. One good advisory service that I was subscribing to at the time recommended that traders go long July and short December cotton, with December selling about 1.70 cents over July. They believed that 1.70 cents a pound was the maximum carrying charge for December over July and thus the trade was "practically risk free." That is, by going short December and long July, I speculated that as the rally lost steam the spread would narrow from 1.70 cents to possibly as low as 1.10 cents. Instead the spread widened to 1.95 cents, at which point the serv-

Intercommodity Spreads. Because certain commodities can be used for the same purpose—such as some of the feed grains—they are by definition and usage competitive and interchangeable to a high degree. Oats and corn, and wheat and rye are two examples of competing commodities in which profitable spread opportunities present themselves from time to time. A profit may be obtained by selling the expensive commodity and buying the cheaper one and then waiting until a more normal price relationship develops.

The margin on intercommodity spreads is not likely to be as low as the margin on intracommodity spreads, usually being equal to the speculative margin on the higher-margined commodity. Thus the margin on a wheat (non-spread margin $500)–corn (non-spread margin $400) spread would probably be equal to the margin on the wheat side, or $500. Unlike intracommodity spreads, there is rarely a price break on commissions on an intercommodity spread.

One of the most popular intercommodity spreads is that involving soybeans and their products: soybean oil and soybean meal. Opportunities for profit arise when the products are selling too dearly with respect to the beans or too cheaply with respect to the beans. If a trader believes that the products are too cheap in comparison with the beans, he simply goes long one contract of meal and one contract of oil and sells short one contract of the beans. Such a spread is called a "reverse crush" spread because it is exactly opposite to the usual position taken by a soybean crusher, who is, as a rule, long the beans (which he needs for raw material) and short the meal and oil (which he usually has available for delivery anyway as a result of his crushing operation). One contract

ice advised immediate liquidation. They believed that some bit of information was missing on the carrying-charge theory and that the safest thing to do was to get out and worry about what was missing later. The smart traders did liquidate but I still believed that the limit on carrying charges was 1.70 cents (even though the market had already widened up to 1.95 cents; this foolish practice is known as fighting the tape). I finally closed out my spreads with December at 2.37 cents over July, suffering a loss of 0.67 cents per pound. A few days later I found out that the contract terms on the December and July contracts were not identical and the carrying-charge limit was closer to 2.80 cents per pound. At which point I was: (1) a few days older; (2) $381 per spread poorer; and (3) a little more cautious in taking positions in surefire spreads.

of oil plus one contract of meal is not what can actually be obtained from crushing one contract of beans, but it is generally close enough to produce a profit if the trader has indeed found a misalignment in prices. Typically, margin on such a spread would be about $1,000. (A closer relationship between beans and their products may be obtained with ten contracts of beans, nine contracts of oil and twelve contracts of meal; margin on this position might be $10,000).

The value of the products relative to the beans is simple enough to calculate. Roughly, a bushel of soybeans will yield 11 pounds of oil, so to obtain the sale value of the oil you simply multiply its price in cents per pound by 11 to obtain the value of the oil in a bushel of soybeans. To obtain the price of meal per pound, one simply divides the quoted price, which is in dollars per ton, by 2,000 pounds per ton and then multiply the resulting figure by 48, which is close to the number of pounds of meal that a bushel of soybeans will yield. Consider the following example. On October 28, 1971, January soybeans were selling for $3.24 per bushel, January soybean oil was selling for 12.90 cents per pound, and January soybean meal was selling for $82.85 per ton. Find the value of the products per bushel of beans relative to the price of the beans.

Value of oil: $0.1290 × 11 pounds/bushel =	$1.4190
Value of meal: ($82.35 per ton/2000 pounds per ton) × (48 pounds per bushel) =	1.9764
Total value of products per bushel of beans	$3.3954
Price of beans per bushel	3.2400
Value of products in excess of the price of beans per bushel	$0.1554

Thus the value of the products is roughly 15½ cents more than the cost of the beans it takes to make them. This number is called the *gross processing margin.* If a trader goes long the products and short the beans, he believes that the value of the products will increase relative to the value of the beans. If a trader goes short the products and long the beans, he believes that the value of the products will fall relative to the price of the beans. In general, whenever this spread sells near zero conversion, or with the products at a discount to the beans, a trader may take up a reverse-crush spread (long products, short beans) with very little risk.

Intermarket Spreads. Because a number of commodities are traded on more than one exchange, it is possible to set up spreads between markets. That is, for example, one can take up a position in the hard red winter wheat traded on the Kansas City Board of Trade versus a position in the soft red winter wheat traded on the Chicago Board of Trade. The fact is that while prices might be related between the prices of the two kinds of wheat, they are not in lockstep, and thus spreads can turn out to be profitable. For example, it is historically true that in the spring the price of Kansas City wheat has a tendency to gain on the price of Chicago wheat. In some cases the commodities traded on one exchange are deliverable against contracts on another exchange; again consider the Kansas City-Chicago wheat example—the hard red winter wheat traded in Kansas City is deliverable against wheat contracts in Chicago.

Generally an intermarket spread requires that two full commissions be paid—one on each contract. Margins, however, are generally shaved so that the total margin required is just about equal to that required on one contract. For example, in the wheat spread mentioned, the total margin would probably not be more than that required on a Chicago Board of Trade wheat contract. A more detailed discussion of this type of spread will be given later in this chapter.

Placing Spread Orders

Initiating a spread position is no more difficult than initiating a straight speculative position. The only difference is that in the event that the trader wishes to obtain his spread at a certain difference in prices he does not state the prices but rather states the difference. For example, suppose the trader wishes to initiate the soybean trade discussed earlier—long July, short September. He would phrase his order to read: "Buy 5 July, sell 5 September wheat, with July 15 cents premium limit." This tells the broker that he is to fill this spread order at any price difference between July and September wheat when July is selling for less than 15 cents over September. The broker now knows that the trader believes that the price differential is insufficient and that the trader wishes to speculate on the possibility that it will widen. The trader could also have found out from the broker where the market was trading and if the differential suited him he could have just placed a market order. Remember that in a spread situation the trader is not concerned with whether this order is executed with July at $3.25 and September at $3.10, or whether it is filled with July $2.50 and September at $2.35; *the price differential is what counts.*

Intermarket spread orders are handled in exactly the same way, except that the market must be included in the order. "Buy 10 Kansas City July wheat, sell 10 Chicago July wheat, with Chicago 7½ cents premium limit." This order may or may not be filled or fillable, considering the distance between the trading floors, and, indeed, some brokers will be reluctant to take such an order. Sometimes intermarket orders like this are filled by specifying the time at which both are to be filled—at the market. For example: "Buy 10 Kansas City July wheat, sell 10 Chicago July wheat—11:25 A.M. market."

Some, but not all, brokers refuse to take stop-loss orders on spreads. Since it always makes me nervous to be in the market without a stop, I find this to be a distinct hindrance. The brokers claim that their floor traders will not accept such orders because they have no time to be computing the differences between the various positions in order to know whether or not to fill a stop. If you plan to be trading spreads—and there are a number of points in their favor as a trading vehicle—then you should trade with a broker who will accept stops on spreads. It is a comforting extra that I believe you should indulge yourself in.

Some Commonly Followed Spreads

In this section several seasonal-type spreads will be considered along with the reasons they generally work—or do not work.

Intracommodity Spreads. As a new commodity trader you may feel you would like to be initiated into the game rather gently. That is, you would like to take up a position that perhaps would not enable you to retire immediately if it worked out, but that, on the other hand, would not send you to the poorhouse if it didn't.

I believe that soybean meal spreads have much to commend them as trading vehicles for a new trader.

In recent years July soybean meal has had a tendency to gain on September meal from late March on. This generally begins after a period of weakness in meal during the late winter months, followed by seasonal strength in June. The seasonal strength is generally more pronounced in the nearby delivery. The position, generally taken up in late winter or early spring, that allows one to benefit from this spread is long July soybean meal and short September soybean meal, with July no more than 60 points ($60 per contract) over September.

The margin requirement on such a spread depends to a large extent on who your broker is. A firm that primarily deals in stocks (a wire house) and handles commodities as a sideline would commonly charge 50 percent of the margin required on a straight soybean meal position, while a firm that specializes in commodities might ask only 20 percent of the margin required on a straight meal position. Which margin you are asked to put up can make a big difference on your rate of return. If the margin on a straight position is $500, then a wire house would ask $250 on a spread while a commodity house would ask only $100. Round-turn commission on both legs of the spread is $44.

This spread has worked unusually well. In a recent fifteen-year period, it was profitable during ten of those years. In nine years the spread has gone into July with July selling at a premium of at least $270 over September. Furthermore, since July has never traded at a discount to September for very long, the risk on the spread is somewhere around $60 per contract plus commission.

Intercommodity Spreads. Spreads between related commodities are just as easy to institute as those between different months of the same commodity. A number of such spreads have been identified and are closely followed by spread traders. Of course, when a spread becomes too popular, it no longer works as well, because the market has a tendency to discount it. One of the more popular intercommodity spreads is the long December wheat-short December corn spread instituted around June 1 and lifted around November 1.

This spread probably works because both wheat and corn prices have a tendency to decline during their harvest periods. The spreader in this case buys his wheat during harvest, hopefully when it is cheap, and sells corn prior to its harvest, hopefully when it is dear. When the spread is lifted in November, corn should be fairly cheap, as its harvest has recently been completed, and wheat should have started to recover from its harvest lows.

The margin required on this position would probably be equal to that required on a speculative position on the higher-margined commodity. A regular round-turn commission on both the wheat and the corn is also required.

The results of a December wheat-corn spread are given in Table 14. The spread was assumed to have been initiated on June 1 and liquidated on November 1. In the ten-year period from 1962 through 1971 the spread was profitable in five years. The maximum profit was about 29 cents, or $1,450 per contract less commissions. Common sense dictates that a stop-loss order on spreads must be used just as if they were speculative positions; I would have set the stop on this spread at 5 cents, so that the most that could be lost on the spread would be $250 plus commissions. If this practice of closing out the spread on a 5 cent adversity had been followed, this spread would have produced a total profit of $2,800 after paying commissions during the ten years from 1962 through 1971. This calculation does not make any allowance for the fact that the spread might have had an adverse move in a year that ultimately turned out to be profitable.

One of the most consistently reliable intercommodity spreads has been the one involving two feed grains, oats and corn. More than half of these two commodities is consumed on the farm directly as feed. In setting up this spread, one must take into account the fact that a bushel of corn averages 56 pounds, whereas a bushel of oats averages only 32 pounds. Thus the spread is normally set up between two contracts of oats for each contract of corn.

How this spread is set up and whether or not it will work depends upon the relative value of oats and corn on April 1, when it is normally instituted. A rule of thumb followed by a number of spreaders is to buy two contracts of December oats and sell one contract of December corn if the premium on two bushels of oats over one bushel of corn is under 15 cents. If the premium is greater

Table 14

The Long December Wheat-Short December Corn Spread

	Closing Prices June 1 (cents/ bushel)	Spread June 1 (cents/ bushel)	Closing Prices November 1 (cents/ bushel)	Spread November 1 (cents/ bushel)	Change in the Spread + = profit - = loss
1971 December Wheat	161.25		159.75		
December Corn	146.00	15.25	114.88	44.87	+29.62
1970 December Wheat	142.00		175.75		
December Corn	122.25	19.75	147.88	27.87	+ 8.12
1969 December Wheat	136.62		135.50		
December Corn	125.62	11.00	118.00	17.50	+ 6.50
1968 December Wheat	145.75		128.75		
December Corn	119.25	26.50	110.88	17.87	- 8.62
1967 December Wheat	177.37		150.25		
December Corn	135.37	42.00	114.13	36.12	- 5.87
1966 December Wheat	178.62		169.12		
December Corn	124.75	53.88	137.12	32.00	-21.88
1965 December Wheat	146.50		164.38		
December Corn	118.13	28.37	114.50	49.88	+21.51
1964 December Wheat	157.63		152.00		
December Corn	118.63	39.00	119.63	32.37	- 6.63
1963 December Wheat	192.00		216.38		
December Corn	116.25	75.75	118.38	98.00	+22.25
1962 December Wheat	223.00		207.38		
December Corn	115.63	107.37	107.63	99.75	- 7.62

than 15 cents, then the oats are sold and the corn is bought. The spread is normally closed out around November 1.

This spread could probably be carried for the margin required on a speculative position in corn. Three commissions would have to be paid—the one on the corn and the two on the oats.

The results of this spread, using the 15 cent rule on April 1, would have produced profits in fifteen years during the twenty-year period of 1952 through 1971. The results of this spread are given in Table 15. The maximum profit in any one year (1971) would have been $1,500 per spread, while the spread would have yielded a net profit of $6,700 over the twenty years using the 5 cent

Table 15

Spread Between December Oats and December Corn

	Closing Prices April 1 (cents/bushel)	Premium 2 bu. oats over 1 bu. corn	Closing Prices November 1 (cents/bushel)	Premium 2 bu. oats over 1 bu. corn	Profit (+) or Loss (-) Long oats/ Short corn	Profit (+) or Loss (-) Long corn/ Short oats
1971 2 bu. Dec. Oats	145.00		147.50			
1 bu. Dec. Corn	143.50	1.50	114.87	32.63	+31.13	
1970 2 bu. Dec. Oats	132.50		158.00			
1 bu. Dec. Corn	118.00	14.50	147.87	10.13	- 4.37	
1969 2 bu. Dec. Oats	136.75		121.00			
1 bu. Dec. Corn	114.50	22.25	118.00	3.00		+19.25
1968 2 bu. Dec. Oats	149.50		134.75			
1 bu. Dec. Corn	127.00	22.50	110.75	24.00		- 1.50
1967 2 bu. Dec. Oats	154.00		143.25			
1 bu. Dec. Corn	142.00	12.00	114.00	29.25	+17.25	
1966 2 bu. Dec. Oats	140.00		151.50			
1 bu. Dec. Corn	120.50	19.50	137.00	14.50		+ 5.00
1965 2 bu. Dec. Oats	140.75		134.75			
1 bu. Dec. Corn	120.62	20.13	114.25	20.50		- .37
1964 2 bu. Dec. Oats	139.00		135.25			
1 bu. Dec. Corn	120.00	19.00	119.50	15.50		+ 3.50
1963 2 bu. Dec. Oats	142.50		142.75			
1 bu. Dec. Corn	113.87	28.62	118.37	24.38		+ 4.25
1962 2 bu. Dec. Oats	149.00		128.75			
1 bu. Dec. Corn	118.00	31.00	107.50	21.25		+ 9.75
1961 2 bu. Dec. Oats	138.50		132.00			
1 bu. Dec. Corn	117.25	21.25	108.50	23.50		- 2.25
1960 2 bu. Dec. Oats	150.50		127.25			
1 bu. Dec. Corn	110.75	39.75	108.37	18.88		+20.87
1959 2 bu. Dec. Oats	137.75		153.00			
1 bu. Dec. Corn	115.50	22.25	109.87	43.13		-20.88
1958 2 bu. Dec. Oats	132.25		130.00			
1 bu. Dec. Corn	117.75	14.50	111.25	18.75	+ 4.25	
1957 2 bu. Dec. Oats	136.25		135.50			
1 bu. Dec. Corn	129.25	7.00	118.37	17.13	+10.13	
1956 2 bu. Dec. Oats	139.25		160.50			
1 bu. Dec. Corn	141.00	- 1.75	138.50	22.00	+23.75	
1955 2 bu. Dec. Oats	135.75		128.75			
1 bu. Dec. Corn	137.87	- 2.13	129.12	- 0.37	+ 1.75	
1954 2 bu. Dec. Oats	147.75		164.75			
1 bu. Dec. Corn	144.75	+ 3.00	156.50	8.50	+ 5.50	
1953 2 bu. Dec. Oats	152.75		156.25			
1 bu. Dec. Corn	156.37	- 3.63	147.87	8.37	+12.00	
1952 2 bu. Dec. Oats	169.00		173.25			
1 bu. Dec. Corn	173.87	- 4.87	166.12	7.13	+12.00	

adversity stop rule. Adverse interim moves have been ignored in making this calculation. If the 15 cent rule is employed, this is probably one of the most reliable spreads in the market.

Intermarket Spreads. This type of spread simply involves the simultaneous purchase and sale of the same commodity in different markets. Some of the most common intermarket spreads are those involving wheat. And one of the most popular of these is the Kansas City vs. Chicago wheat spread that is generally put on in midwinter and lifted around June 1; the July contract is generally used with the trader going long Kansas City wheat and short Chicago.

There are fundamental reasons why this trade seems to work well, but before getting to them, first consider what is the difference between the two wheat contracts other than the location of trading. Normally soft red winter wheat is delivered against Chicago contracts. This wheat is low in protein content and is especially suitable for making pastry, crackers and cakes. It is grown largely in Ohio, Indiana, Michigan, Illinois and Missouri. The Kansas City contract calls for hard red winter wheat, which is grown largely in Oklahoma, the Texas panhandle, eastern Colorado, Nebraska and Kansas. It is especially suitable for making bread flour. Both of these crops are sown in the fall, the seeds lie dormant all winter, and then the crop is harvested during early summer. The harvesting of the hard red winter wheat begins in late May, about a month before the beginning of the soft red winter wheat harvest.

Geography dictates that much of the hard red winter wheat is exported through the Gulf Coast ports, while the soft red winter wheat is shipped out of the Great Lakes ports. Transportation costs argue against the shipment of one class of wheat out of one harvesting region to another. However, *hard red winter wheat may be delivered against Chicago contracts.* At a certain price differential such a shipment becomes attractive. This differential is believed to be in the neighborhood of 13 cents per bushel. This is an important fact because it limits the risk a trader may be exposed to in taking up this spread. That is, Chicago probably will not sell for more than 13 cents per bushel over Kansas City wheat, or else hedgers will begin to deliver Kansas City wheat to Chicago at a guaranteed profit.

There is no limit, however, to how much of a premium Kansas City wheat can command over Chicago wheat. Historically it has been noted that the Kansas City July wheat future has a tendency to lose ground with respect to the Chicago July futures contract during the fall and early winter. This is believed to happen because speculators generally prefer trading in the Chicago market to trading in the Kansas City market. This preference tends to keep Chicago prices higher than Kansas City prices. In late winter and early spring this pattern seems to reverse as the milling trade becomes active in the Kansas City market, causing it to become stronger relative to Chicago.

Figure 28 illustrates how these factors have operated from 1957 through 1971 by means of an envelope of prices. Eleven of the fifteen years are contained totally within the envelope. The exceptional years of 1958, 1963, 1970 and 1971 are shown by dotted lines on the chart. This spread, even with the exceptions included, has never failed to produce a gain sometime between the winter entry point and the spring close-out. It is interesting to note that if one had entered this spread on January 15 and had offset it on June 1, profits would have accrued in ten out of fifteen years. The maximum gain would have been 10¾ cents while the maximum loss 3 cents. The largest intermediate loss would have been around 5 cents.

A similar type of spread on May wheat, traded on the Chicago and Minneapolis exchanges, has been studied. It too has worked out profitably in a high percentage of the years considered.*

When Not to Spread

Most people who are new to commodity trading learn about spreads at the wrong time in their trading experience—they learn about them at the time of a margin call. The story generally goes something like this:

You bought, for either technical or fundamental reasons, four contracts of January orange juice at 62 cents per pound. You put up a margin of $600 per contract, or $2,400 in all. The broker has just telephoned to inform you that orange juice has closed at

* Frederick T. Clifton, "Wheat Spreads," in *Guide to Commodity Price Forecasting* (New York: Commodity Research Bureau, Inc., 1965).

FIGURE 28. The historical relationship that exists between the July wheat contract traded in Kansas City and the one traded in Chicago. Usually the price of the Kansas City July wheat contract gains on the price of the July Chicago wheat contract from early spring until the contract expires. In 1970 and 1971 the spread failed to work to any degree; however, for 15 years it was remarkably reliable, as shown by the heavy black lines bounding the price differences for the two contracts from 1955 to 1969.

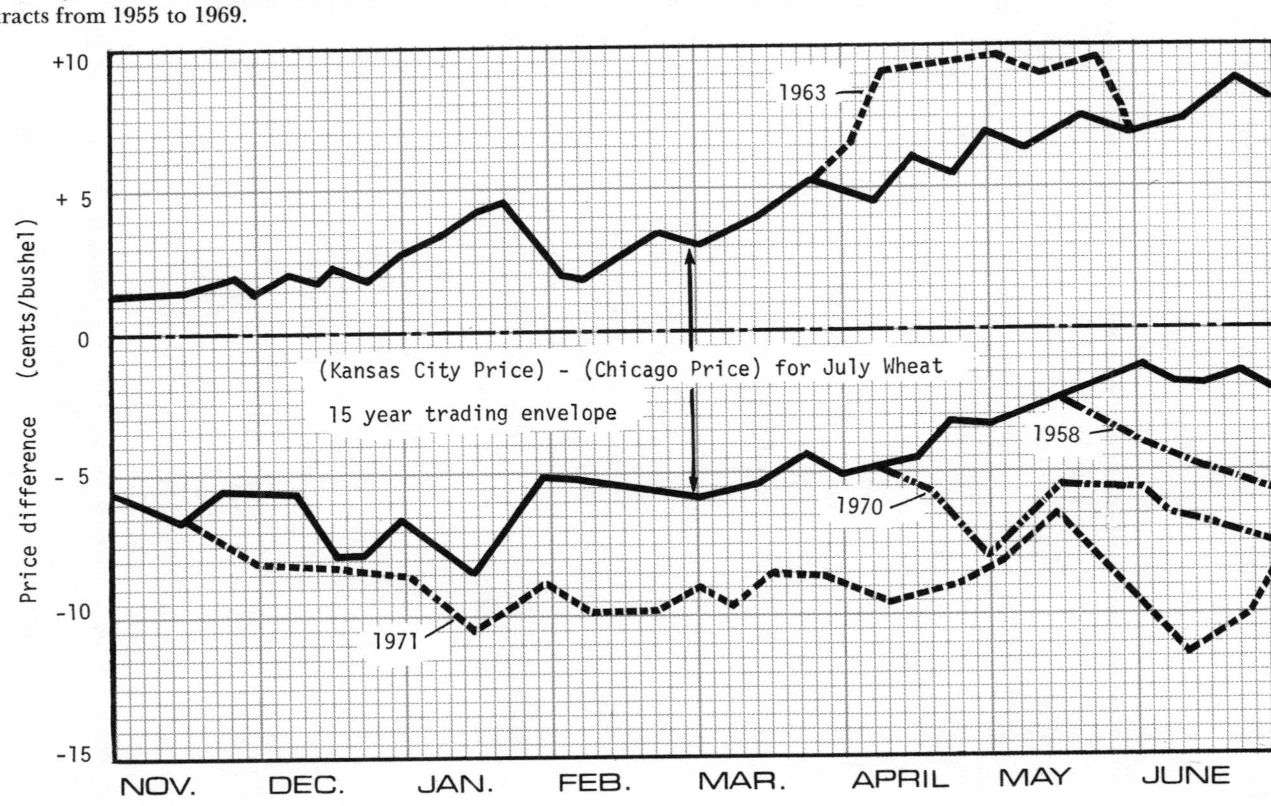

60 cents, which gives you a loss of $300 per contract, or $1,200 on your four positions. (Each 1-cent move on an orange-juice contract is worth $150.) He also informs you that the margin clerk requires that you maintain an equity of at least $450 per contract, and since your equity is down to $300 per contract you are short a total of $600 on your four orange-juice contracts. Having made that cheerful calculation for you, your broker says that you should inform him before the market opens in the morning as to what action you are planning to take. There are three possibilities open to you:

1. Supply the additional $600 margin as requested.
2. Close out all, or part, of your position.
3. Turn your speculative long position into a spread by selling, for example, four March contracts which thus team up with your four January longs to create the spread.

Let us examine each of these alternatives in turn. Of course, you don't have the additional $600—traders never do when margin calls arrive.* If you had another $600 you probably would have bought five contracts instead of four anyway. (It was your plan to retire permanently from work on the profits from your orange-juice "killing.") That takes care of the first option.

Option number two makes a lot of sense, and, in fact, you should have done that as soon as your position moved against you by 1 or 1¼ cents, thereby never exposing yourself to a margin call. The disadvantage of this option is almost too sad to put into writing. You have to admit to yourself, your broker, your accountant and, if you are not cagy, your spouse, that you made a bad trade and lost quite a bit of money. Most new commodity traders feel that as long as a loss is not realized it has not really occurred and there is always the hope that the market will turn around and turn the trade from a bad one to a good one. It rarely does, but hope springs eternal anyway. Be that as it may, most inexperienced traders won't be able to turn their unrealized losses into a realized one. The ability to do that comes with a little practice.

The third option dawned on you when you were examining the margin sheet given to you by your broker. It showed that the margin on an orange-juice spread was only $200 per contract. When you read that, it occurred to you that your problems were solved,

* Not only do you not have the $600; you are not sure you have enough to meet the monthly mortgage payment. You could offer the brokerage house your kids, but they bring very little—probably because supply exceeds demand.

because as soon as you sell the March contracts against the January your margin requirements on the four spreads drops immediately to $800. You call your broker and instruct him to sell the four March contracts, and you breathe a sigh of relief. Unfortunately, you have solved nothing by this action. While it is true that you have satisfied your margin call, you could also have satisfied it by simply selling out. If orange juice continues to fall in price, whatever you make on the short leg of your spread, you will probably lose an equal amount on the long side. Thus, if orange juice drops 2 more cents and you decide to cover your short sale, you will immediately be faced with a margin call again for $600. There are only two things that might help you here—March might fall further than January and thus the spread would work in your direction. However, keep in mind that you did not go into this spread for fundamental or technical reasons—only for expediency—which is surely the worst reason for taking any position in the market. The other slim reed that you might lean on is that you might cover your short sale in the morning and then hope for a rally during the day so that at the close you could then offset your long position at little or no loss—thereby beating the margin clerk to a second call. It might happen. It might also snow in August.

The moral of this story should be clear. Never use a spread as a method of trying to save a bad speculative position. It will simply generate commissions (in this case an additional $180) for your broker and delay the day of reckoning.

Conclusions

Spreads can produce dramatic profits on small margins. It is, however, those small margins which can entice a speculator into overtrading his account. Remember, spreads do not *have to move* in your favor—they can, unless restricted by carrying-charge limitations, move against you with sickening speed. Thus there are three important rules that must be obeyed at all times in trading spreads: (1) Do not overtrade your capital; (2) Decide in advance exactly how much you are willing to lose on that position and set a stop-loss accordingly; (3) Never use a spread to bail you out of a bad speculative position. Follow these three rules and you may trade spreads in peace—and sometimes, even, with profit.

CHAPTER **13**

Advisory Services

Many receive advice, few profit by it.
—Publilius Syrus

□

Publilius Syrus's quotation is probably an overstatement of the situation that exists between commodity traders and the advisory services that they use. But it might not be too far from the mark. Am I implying that traders should shun advisory services then, and depend solely upon themselves or their brokers for taking up positions? Well, not exactly. But there are some things that every new commodity trader should know about advisory services. Such knowledge could save the trader time, aggravation and money.

Reasons for Using an Advisory Service

If Publilius is right, and few people do indeed profit from the advice they receive, why bother to subscribe to a service at all? Because even if a service's advice is not *always* correct, and no advisory service ever is, there are still a number of important reasons why you should give serious consideration to using one.

First off, probably all successful traders utilize some kind of a trading plan. As a new trader you probably do not have any specific method of trading in mind, and yet without one you will, like it or not, be depending upon blind luck. It is just as impossible to be right on every trade in the commodities market as it is for a gambler to be right on every roll of the dice or every deal of the cards. The random variations simply will not permit it. The speculator can never know in advance all of the contingencies that will determine the next price change, just as the gambler is not sure where the forces on a roulette table will bring the ball to rest.

However, by following a trading plan that has some logic behind it the speculator can hope to have the odds on his side in the long run—something a gambler can never expect to have. A good advisory service can provide a speculator with such a plan. Because the recommendations of most services have at least a modicum of rationality behind them, a new trader will not be nearly so tempted to jump from one position to another with nothing more than a gut reaction to justify his actions. That is, the regular use of a good advisory service can help to isolate you from your own emotions.

Most of the readers of this book will not be full-time commodity speculators, which means that they have other things to do during most of their waking hours. This provides the second major reason why a trader should consider using an advisory service. Such a service can save a trader a tremendous amount of time. Time is saved, no matter whether you are trying to prepare your own supply-and-demand estimates, if you are a fundamentalist, or whether you are a technician who must update either charts or calculations which are needed to make trading decisions. If you place any value on your time at all, an advisory service will pay for itself in a few weeks. Thus an advisory service serves three main purposes: (1) It gives you a trading plan; (2) It instills discipline and acts to save you from your own emotions; (3) It saves time.

What an Advisory Service Cannot Do

It cannot make you a fortune between now and the end of the year. As pointed out earlier, no service is right 100 percent of the time. Many of them are happy to be right 50 percent of the time—by right I mean that the trades they recommend at least make commissions. However, of those five trades out of ten that they call correctly, they would hope to have 75 to 150 percent profits on three of the five positions taken. On the five on which they are wrong, most of them would advise setting stops that precluded the losing of more than one-third of the margin supplied. In actual dollars let us see how this works out. Assume that 100 percent profit is made on the three good trades, commissions only are made on two other trades, and the five bad trades result in a net loss of one-third of the margin. Furthermore, assume that the margin is $600 per position. Then for ten trades:

3 trades at 100 percent profit or $600 each	=	$1,800
2 trades—break even	=	0
5 trades of 1/3 loss of margin or $200 each	=	—1,000
Net profit on 10 trades		$ 800

Now suppose a trader was in two of these trades at a time that would require $1,200 in margin money plus a cushion of at least another $800 for a minimum working capital of $2,000. If he withdrew any profits that caused his working capital to exceed $2,000, then an advisory service which was able to be very right three out of ten times would produce on average a net return of 40 percent on the invested capital. One serious criticism of this analysis is that if the five bad trades were to happen successively the working capital would be reduced to $1,000 before a good trade might come along. Of course, the only way to protect against that is to start with more capital.

By the way, this little analysis is important for another reason: it puts the lie to the old saw that "you can never go broke taking a profit." If a trader had decided that $200 was a "reasonable profit" on the three good positions and closed them out at that point, then he would quickly exhaust his capital as he accrued the more numerous $200 losses. The one rule of commodity trading that experienced traders try to convince novices of is—let your profits run, and cut your losses. It sounds so simple, and yet as a rule it is rarely followed by newcomers to trading. There are probably many reasons why they do not follow it but the one that seems most logical to me is that most traders want to be able to brag (even if it is just to themselves) about a winning trade that they have all wrapped up. And, of course, the only way one is indeed certain of a profit in commodity trading is to close out a profitable position. The argument for closing out a trade is that it does not hurt to leave a little for the next fellow, but remember, on the bad trades the trader left $200 per trade on five trades for the next fellow. So why shouldn't he wait around for a 100 percent return on three out of ten trades?

Long-time observers of commodity trading have noted that every year somewhere between ten and fifteen commodities will have sustained bull or bear moves—moves that are so strong that even if one catches only part of them they will produce substantial profits. Most people who run commodity services feel that if they can catch half of those moves for a substantial part of their ride, they will have earned their fees. At the same time they hope to get their clients to stop-out their losses while they are still modest. That goal is not an unreasonable one, although it may not sound like the royal road to retirement with a bottomless purse. Any advisory service that can deliver seven or eight sustained moves each year for its clients is doing reasonably well.

Different Types of Advisory Services

It is safe to say that there is an advisory service somewhere that will suit any taste except the one that demands that the service never be wrong. There are services that discuss commodities in general: ". . . Silver appears to have hit a bottom, watch for a spot to take up new long positions"; and there are services that specify everything: ". . . Long September silver at 1.3180 per ounce before 11 A.M. on Monday only." The first type of service presumes that its subscribers have been following the silver market rather closely and are familiar enough with the various contracts and prices to know what looks like a "good spot to take up a new long position." The second service assumes that its subscribers know nothing about the various contracts and that they wish to be told what, when and where to buy. New traders generally prefer the latter-type service, but they should not expect too much. Just because a service makes all those specific recommendations does not mean that it is going to be any more correct than a service that makes general recommendations. A specific recommendation does not produce a specific profit any more than a general recommendation will produce a general profit; both types of recommendations can produce miserable losses, however.

Fundamental Services. Appendix C is an annotated list of advisory services. It describes briefly how each service that is listed basically arrives at its recommendations—that is, whether it uses mostly technical or fundamental methods, how often the service appears, what it charges, and other pertinent factors. You will note that most of the services listed are technical rather than fundamental in nature. This is so because in most cases fundamental forecasting is more difficult to do and inherently more subjective in nature. After all, it is far easier to arrive at a recommendation for the sale of March corn based on the observation that an apparent head-and-shoulders formation has been completed, or that the 3-day moving average crossed the 10-day moving average, than it is to forecast a surplus of corn based on future consumption for eight months in advance. Nevertheless, many of the fundamental services do well in their forecasting on a long-run basis because when they latch on to a good position they have a tendency to stay with it much longer than do technical services.

On the other hand, sometimes fundamental services are more apt to let a position move against them to a much greater extent than a technical one simply because they believe that ultimately supply and demand must determine a price close to the one that they have forecast. Trading on fundamentals, then, can require a much stronger stomach under adverse price moves. However, for the trader who wants to trade infrequently and add to a good position as it is confirmed in the marketplace, a fundamental advisory service is probably the best type to subscribe to. Moreover, it is generally the fundamental services that follow spreads and make recommendations on taking up such positions, since the price movement of spreads is more dependent on fundamental factors than on technical ones.

Technical Services. The most popular type of advisory service today is the technical service. In the last few years the number of technical advisory services publicly offering their wares has increased markedly. The reason for this appears to be the availability of relatively cheap time that is now available on large-scale digital computers. Such time makes the analysis of tremendous amounts of price, open interest and volume data a relatively easy job even if as many as 50 or so contracts are being followed at once. It is sad but also true that the availability of such computer time and the resulting analyses have not produced tremendous profits for followers of purely technical advisory letters. People, not computers, still make markets and therefore markets remain in many cases as unpredictable as . . . well . . . people. One is never certain whether or not on any given day it will be the technical factors or the fundamental factors that will hold sway during that day's trading. Therefore, while technical reasons might cause you to go short at the opening, the announcement during the day of a big overseas grain sale could easily offset the technical factors that indicated a weakness in futures prices.

Technical services, for the most part, are very specific about where to take up positions and where to close them out. It is this reason, more than any other, that gives them their "security blanket" aspect. All they say is that you should follow their recommendations and in the long run you will get your three or four big winners out of ten. Of course, you must be prepared to sustain a few losses on the way. Since technical services almost invariably are trend followers—that is, they make a recommendation after they believe a new price trend has started—the good ones do catch many of the yearly major moves. The very fact that they do use trend-following methods means that they must join a trend after it begins—that is, there has to be a trend for them to recognize—and they leave a trend only after it has already peaked or troughed, which is how they get a signal to close out a position. Naturally, the larger the sustained move, the more of it a technical service will capture.

On the other hand, all commodities undergo periods without any pronounced trend to characterize them. The more refined the technical approach used by the service, the more likely it is that it can avoid taking positions in a commodity that is not going anywhere—up or down. (Recall Figure 19, which illustrated such a contract in the November 1971 Maine potatoes contract.) Nevertheless, even the best technical services are whipsawed every year on a number of contracts. There is no way to completely avoid this problem except to refuse to trade—but there is no fun and certainly no profit in doing that.

Services that Combine Fundamental and Technical Analysis. It has probably occurred to you that all one has to do in order to get the best of all possible worlds is to subscribe to a service that combines fundamental and technical methods in making its recommendations. The idea is very appealing, and a number of services do use both techniques. And just as you might have already guessed, this combined method works sometimes and sometimes it doesn't. There are also services that use contrary opinion along with technical and fundamental methods in arriving at a market judgment. One service provides its subscribers with three moving averages, point-and-figure analyses, price, volume and open-interest momentum, resistance and support zones, a contrary-opinion index, and a factor that includes opinions of floor traders.*

Again and again we come back to the fact that no matter how many different types of inputs are thrown into the mix, no service is going to be right all the time. Indeed, none that I know of claims to be right more than about 60 percent of the time. This is the most important thing to keep in mind about services: They are fallible and they do make mistakes—almost every day. To expect something different is a very unrealistic attitude to begin trading with. Remember that if the owner of an advisory service could be right more than 60 percent of the time he would not be running an advisory service—as I said earlier, he would be on his yacht taking in the Caribbean sun and buying and selling for himself.

What Do They Cost?

The only time an advisory service seems cheap is when on the day you receive the first issue of your subscription you take up a position recommended by the service and it produces $1,000 profit in three weeks. Unfortunately that does not happen very often, and therefore services seem expensive when you start to subscribe to them. They seem expensive for one of two reasons: (1) You have been trading without a service and losing the shirt off your back and are therefore low on cash; or (2) You have not traded at all and you have to give up some of your trading capital to begin the serv-

* I have omitted a few of the other factors supplied in order to keep the list reasonably short.

ice. In either case the service seems high when you go to pay the bill.

Most advisory services charge between $100 and $250 per year, with lower rates, of course, for three- and six-month trials. This cost, which is between 30 cents and 75 cents per day, is not unreasonable if they help you to avoid only a few mistakes and help you to catch a few substantial moves. Moreover, the cost of a service is an acceptable tax deduction if you itemize expenses. You would be well advised not to pick a service on the basis of cost alone, but instead to pick one on the basis of how it suits your temperament and how good a job the service actually does in its recommendations.

Before you subscribe to any advisory service, ask to see a recent track record that covers at least six months and preferably a year of recommendations. This track record should include all recommendations made by the service indicating the net profits and losses that would have accrued to a trader who had been reasonably diligent in following that service's recommendations. For it is the track record that should weigh most heavily in your mind on whether or not you should subscribe to that service. Indeed, that is the proof of the pudding. If the service does not wish to supply you with such a record, for whatever reason, that should give you pause about that service's past ability to forecast price movements. If they say they are going to do better next year because they have changed their system and therefore last year's record is not really representative, wait until next year and then ask to see their record. The track-record factor cannot be overstressed, and I for one firmly believe that if more traders insisted upon track records before subscribing there would be fewer services with poor track records to pick from.

Most services come out with a weekly letter, though a few of them offer a daily advisory bulletin. Now that long-distance calls can be made at such low rates—especially in the evening—many services offer a telephone recorder to update the weekly letter. The overnight shift in opinion on a given commodity that sometimes occurs almost demands some rapid method of informing subscribers of changes in opinion on a position. Some services also accept paid telephone calls from subscribers who want advice on a position they are holding or wish to hold. This can be a useful addition for a new trader.

It should also be pointed out that nearly all the major brokerage houses—wire houses and houses that specialize in commodity trading—publish their own advisory letters. These letters are generally free to commodity-trading customers. Sometimes a house will publish both a technical letter and a fundamental letter, and sometimes it will publish one letter on the so-called New York commodities—copper, cocoa, silver, cotton, etc.—and another on the Chicago commodities—that is, those commodities traded on the Chicago Board of Trade and the Chicago Mercantile Exchange. Some of these letters are quite good; some are simply collections of rumors passed around by floor traders, sometimes backed up by simple bar-chart analyses. You should certainly read what your brokerage house sends you and compare its recommendations with those of any advisory services you subscribe to. It may turn out that what your broker is sending you for nothing is better than what you are paying for.

When all the factors are considered, I believe that, in general, a new trader will have a better chance of success if he subscribes to a service that has proven itself over time to be a reasonably good forecaster of price change. That proof should be in the form of a complete track record covering at least one year of trading.

CHAPTER **14**

The Eight Commandments of Sensible Speculation in Commodities

□

In the preceding thirteen chapters, both the mechanics and some of the techniques of commodity trading have been described. Whenever possible I have tried to point out the risks in taking certain kinds of actions and positions. I have tried to make clear that commodity trading is a risky business—riskier in many respects than the purchase of stocks or bonds, which can be put away and forgotten for months or even years at a time. But by and large, the daily opportunities for profits available in the commodity markets are unequaled by any other form of legal speculation. Concomitant with the opportunities for profit are, of course, the opportunities for loss.

This book has been written to help you make the most of the profitable opportunities while limiting, insofar as possible, your losses. Down through the years individual commodity traders have developed a set of rules that seem to work well in producing profits and minimizing losses. I have borrowed some ideas from these rules and then added other ideas based on my trading experiences to produce another set of rules better suited to beginning traders. After you have some trading experience of your own, you may choose to modify these guides to suit your own taste. (I hope you do, because as your account balance grows, some of these rules will no longer be strictly applicable.) Following them will not guarantee that you will make a profit—I am afraid that is something no set of guidelines can do. However, following these rules will certainly improve the probability of your making a profit by a significant amount. After you have studied these guides you may decide that one or more make no sense for you, or that they should be modified in some way. Fine. You should feel free to change them to suit your own needs and tastes. But before you do, I hope that you will give this set a fair trial.

Rule Number 1. Decide on a Trading Plan (and Follow It)

Well, you have finally decided to risk a few dollars in the commodity market. Your other duties where you work or at home prevent you from spending the time it takes to make detailed supply-and-demand estimates for the several commodities you are interested in. While you can manage to keep a few bar charts up to date, you don't have the inclination to compute several moving averages daily.

It is for this reason that you decide to subscribe to an advisory service. Let us suppose it is a technical service with a reasonably impressive track record which has caused you to subscribe to it. Generally what happens next is something like this: The first three trades your service recommends go against you and you take your losses with a certain amount of uneasiness. On two of those recommendations your broker wanted you to go the other way. That is, if the service wanted you to go short March corn, he wanted you to go long. Thus, after three trials, your broker has been right two out of three times. He then proposes that you give up on the service's recommendations and try his. On the next three trades your broker is wrong twice, and your advisory service is right on two of *its* three recommendations. You have now traded six times, and you have a disastrous trading record because you have been whipsawed between two sources of information. If the service convinced you to subscribe because of its good track record, why didn't you give their trading plan a reasonable trial? If your broker had shown you a reasonable track record—which is highly unlikely, since brokers rarely keep a record that shows both winners and losers—then perhaps you should have followed your broker's recommendations rather than subscribed to an advisory service in the first place. Unfortunately your present strategy has managed to get the worst of both worlds.

I will admit that a broker's recommendations on the telephone may have more immediacy and may be far more persuasive than the recommendations you receive in your weekly or daily letter from your service. But the important thing is that you evaluate the trading plans of both, make your choice, and then give whichever plan you have chosen a reasonable chance to prove itself right—or wrong.

Thus the consistent following of Rule Number 1 will play an extremely important role in your success or failure in the commodity market. Chances are that if you succumb to whipsawing on more than two or three sets of trades you will be forced out of the commodity market—at least temporarily. Not only will it probably cause you to lose a lot of money but it will also produce internal conflicts resulting from the fact that you are not quite sure whose advice you should be taking on the next trade. The rule then is a simple one: Adopt a trading plan based on whatever rational techniques appeal to you and then follow it for a reasonable period of time in order to give it a fair test.

Rule Number 2. Do Not Overtrade Your Margin

The purpose of margin is to keep traders honest. It assures your broker that, if prices move against positions you have taken, you have the resources to cover any losses you might sustain. In a completely honest world in which traders would not take on more positions than they could financially be responsible for there would be no need for you to put up any initial margin money. But, alas, we do not live in such a world. Not only do most new traders need margin in order to discipline themselves; they must learn to not overtrade what margin they have.

Suppose you have assembled $3,000 worth of risk capital to begin trading with. It seems like a lot of money and you just know you can turn it into $6,000 in two months. Your advisory service recommends that you go short wheat (say that the margin on a wheat trade is $600 per contract). So you call up your broker and tell him to sell you five May wheat contracts at, say, $1.58½ per bushel. Your margin is now 100 percent committed on the wheat. If wheat prices should rise by 2 cents per bushel, you would sustain a loss of $100 per contract. Your equity then is reduced to $500 per contract, which is the maintenance margin level—that is, if your equity falls below $500 you must supply enough margin to bring it back up to $600. That means a margin call. Because you committed all of your margin you could only sustain a 2 cent adversity without being asked for additional margin or without being forced to reduce your position.

The obvious solution to this problem, of course, is to sell only three wheat contracts to begin with, thus leaving $1,200 of cushion in your account to take care of adverse price movements. Unfortunately, most new traders believe that they are not getting their money's worth unless every cent is tied up in a position. This example raises another question: How much of a new trader's margin should be tied up in a single position? This point will be more fully explored in Rule Number 3.

You must take my word that it is no fun having your name on top of the file on the margin clerk's desk.* It has happened to me too many times, and I can assure you it takes all the pleasure out of trading.†

Rule Number 3. Set a Risk Limit for Each Trade

Let us consider your first position in the commodity market again where you sold May wheat at $1.58½ per bushel. You hang up the phone with a curious feeling of satisfaction and fear. In my opinion, the first few days in a new position are the scariest—for in most cases it is during this time that you will find out if your position is a good one. In most cases prices will either start to move against you or with you in fairly short order. But until you get that first

* Another of the consequences of the availability of low-cost computation time is that brokerage firms can run a margin check every night after the markets close, with very little effort and cost. In the old days a delinquent account might escape the margin clerk's attention for a few days—with unforeseen consequences, both good and bad, for the trader. Nothing escapes the attention of that tireless indefatigable IBM machine in the back room—ever.

† Or sleeping or almost anything else you can think of.

clearcut sign you will, naturally enough, have some doubts about the wisdom of your position.

But a lot of the anxiety of commodity trading can either be eliminated or reduced if you decide at the time you enter a trade exactly how much of your margin money you are willing to risk on that position. This decision should be an explicit one and not a fuzzy figure in your head of, say, "about $350." The trouble with "about" figures is that they have a tendency to encourage self-deception. They cause traders to wait for the market to prove them right. The market rarely accommodates such traders but, on the contrary, has a distinct predilection for proving certain types of traders to be fools.

Let us examine the imaginary wheat position you just assumed. You have not explicitly decided on how wrong you are willing to be, but you tell yourself that if the market rises 3½ cents ($175) you will think seriously about covering your short position. The market then backs and fills for a few days, closing a week after you took up your position 3 cents above where you sold it. About noon of the next day you call your broker and he tells you that the grains were strong during the morning and that May wheat was up another 1½ cents. The market has now moved against you by 4½ cents and you are still holding on to your position like a security blanket. It isn't and never can be. Your wheat contracts are pieces of paper, incapable of knowing or caring who owns them. They have no emotional ties to you so why should you have any emotional ties to them? By the close wheat is up another 1 cent and the market has moved against you 5½ cents ($275) plus a commission of $30 or $305 per contract in all. If you initially supplied $600 in margin, you are in the unhappy position of just having seen 50 percent of it evaporate. What to do? You are too unhappy to laugh and too old to cry.

The mistake here is a common one. You should have sat down with pencil and paper before you entered the position and decided on your risk. Some traders say they will risk 30 or 35 percent of their initial margin. In the wheat example, that would be $150 plus commission. You decide in advance that if the market goes against you by that amount you will bail out—no ifs, ands or buts. Other traders calculate, for example, the ten- or twenty-day moving average of closing prices and state that if the market penetrates that price they will close out their position immediately. Another method frequently used by traders is to draw a trend line on a bar chart of prices, as was explained in Chapter 9, and then they use that line as the limit of their risk; any penetration of that line and they automatically close out their position. Whatever method is chosen it must be adhered to without compromise. Compromises become extremely plausible in the trader's mind when prices start to move against him because he just knows that the market will turn very soon. But remember, there is no law that says this has to happen. On the contrary, prices have a tendency in the commodity market to keep moving in a certain direction once they have started that way.

In summary then you must decide on your risk level in advance and adhere to it. Sticking with a position after it has moved against you is called in the commodity market being a "hero." There are very few heroes who survive either wars or commodity trading. The one sure way to maintain your official standing in the Cowards' Club of America is to use stop-loss orders—which are the subject of the next rule.

Rule Number 4. Do Not Trade Without Stop-Loss Orders

Actually this rule is part of Rule Number 3: setting a risk amount on every trade. A sensible commodity speculator not only determines in his head what he is willing to risk but actually places a stop-loss order to insure that no more than that amount is actually lost. It always seems to me that once I place my stop-loss order I have transferred most of my worries from my head to the floor broker's head. If my order is filled and I am taken out of my position with a loss, I am not exactly happy about it, but I have built that loss into my trading plan and it certainly won't cause me to stop trading.

Many new traders do set stops and then commit one of the cardinal crimes of commodity trading—they move the stop away from the price. Consider the wheat example again. You sold a May wheat contract at $1.58½ and you set your stop-loss order 3½ cents higher at $1.62. Prices then rally to $1.61. Such price action might sorely tempt you to move your stop to $1.64. But don't do it. If the price moved against you by 3½ cents, there is nothing to stop the market from moving against you by 7 cents. Once you begin to move stops away from the current price, you have invited disaster to join you as a trading partner.

However, stops can be moved the other way—that is, closer to the current price. This is not a bad idea when a position is beginning to show an appreciable profit. Say that May wheat has now dropped to $1.44, which gives you a gross profit of $725. Suppose, further, that you had been using the twenty-day moving average as your stop-loss point and that this average has now fallen to $1.49. The sluggish 20-day moving average is 5 cents higher than the current price because prices have been dropping quickly and thus the moving average has not been able to keep up with the steep drop in current prices. With 5 cents separating your stop and the current price, you are risking $250 of your profit. Under these circumstances I see no harm in reducing the risk to your profit by moving your stop to someplace like $1.46½ or just 2½ cents above the close. Of course, the closer you put the stop the more likely you are to be stopped out of your position by a minor rally created by traders who now think: (1) wheat is cheap; or (2) by shorts who are buying in and taking profits. In general I prefer to be taken out of a profitable position by a stop because neither I nor anyone else (including your broker) has any idea how far a price trend will persist. Some traders set profit objectives but I believe that action is setting a limit in the wrong direction. Losses should be limited—profits should not.

On page 59 I mentioned a stop-loss order that is filled only on the close. I believe such an order can be profitably used in two circumstances. Just after you have entered a position, when the 20-day average (or any other stop point you might be using) might be close to your position, you might choose to use an on-the-close stop. Say that the twenty-day moving average was at $1.60 when you shorted wheat at $1.58½. You might decide that if prices closed more than ½ cent higher than the twenty-day moving average you would want to be out of your position. Thus you would set a stop to buy one May wheat contract at $1.60½ on the close only. Thus if during the day prices moved up above $1.60½ but settled back down at the close under that price you would hold on to your position. Only if prices were to close above $1.60½ would you be taken out of your short sale. Keep in mind, however, that an on-the-close order has an additional risk that an ordinary stop does not have. It does not limit your loss to any certain amount. You will be stopped out if wheat closes at \$1.60⅝ or if it closes at \$1.65½. In the first case you would lose \$136.25 while in the second you would lose \$380. This point should be thoroughly understood before an on-the-close order is utilized. An on-the-close order can also be used when holding a good profit on a position. In this case it can be set fairly close to the previous day's close, and only if prices were able to close beyond the stop would you be taken out of your position.

In summary, then, it is preferable to close out both losing and profitable positions with stop-loss orders. This rule guarantees that you will be following what is probably the oldest maxim of commodity traders extant: "Take your losses when they are small and let your profits ride."

Rule Number 5. Diversify Your Positions

Since nearly all commodity traders at one time or another dream of making that one big trade that will put them on Easy Street, they become subject to the temptation of going for broke. More often than not, that is exactly where they wind up—broke. This leads us to Rule Number 5. Do not under any circumstances place all your trading capital on a single position. A reasonable rule of thumb to follow is never to put more than 40 percent of your speculative funds into any one position. This rule can save you from a trading disaster of the highest order. An example should make this clear.

Suppose that when you got the signal to sell May wheat you were holding no other positions and had \$3,000 in your trading account. Suppose further that the margin on a wheat contract was \$600 at that time. So you decided to sell four contracts short, thus obligating \$2,400 of your \$3,000 in capital. (At least you followed Rule Number 2 and did not sell five contracts.) You also followed Rules Number 3 and 4 and decided you wanted to risk no more than 4 cents on your position so you set a stop-buy order at \$1.62½. Then suppose that you did indeed get stopped out at \$1.62½; your loss was then $800, plus $120 in commissions, giving a net loss of $920 or almost a third of your trading capital. With a total trading capital of $3,000 no more than two wheat contracts should have been taken, which would have limited your loss to $460.

Of course, it is easy to argue against this position by pointing out that had prices moved in a favorable direction the trader with four contracts would have been able to increase his trading capital by a substantial amount. The point to keep in mind, however, is not what happens if a position moves in your favor, but what happens if it moves against you. All of us can learn to live with and trade with more capital. It is much more difficult to trade on substantially less capital. Always prepare yourself for the worst, and then you can have nothing but pleasure when things go your way.

By diversifying your account so that you are holding at least three different positions you improve the odds of always holding at least one profitable position, which can be mighty helpful in keeping your spirits up on those days when the other two trades are moving against you. In fact, if you have sufficient trading capital I see no harm in holding five or even more positions.

It should be pointed out that this idea is contrary to the recommendations of most commodity speculators. They reason that the average trader cannot possibly do a good job of following more than three commodities. This argument makes no sense to me, for if a trader is using an advisory service, then he is letting them do the tracking and he is simply following their recommendations. All he must do is simply look after keeping the stops adjusted properly. I agree that if you are working without an advisory service, looking after three trades will give you more than enough to do and you should not try to follow more than that.

In summary, then, this rule recognizes that many positions will not work out as expected, but by taking three or more different risks at a time the probability of being able to close out a successful trade at frequent intervals will be increased.

RULE NUMBER 6. DO NOT PYRAMID

Of all the rules that lead to sensible speculation for beginning commodity traders, I believe this is the one that most experienced traders would reject out of hand. They would reject it because it involves a technique they frequently employ—that technique is called pyramiding and it works like this:

Suppose a large trader with ample capital believes May wheat is too high, just like you do. Instead of selling two contracts at $1.58½ he sells ten contracts. He puts up $6,000 margin on the ten contracts. Prices ease, as he expects, to $1.55 giving him a profit of 3½ cents per bushel; he now sells five more contracts short at that price. Now, however, the broker does not ask him to put up an additional $3,000 for the five new contracts, but only $1,250, as the trader has accrued a $1,750 profit (3½ cents/bushel × 5,000 bushels/contract × 10 contracts) on his original short sale of ten contracts. Prices continue to ease so our happy pyramider sells three more contracts short at a $1.52. This time the broker asks him to put up no more additional funds because when prices fell 3 cents from $1.55 to $1.52 the trader accrued 45 cents more profit on his fifteen contracts, or $2,250, which more than meets the margin requirement on the three new short sales at $1.52. It should be obvious that the profit possibilities from pyramiding are enormous. If prices continue to fall and the trader is able to close out his positions at $1.44, his net profit on his eighteen contracts is $10,660 on a total investment of $7,250. So why shouldn't you do it if the big boys do it all the time?

The answer to that question has to do with pyramid building. Even a casual observer of pyramid construction notes that the base is wider than the top. One of the things you are in no position to do is to make the base of your position very wide; if you do you will violate Rule Number 5, which says you should diversify your positions. For if you start out with only one or two positions for the base of your pyramid you must either put up more margin to add another contract or else wait until the trade has moved substantially in your favor. These two restraints lead me to believe that it is not impossible for a small trader to pyramid, but it does require a steady hand and a strong stomach.

If you had shorted two wheat contracts at $1.58½ you would be in a position to short another one without additional margin at $1.52½, at which point you would be holding a $600 paper profit. If prices were to move up only 2 cents to somewhere above $1.54½ you must then be prepared to answer a margin call, for at that price your equity is just $1,500, which is the minimum required on the three contracts. Since all commodity prices bounce around a good bit, a 2 cents adverse price movement should be expected. Therefore unless you can supply the additional margin or are willing to sell out your additional position, you should not have added another contract at $1.52½.

Pyramiding, then, is for traders who have more resources than most of the small traders for whom this book is written. If, however, after several years of trading, the equity in your account has increased by several times, then I can see no harm in a modest amount of pyramiding as long as the other rules set forth in this chapter are scrupulously followed. Therefore I will now rephrase Rule Number 6 to reflect this exception to my ban on pyramiding: Traders with small accounts should never pyramid; traders who have access to additional capital can pyramid on a modest scale.

Rule Number 7. Ignore Well-Meaning but Irrelevant Advice

Once you start commodity trading you will find advice of all kinds pouring in on you from almost every direction—from friends, your broker, unsolicited mailings from advisory services you don't subscribe to, and even from your spouse. The only thing I can tell you is to ignore it—shut it all out and pay no attention to it. It will only confuse you and probably cost you money to boot. Not that it will always be bad advice. On the contrary, sometimes it will be quite good—but sometimes it *will* be irrelevant, and since you are in no position to sort out the bad from the good, the only safe thing to do is to ignore all of it. If you have subscribed to an advisory service with an established track record, why should you listen to people or sources whose track record is unknown to you?

In Chapter 12 I mentioned a spread position I was holding during a bull market in cotton. The spread, as you will recall, moved against me, and my advisory service recommended that all such spreads be closed out immediately. At the time I was holding these cotton spreads with a partner. My partner was raised on a farm in the Midwest and he believed that he was extremely knowledgeable in the ways of commodity trading and prices. Unfortunately, I also believed that he was extremely knowledgeable in these areas. It only took a little encouraging on his part to convince me that we should not close out our cotton spreads as the advisory service recommended. So we hung on another three or four days, which cost us an additional $200 per spread as the spread proceeded to widen, even though my farm-raised partner said it would not, right up until the moment we sold out rather than answer a margin call.

Sometimes your broker will advise you not to take a position that your advisory service recommends. At the very least you should probably listen to your broker's reason,* but once again I believe you will have to follow the advice of the information source with a proven record—which should be your advisory service or you yourself, if you have developed your own method whose reliability you have established. This rule could also be paraphrased to read: Save me from the good intentions of my friends.

Rule Number 8. Remove a Portion of All Profits from Your Account

If you follow religiously all of the preceding seven rules given in this chapter I believe you will find that profits will begin to accrue in your account. When that happy event begins to take place you will be faced with the kind of problem all speculators enjoy working on. That is, what do you do with the profits? Do you let them accumulate in the account where they may be added to your trading capital so that bigger and bigger positions may be assumed? Or do you take them all out as they occur so that the capital available for trading remains constant?

I believe the best thing to do is take out a portion of all profits as they occur. Some traders like to remove half, others three-quarters. You may then have the pleasure of putting this portion of your profit to work in a less volatile area of the market—say, good-grade corporate bonds, or municipal bonds if you are in a higher tax bracket. Or you might choose to put this money into a savings account or simply apply it against your home mortgage if you have one. The advantage of the latter is that once you have done it you would have a lot of trouble getting at the money to put it back into

* One wag probably overstated the case when he stated that the only sure tip he ever got from his broker was a margin call.

commodity trading if you decided you wanted to go after a "big killing." (A commodity trader must be constantly on the lookout for ways to save himself from his own emotions—you remember the important ones: fear and greed.)

You might wish to spend your profits on a vacation or remodeling the house—items which the regular budget generally is hard put to fund. The important point is that you should take a portion of your profits and do things that you ordinarily would not be able to do.* In that way commodity trading will provide a daily source of excitement, an intellectual challenge, and an income to do things that your regular income will not permit. What more can you ask for?

Summary

The rules are clear and I believe they are well tested by time. You should verify that every trade and your whole account are in compliance with the eight rules at all times. You should also bear in mind that violation of any of the first six rules can invite a disaster of such a large magnitude as to remove you from the commodity markets for a considerable period of time. I believe these rules to be so important to your trading well-being that I will repeat them here:

1. Decide on a trading plan—and follow it.
2. Do not overtrade your margin.
3. Set a risk limit for each trade.
4. Do not trade without stop-loss orders.
5. Diversify your positions.
6. Do not pyramid ever (or almost ever).
7. Ignore well-meaning but irrelevant advice.
8. Remove a portion of all profits from your account.

* The story is told of the former *bon vivant* who had run through a considerable sum of money in a rather short period of time. One of his friends asked him what exactly had happened to all that money his mother had left him. He thought a moment and then he answered, "Well, I spent some of it on beautiful women; quite a bit of it was used up when I went to the racetrack every day; and, of course, I like to eat and drink very well, so I did." He then added, "I guess I just spent the rest foolishly."

Epilogue

□

If you started to read this book because you hoped that commodity trading would be an easy way to achieve substantial wealth in a short period of time you are probably disappointed. I believe that I have made it abundantly clear that it is not; I have tried to make clear that it is a speculative activity which can produce both substantial profits and substantial losses for those who engage in it. This book, if closely followed, in my opinion will help you to capture some of those profits and keep your losses small. The book is designed to help the trader who goes into the commodity market with an eye to the long run—the trader who expects to be in the market next year at this time; it is not designed to be very useful to the trader who wants to make a killing—who wants to make that one trade that will enable him or her to retire on Easy Street. There is no book that can help that kind of trader.

Many things about commodity trading make it an attractive activity. The one thing, undoubtedly, that brings most people to it is the chance to reap big profits from a small investment. But there is another benefit that can be even more important than making money. Commodity trading forces those who undertake it to examine themselves in a very careful manner. First they must test themselves to see if they can live in relative peace with those two constant companions who are the silent partners of every commodity trader: fear and greed. A trader must come to know himself more thoroughly than most people care to. Self-knowledge is like a very powerful searchlight—it can show us things in ourselves which we would rather not see, but which, once aware of, can lead us to an inner peace not available by any other means. I am certain that Sören Kierkegaard did not have commodity traders in mind in 1847 when he wrote his journals. Yet one line from those journals makes a very powerful argument for the activity described in this book:

> The majority of men are subjective towards themselves and objective towards all others, terribly objective sometimes—but the real task is to be objective towards oneself and subjective towards all others.

I believe that commodity trading is the ideal way to achieve Kierkegaard's worthy goals. I hope you agree and give it a try.

APPENDIX A

A Brief Glossary of Terms Used in Commodity Trading

ACTUALS: The physical commodities themselves as distinguished from a futures contract for those commodities.

ARBITRAGE: The simultaneous sale of cash commodities or futures in one market against the purchase of cash commodities or futures in the same or a different market. The purpose of such transactions is to profit from a discrepancy in price between the two markets. See also *Hedge* and *Spread.*

ASK: An offer to sell at a designated price.

BASIS: Generally used to mean the difference in price between the spot or "cash" price and the price of the nearest futures contract. It can also be applied to the difference between the cash price and more distant futures contracts.

BEAR: One who believes prices will go lower. When used as an adjective it means declining prices, as in *bear market.*

BID: An offer to buy at a designated price.

BREAK: A sharp price decline.

BULGE: A sharp advance in price.

BULL: One who believes prices will go higher. When used an an adjective it means advancing prices as in *bull market.*

BUY ON THE OPENING OR CLOSE: An order to buy at the beginning or end of a trading session.

CARLOAD: An amount of grain usually somewhere between 1,400 and 2,500 bushels.

CARS: A slang expression used by commodity traders as a synonym for contracts. Probably comes from *carload.* Five "cars" of silver simply means five contracts of silver.

CARRYING CHARGES: The cost of holding an actual commodity in storage over a period of time. Such charges generally include storage, interest and insurance.

CASH COMMODITY: The actual or physical commodity. Goods available for immediate delivery.

CASH PRICE: The current price of the cash commodity of a designated quality available for immediate delivery.

CLEARINGHOUSE: The name given to the association of exchange member firms through which they can have trades either offset or cleared, and through which financial settlement is also made. In some cases the clearinghouses also serve as depositories for maintenance margin.

CLOSE: (1) The end of a trading session; (2) The period at the end of a trading session during which all trades are officially declared as having been executed "at or on the close." There may be simultaneous acceptance of "ask" and "bid" prices at the close, resulting in a *split close.*

COMMISSION HOUSE: A firm that buys or sells for the accounts of its customers. Also called a broker or brokerage house or sometimes a *wire house.*

COMMODITY CREDIT CORPORATION (CCC): That part of the U.S. Department of Agriculture which functions as the holding and marketing agency in connection with administered farm commodities. See *Government Support Program.*

COMMODITY EXCHANGE AUTHORITY (CEA): A department of the U.S. Department of Agriculture set up by Congress to regulate trading in certain commodity futures.

CONTRACT: In futures trading, the unit of trading established by the exchange for each commodity traded. For example, in grains one contract is 5,000 bushels, in plywood it is 69,120 square feet of ½-inch-thick plywood, and so forth.

CONTRACT GRADES: The grades of a commodity that are eligible for delivery against a futures contract. The rules of the exchange for each commodity traded may permit other grades besides the basic grade to be delivered at a premium or discount to the basic grade price.

CORNER: To secure such a strong control of a commodity or security that its price can be manipulated.

COUNTRY ELEVATOR: A grain elevator that is generally located near where the grain is actually grown. Farmers frequently sell or store their grain in these elevators.

COUNTRY PRICE: The price farmers receive when they sell their commodity in an area removed from the central market. It is frequently quoted as so many points or cents "on" or "off" a certain futures price.

CREDIT BALANCE: What the broker owes the customer.

CROP YEAR: The accounting period used for statistical and reporting purposes. The crop year generally begins with the first of the month during which the bulk of the crop is harvested, and it extends to the same date next year. For example, the crop year for wheat, oats and rye in the U.S. begins on July 1 and extends through June 30 of the following year.

CRUSH SPREAD: A spread that involves the simultaneous purchase of a soybean futures contract and the sale of a soybean meal futures and soybean oil futures contract.

COVER: The process of closing out a short position by making an offsetting purchase.

DAY ORDER: An order to buy or sell, good for the day it is entered only. If not filled it automatically expires at the close.

DAY TRADER: A trader who carries no open positions overnight.

DEBIT BALANCE: What the customer owes the broker.

DELIVERY MONTH: The calendar month during which the futures contract expires.

DELIVERY NOTICE: The notification given to the clearinghouse by a short seller of a futures contract declaring his intent to deliver the actual commodity.

DELIVERY POINTS: Those locations designated by a commodity exchange at which the commodity specified in a futures contract may be delivered to fulfill the terms of the contract.

EVENING UP: Closing out all open positions by offsetting purchases and sales; frequently done in order not to carry positions overnight or over weekends or holidays.

EXECUTION: The actual filling of a customer's order. Executions are done by a *floor broker* in the trading pit for others or for himself.

FARM PRICES: The prices actually received by farmers for their products as reported each month by the U.S. Department of Agriculture.

FARM STOCKS: The grain stocks held by farmers.

FILL OR KILL ORDER: A commodity order that demands immediate execution at the price stated or else it is automatically canceled. Sometimes called a *quick order*.

FLOOR BROKER: A member of an exchange who, in the trading pit, executes buy and sell orders for others. At times he may trade for his own account.

FLOOR TRADER: A member of an exchange who trades only for his own account in the pit.

FREE BALANCE: Margin funds on deposit with a broker, which are not committed against existing open positions.

FREE SUPPLY: The quantity of a commodity available for commercial sale; does not include Government-held stocks.

FUTURES: Contracts to buy and receive or to sell and deliver a commodity during a specified future month with the terms of the contract specified by the futures exchange on which the contract is traded.

GOOD-TILL-CANCELED ORDER (G.T.C.): An order to buy or sell which remains in effect until either filled, or canceled by the customer.

GOOD-THE-WEEK ORDER (G.T.W.): An order to buy or sell which remains in effect until it is either filled or until trading ends on the last trading day of the week.

GOVERNMENT SUPPORT PROGRAM: A program authorized by Congress by means of which the Department of Agriculture is supposed to stabilize farm prices. This program is carried out, for the most part, by making loans to producers at stated prices. Up to a certain date for each crop, the farmer can, if he chooses, take his crop out from under loan and sell it on the free market. If free market prices are low, farmers will let the Government keep the crop and default on the loan. In essence, the farmer sells his crop to the Government at the loan rate. The Government program has a tendency to take a commodity out of the market at a time when the supply of that commodity is substantially in excess of demand. Farmers who participate in this program generally have their acreage limited for each of the Government-supported crops.

HARDENING: A term used to describe a slowly advancing market.

HEAVY: A market in which sell orders seem to be more numerous than buy orders—a weak market.

HEDGE: A commitment in the futures market which is established to offset a cash commodity position. If a dealer is holding wheat in his elevators he might wish to institute a *short hedge* by selling wheat futures contracts to protect himself from a decline in wheat prices. Likewise, a grain exporter might have arranged to sell for cash wheat which will be exported some months in the future. He owns no wheat now, but on the day he arranges his sale for export he purchases wheat contracts which will mature just before he has to load his grain for shipment. The exporter has now protected himself with a *long hedge* against a price rise that might have wiped out any profit he had on the cash sale.

INITIAL MARGIN: The amount of money required to take up a newly established futures position.

INTERCOMMODITY SPREAD: A position between two related commodities; for example, a long wheat and a short corn position is an intercommodity spread.

INTERMARKET SPREAD: A position in the same or almost the same commodity traded on two different exchanges; for example, long Kansas City and short Chicago wheat constitute an intermarket spread.

INTRACOMMODITY SPREAD: A position in the same commodity but different months on the same exchange; for example, long February, short August frozen pork bellies represents an intracommodity spread.

INVERTED MARKET: A market in which the nearby futures are selling at a premium to the more distant futures.

LAST TRADING DAY: The last day during which trading in a futures contract is permitted during the delivery month. All contracts which have not been offset by the end of trading on that day must thereafter be settled by delivery or agreement.

LIMIT ORDER: An order by the customer to his broker which restricts the broker to buy for not more than, or sell for not less than, a stated price.

LIMIT (UP OR DOWN): The maximum price advance or decline from the previous day's settlement price that is permitted in one day's trading session as set forth by the rules of the exchange.

LIQUIDATION: The closing out of a long position by making a sale.

LOAN PRICE: The price at which farmers may obtain crop loans from the Government. See *Government Support Program.*

LONG: One who has bought a futures contract and who has not yet closed out this position through an offsetting sale. One can also be long the cash commodity.

LONG HEDGE: See HEDGE.

LONG SQUEEZE: A market situation in which longs are forced to liquidate their positions because of falling prices.

MAINTENANCE MARGIN: The amount of money required by a clearinghouse to retain a futures position. It is less than the "initial" margin and allows the flexibility needed to permit minor price fluctuations. For example, the initial margin on a live-cattle contract might be $400 while the maintenance margin might be only $250.

MARGIN: Money deposited by buyers and sellers of a futures contract to ensure fulfillment of the contracts. It acts as a performance bond rather than as a down payment.

MARGIN CALL: A request for funds to margin a newly established position (initial margin) or, more commonly, a call for additional funds to bring the margin on an old position back up to the initial-margin level.

MARKET-IF-TOUCHED ORDER (M.I.T.): An order to buy or sell at the market immediately if an execution takes place at a certain price stated in the order. Such an order might read, for example "Buy 10 May oats 76½ MIT." Thus if a trade in May oats takes place at \$0.76½ (or even if the market skipped \$0.76½ and jumped from \$0.76⅜ to \$0.76⅝), the M.I.T. order would be filled at the best price then available.

MARKET ORDER: An order to buy or sell immediately at the best possible price.

NEGOTIABLE WAREHOUSE RECEIPT: A certificate issued by an approved warehouse that guarantees the existence and the grade of a commodity held in store.

NOMINAL PRICE: Sometimes used to give an approximate idea of price level when no trading has actually taken place at that or any other price. A price in name only.

NON-RECOURSE LOAN: The type of loan that the Government makes to farmers under its price-support program. In the event that the farmer defaults on the loan, the Government has no recourse against the farmer if the security the farmer has put up (his crop) fails to bring the amount of the loan when sold.

NOTICE DAY: The day on which notices of intention to deliver may be issued.

NOTICE OF INTENTION TO DELIVER: A certificate supplied by a short seller indicating his intention to fulfill his contract obligation by delivering the actual commodity.

OFFER: Expression of a willingness to sell.

OFFSET: Closing out of an existing long or short position by making an appropriate sale or purchase.

ONE-CANCELS-THE-OTHER ORDER (O.C.O.): A contingency order in which one part is automatically canceled as soon as the other part is filled.

OPEN INTEREST: The number of futures contracts (or, in the case of the grains, the number of bushels represented by those contracts) that the clearinghouse books show to be open at the close of each market day. The open interest shows the total position on one side of the market only, since the long interest must always equal the short interest.

OPENING: The official beginning of a trading session.

OPEN ORDER: A good-till-canceled order.

OVERBOUGHT: A market that has outrun its support and thus is vulnerable to a downside correction.

OVERSOLD: Just the opposite of overbought. Such a market is vulnerable to a sharp upside correction.

PAPER LOSSES OR PROFITS: Losses or profits on positions which have not been closed out and hence have not been realized yet. Margin requirements are adjusted according to paper profits and losses, so to a certain extent they are real.

PARITY: A price that is presumed to put farm commodity prices on a par with other prices in the economy. The price is usually determined by a formula which takes into account relative prices in a past period considered to have been normal.

PENETRATION: A move through a previously established resistance level. Chartists believe that penetration of such a level means that the current trend will continue.

PIT: The designated locations on the trading floor where futures trading takes place in particular commodities.

POSITION: To be either long or short in the market.

PREMIUM: The amount that a given futures contract or actual commodity sells over another futures contract.

PUBLIC: Private individuals who trade in futures contracts through brokerage houses, in contrast with trade participants who frequently are hedging their cash positions and floor traders who trade full time to earn their living.

PURCHASE AND SALE STATEMENT (P & S STATEMENT): The statement sent by a broker to a customer when the customer's position has been reduced or closed out. This statement shows the commodity traded, the size of the position, the dates and prices at which the position was acquired and closed out, the amount of the commission, and the net profit or loss on the completed transaction.

PYRAMIDING: The technique of using profits to increase a position in a commodity.

RALLY: A price rise in a market that is generally falling.

RANGE: The high and low prices for a specified period of time.

REACTION: A price fall in a generally rising market.

REALIZE: The act of turning paper profits or losses into actual profits or losses.

REGULATED COMMODITIES: Those commodities over which the Commodity Exchange Authority has supervision are termed "regulated." The CEA acts to ensure that an orderly market prevails and on occasion investigates abnormal price movements in the regulated commodities.

RESTING ORDER: See OPEN ORDER.

RING: See PIT.

ROUND TURN: The completion of both a purchase and an offsetting sale, or vice versa. Sometimes used to refer to the commission charged for buying and selling a contract.

SCALPER: A speculator operating on the trading floor who buys and sells for his own account with great rapidity and who is willing to accept small profits (and even smaller losses). He supplies the market with liquidity.

SETTLEMENT PRICE: A price set by the clearinghouse at the end of each trading session which is used to adjust the margins between clearing members and the clearinghouse. The price is usually the same as the closing price, or if there is a range in the closing prices, it might be midway between the high and low price of the range.

SHORT: One who has sold a futures contract and is obligated to deliver under the terms of the contract or close it out by means of an offsetting purchase.

SHORT HEDGE: See HEDGE.

SHORT SALE: The process of selling a futures contract in expectation of buying back or offsetting the sale at some time in the future at a lower price.

SHORT SQUEEZE: A sharp run-up of prices that forces shorts to make offsetting purchases in order to avoid larger losses.

SOLD-OUT MARKET: A market in which weakly held longs have been forced out.

SPECULATIVE POSITION: An open position held by a trader that is unhedged.

SPECULATOR: One who voluntarily accepts the risks associated with the ownership of a commodity and relies on a price change in the commodity to produce a profit, or risk premium, for his efforts.

SPLIT CLOSE: A closing quotation that consists of two prices, caused by simultaneous transactions at the close between two separate sets of floor brokers.

SPOT COMMODITY: See CASH COMMODITY.

SPREAD: The simultaneous purchase of one futures contract against the sale of another futures contract of the same commodity but with a different delivery month, or of a different commodity in the same or different markets.

STOP ORDER OR STOP-LOSS ORDER: An order entered to buy or sell when the market reaches a specified point. A stop order to buy becomes a market order the instant a contract sells (or is bid) at or above the stop price. A stop order to sell becomes a market order when a contract sells (or is offered) at or below the stop price. Such orders are used to limit losses or protect profits.

SWITCH: The simultaneous closing out of one futures position and the reinstatement of it in another. For example, in June one might want to close out a long position in June hogs and switch into a July hog contract in order to avoid having to accept delivery.

TENDER: To deliver a commodity against a futures contract.

TERMINAL ELEVATOR: A grain elevator located at or near a major agricultural marketing center.

TRADING LIMIT: The maximum position under the Commodity Exchange Authority that may be held or controlled by one person.

VISIBLE SUPPLY: The amount of a commodity in storage facilities and at major marketing centers.

VOLUME OF TRADING: The purchase and sales of a commodity future during a specified period of time. Because purchases must equal sales, only one side of a transaction is shown in the published reports.

WAREHOUSE RECEIPT: A document which declares that a certain amount of a specified grade of a commodity is in storage in a designated warehouse. This receipt is a negotiable document showing ownership and may be used to satisfy the delivery requirements of a futures contract if the warehouse issuing the receipt is approved for delivery purposes by the exchange on which the contracts are traded.

WEATHER MARKET: A market subject to sharp price movements based largely on weather reports or weather prospects. Such markets occur when traders believe that the weather will have a big influence on the supply of a commodity.

WIRE HOUSE: A commission house with branch offices connected by telephone, teletype or other communications facilities.

APPENDIX B

Sources of Statistical Information

Following is a partial list of sources of information on various farm products. A complete list of all regularly appearing Government reports pertaining to agricultural products may be obtained from the Statistical Reporting Service, U.S. Department of Agriculture, Washington, D.C. 20250.

Grain Market News, Grain Division, Consumer and Marketing Service, Independence, Missouri 64050. No charge. A weekly publication that carries both weekly and monthly statistics on stocks of various grain commodities owned by the Government. It is an excellent source of information on supply-demand data. It includes a summary of the week's markets and information on export activity. Reports on estimated production released monthly during the growing season, as well as the quarterly reports on stocks in all positions, are included in this publication.

The Feed Situation, OMS Information Division, U.S. Department of Agriculture, Washington, D.C. 20250. No charge. This report is published five times a year and gives a review of market supply-and-demand situations and price prospects. It gives statistics on feed grains under loan and Government-owned stocks as of the first of each quarter.

Chicago Board of Trade Statistical Annual, 141 West Jackson Boulevard, Chicago, Illinois 60604. This publication includes daily market quotations, daily trading volume and daily open interest for all futures contracts traded on the Chicago Board of Trade. It also gives crop production for all grains for the past ten years, cash grain prices and supply-demand tabulations and other pertinent statistics.

USDA Crop Production Report, OMS Information Division, U.S. Department of Agriculture, Washington, D.C. 20250. No charge. Released around the tenth of each month, it is the accepted authoritative source of planting data such as intentions, acreage, yield and crop size.

A special report of a similar nature that receives close attention from grain traders is published around March 15 of each year by the USDA and is called the *Prospective Plantings Report.* It reveals farmers' intentions on planting for the coming season.

Quarterly Stock of Grains in All Positions Report, OMS Information Division, U.S. Department of Agriculture, Washington, D.C. 20250. No charge. Released about the twenty-second of January, April, July and October, this report provides analysts with a breakdown of the ownership of the stocks of all major grains by size and location. This report can have a dramatic effect on prices both immediately and long term as its contents are analyzed by farmers, the trade and speculators. Holding open positions as this report is being released can be hazardous and/or profitable.

Commitments of Traders in Commodity Futures, Commodity Exchange Authority, 141 W. Jackson St., Chicago, Illinois 60604. No charge. Reports the open interest of holders of both long and short positions divided into groups of large traders and small traders. (A large trader is generally considered to be one who holds more than 40 contracts of a grain or 25 contracts of the other major agricultural commodities.) In the case of large traders, their positions are further classified as to whether they are straight speculative positions, spread positions or hedged positions.

Livestock and Meat Situation Report, OMS Information Division, U.S. Department of Agriculture, Washington, D.C. 20250. No charge. Published six times a year, this report includes historical summaries of livestock data and professional comments on general economic conditions affecting the various livestock and meat markets.

Hogs and Pigs Crop Report, OMS Information Division, U.S. Department of Agriculture, Washington, D.C. 20250. No charge. A monthly publication giving the number of sows farrowing, pigs per litter, total pig crop, animals kept for breeding, and the number of animals intended for market, broken down into various weight classes. A very closely watched report by live hog and belly traders. This report can produce very sharp swings in market prices.

Livestock Slaughter and Meat Production, OMS Information Division, U.S. Department of Agriculture, Washington, D.C. 20250. No charge. Published at the end of the month, this report gives the slaughter and meat production for cattle by numbers and by weights for the previous month.

Cold Storage Report, OMS Information Division, U.S. Department of Agriculture, Washington, D.C. 20250. No charge. Released about the middle of the month, this publication reports cold-storage holdings as of the first of the month in pork bellies, broilers, eggs, and frozen orange-juice concentrate. Data contained in this report can also have a sharp effect on the prices of the commodities covered.

Livestock, Meat and Wool Market News, Livestock Division, Consumer and Marketing Service, U.S. Department of Agriculture, Washington, D.C. 20250. No charge. Published weekly, this report is a current source of information for weekly and monthly slaughter, for weekly bacon slicings and for the hog-corn ratio.

Chicago Mercantile Exchange Year Book, Chicago Mercantile Exchange, 110 North Franklin Street, Chicago, Illinois 60606. Lists the daily prices, volume and open interest of each futures contract traded during the year, as well as cash daily prices for commodities traded on the Chicago Mercantile Exchange.

Cotton Production Reports, OMS Information Division, U.S. Department of Agriculture, Washington, D.C. 20250. No charge. This report, issued in January, March, May, August and October, is considered to be the most useful report available to the cotton trader. It includes a broad assessment of the cotton market as well as historical data.

Fats and Oils Situation Reports, OMS Information Division, U.S. Department of Agriculture, Washington, D.C. 20250. No charge. Published five times a year, this report provides professional comments on general economic conditions as well as those factors believed to influence soybean yield, disappearance by crushing and export, processor's margins, Government programs and the like. Includes abundant statistical information on soybeans, soybean oil, and other fats and oils.

Crop-production reports and situation reports on frozen orange-juice concentrate, eggs and poultry, are also available from the U.S. Department of Agriculture.

The *Commodity Year Book,* Commodity Research Bureau, Inc., 140 Broadway, New York, New York 10005. This book appears about midyear and gives a complete statistical rundown on more than 100 basic commodities. It normally includes at least 100 charts showing long-term price trends and hundreds of statistical tables. Probably the most complete review of commodity information available in a single volume.

APPENDIX C

Annotated List of Advisory Services

Listed below in alphabetical order are 28 advisory services that have come to my attention. There are, no doubt, others that I am not aware of. Thus the list is in no sense to be considered complete. Addresses and rates are based on the latest information available to me and are, of course, subject to change. Services come and go and some of these may no longer exist by the time this is published. Based on a personal examination of its market letter, I have tried to describe the way I believe each service arrives at its trading decisions. My interpretation may be in error. I have also indicated those services for which I have seen a *complete* track record based on *recent* trades. Many of the services listed here will send a sample issue on request.

Active Cycles, P.O. Box 1683, Studio City, California 91604. Subscription rate: 2 months, $25. Track record available on request. A weekly technical advisory service that covers practically every actively traded commodity in the U.S. and Canada.

Berkley Associates, 132 West Broadway, San Diego, California 92101. Subscription rates: 2-month trial service, $15; other rates supplied on request. Track record on various trading methods supplied on request. This is not an advisory service in the ordinary sense of the word but a series of 31 methods used for trading various commodities based at least in part on seasonal considerations. Each method of trading is sold separately.

Chartcraft Commodity Service, Larchmont, New York 10538. Subscription rates: $120 per year. A point-and-figure chart service that provides buy and sell signals and reversal points.

Clayton Commodity Service, 7 North Brentwood Boulevard, St. Louis, Missouri 63105. Subscription rates: 3 months, $75; 6 months, $100; 1 year, $150. Weekly publication is called *Commodity Comments* and periodically publishes *Formula Trading Guides.* Track record available on request. This service leans heavily on fundamentals and historical price trends. The Clayton Commodity Service is closely associated with a commodity brokerage house.

Commodex, 90 West Broadway, New York, New York 10007. Subscription rates: 1 month, \$10; 6 months, \$150; 1 year, \$250. Daily letter. This service is 100 percent technical, basing its trading recommendations on a method that integrates price change, change in open interest and change in volume. Normally tracks two or more contracts in 20 different commodities. Uses a moving average to set trading stops.

Commodity Advices Point and Figure Technique, Morgan, Rogers and Roberts, Inc., 150 Broadway, New York, New York 10038. Subscription rates: \$25 per month. A specific technical advisory service issued twice each week, which attempts to call to the attention of its readers the few commodities offering the best opportunities for good percentage trades. Uses point-and-figure techniques exclusively.

Commodity Chart Service, Commodity Research Bureau, Inc., 140 Broadway, New York, New York 10005. Subscription rates: 1 trial issue, \$5; 3 months, \$65; 6 months, \$115; 1 year, \$200. A weekly chart service that supplies bar charts on all commodities traded in North America as well as on certain London commodities. Charts show volume and open interest and come with a computer trend-analyzer service. A summary of the Commodity Exchange Authority open-interest data as to large and small traders is also included. Some spread charts are in each issue.

Commodity Charts by Futures Publishing Company, 624 South Michigan Avenue, Chicago, Illinois 60605. Subscription rates: 3 months, \$51; 6 months, \$84; 1 year, \$150. This service supplies each week a complete set of price charts on more than 60 contracts. The charts show a daily price bar, open interest and volume data. Recommendations are based on technical considerations.

Commodity Computer Report, Scientific Investment Research, 526 North Rose Lane, Haverford, Pennsylvania 19041. Subscription rates: 4½-month introductory trial, \$17. Current track record available. A weekly advisory service utilizing a computer technique to predict trends in commodity prices.

Commodity Futures Forecast, 90 West Broadway, New York, New York 10007. Subscription rates: 1 month, \$25; 6 months, \$125; 1 year, \$200. Weekly letter. This service uses a combination of fundamental and technical information to make its recommendations.

Commodity Futures Statistics Service, P.O. Box 799, Wall Street Station, New York, New York 10005. Subscription rates: short trial, \$12; 3 months, \$36; 6 months, \$68; 1 year, \$120. Weekly letter plus telephone recorder service. Track record available on request. Utilizes a computer-based technical system to make its recommendations.

Commodity Research Institute, 141 West Jackson, Room 855, Chicago, Illinois 60604. Subscription rates: 2 months trial, $20; 6 months, $75. Track record available on request. Weekly letter plus telephone recorder service. This service utilizes a technical method to make its numerous recommendations.

Commodity Timing, P.O. Box 2176, Carmel, California 93921. Subscription rates: 2-month trial, $20; 6 months, $60; 1 year, $100. A weekly letter plus telephone recorder service. Track record available on request. This service uses a timing index based on both fundamental and technical considerations. The technical index is based on price and volume momentum.

Commodity Trend Service, 518 Empire Building, Columbus, Georgia 31901. Subscription rates: 1 month, $35; 3 months, $95; 6 months, $150. Combines vertical line charts, seasonal charts, contrary-opinion and statistical analysis to arrive at recommendations.

Daily Commodity Computer and Analyzer, Commodity Research Bureau, Inc., 140 Broadway, New York, New York 10005. Subscription rates: 1 month, $59; 3 months, $155; 6 months, $275; 1 year, $485. A computer-based daily report covering all actively traded contracts. Track record available on request. The service is completely technical and integrates price information, market volatility, timing factors and the like, along with moving averages, in arriving at its recommendations.

The Daily Commontrace, 500 Northern Boulevard, Great Neck, New York 11021. Subscription rates: 1 month, $30; 3 months, $80; 6 months, $145; 1 year, $250. A daily letter and telephone advisory service. A weekly summary is also given to subscribers. A technical service utilizing a computer to assist in making trading decisions.

Dunn & Hargitt Commodity Service, P.O. Box 101, Lafayette, Indiana 47902. Subscription rates: 3 months, $55; 6 months, $95; 1 year, $170. Weekly letter and charts, with telephone service. Track record available on request. This service basically uses a technical method to make its recommendations.

Futures Market Service, Commodity Research Bureau, Inc., 140 Broadway, New York, New York 10005. Subscription rates: 3 months, $22; 6 months, $40; 1 year, $75. The weekly "blue sheet" is one of the oldest advisory services around. Generally makes its recommendations on fundamentals.

Green's Commodity Market Comments, P.O. Box 174, Princeton, New Jersey 08540. Subscription rates: 6 months, $75; 1 year, $120.

Weekly letter. Pays close attention to international monetary developments and the supply-and-demand statistics for precious metals.

International Grain and Commodity Service, 53 West Jackson Boulevard, Chicago, Illinois 60604. Subscription rates: 3 months, $80; 6 months, $130; 1 year, $220. Service includes a daily report on prices, volume and open interest on 32 commodities and spread differentials on a selected number of spreads. A weekly report includes a commodity analysis, buy-sell recommendations, an analysis on a single commodity and various charts. There is also a monthly report of prices and several additional charts. This service utilizes both technical and fundamental methods to arrive at recommendations.

Keltner Commodity Letter, 1004 Baltimore Avenue, Kansas City, Missouri 64105. Subscription rates: 3 months, $25; 6 months, $45; 1 year, $85. A highly respected weekly letter whose recommendations are generally based on fundamentals. This service concentrates on agricultural commodities especially the grains and the soybean complex.

Market Vane, 431 East Green Street, Pasadena, California 91101. Subscription rates: 3 months, $60; 6 months, $110; 1 year, $200. Track record available on request. Weekly letter and daily telephone recorder available. This service basically uses technical and fundamental indications but makes many of its recommendations on the theory of contrary opinion.

M.B.H. Commodity Advisors, Inc., Box 353, Winnetka, Illinois 60093. Subscription rates: 5-week trial, $9; 13 weeks, $65; 26 weeks, $115; 52 weeks, $190. Current track record supplied on request. A weekly letter that makes recommendations on long-term trades and short-term trades with specific profit objectives given for each trade. Stops are also suggested along with the estimated risk for each trade. Service uses a parametric index to estimate the effect of supply and demand on price.

Parris & Company Commodity Service Letters, P.O. Box 2471, Fort Lauderdale, Florida 33303. Subscription rates: 3 months, $40; 6 months, $75. A weekly letter that specializes in spreads. Utilizes both fundamental and technical information to take up positions. Depends heavily on point-and-figure techniques to enter and close out positions.

SMR Commodity Chart Service, Security Market Research, Inc., P.O. Box 14096, Denver, Colorado 80214. Subscription rates: 3 months, $60; 6 months, $110; 1 year, $200. A weekly timing service that utilizes a technical method to recommend trades.

Special Trading Situations Bulletin, 1631 Kingston Road, Placentia, California 92670. Subscription rates: 3 months, $55; 6 months, $105; 1 year, $195. Weekly letter and telephone recorder service. Utilizes many different types of information to arrive at recommendations on both straight speculative positions and spreads. Some of the inputs utilized include moving averages, point-and-figure techniques, resistance and support levels, contrary opinion, floor traders' opinions, and price volatility.

TARA Inc., 2315 50th Street, Suite I, Lubbock, Texas 79412. Publishes five advisory services. A weekly cattle letter which costs $225 per year, and a monthly cattle letter at $60 per year. A weekly hog and pork letter at $200 per year and a monthly hog and pork letter at $60 per year. A weekly technical letter on all major commodities at $100 per year. The hog and cattle recommendations are based on fundamentals and point-and-figure analysis. The weekly technical letter on all major commodities appears to be based on point-and-figure analysis. Personal telephone consultation available.

The Weekly Commodity Guide, 1330 Beacon Street, Boston, Massachusetts 02146. Subscription rates: Trial subscription, $5; 3 months, $35; 6 months, $60; 1 year, $100. Weekly letter plus occasional collect telegrams if desired. This service uses fundamentals, technical factors and prevailing market psychology.

Index

☐